I0890206

# American Audacity

## WRITERS ON WRITING

Jay Parini, Series Editor

A good writer is first a good reader. Looking at craft from the inside, with an intimate knowledge of its range and possibilities, writers also make some of our most insightful critics. With this series we will bring together the work of some of our finest writers on the subject they know best, discussing their own work and that of others, as well as concentrating on craft and other aspects of the writer's world.

Poet, novelist, biographer, and critic, Jay Parini is the author of numerous books, including *The Apprentice Lover* and *One Matchless Time: A Life of William Faulkner*. Currently he is D. E. Axinn Professor of English & Creative Writing at Middlebury College.

### TITLES IN THE SERIES

*Michael Collier*
Make Us Wave Back: Essays on Poetry and Influence

*Nancy Willard*
The Left-Handed Story: Writing and the Writer's Life

*Christopher Benfey*
American Audacity: Literary Essays North and South

# American Audacity

## Literary Essays North and South

*Christopher Benfey*

The University of Michigan Press
*Ann Arbor*

Copyright © 2008 by Christopher Benfey
All rights reserved
Published in the United States of America by
The University of Michigan Press
Manufactured in the United States of America
♾ Printed on acid-free paper

2011 2010 2009 2008 4 3 2 1

No part of this publication may be reproduced, stored in a retrieval system, or transmitted in any form or by any means, electronic, mechanical, or otherwise, without the written permission of the publisher.

*A CIP catalog record for this book is available from the British Library.*

Library of Congress Cataloging-in-Publication Data

Benfey, Christopher E. G., 1954–
American audacity : literary essays North and South / by Christopher Benfey.
p. cm. — (Writers on writing.)
ISBN-13: 978-0-472-11626-3 (cloth : alk. paper)
ISBN-10: 0-472-11626-6 (cloth : alk. paper)
1. American literature—History and criticism. 2. Regionalism in literature. 3. National characteristics, American, in literature.
I. Title.
PS169.N35B46 2007
810.9—dc22 2007030972

# Contents

## Part III: The Union Reconsidered

# Introduction

THIS SELECTION OF ESSAYS covers roughly ten years of work. During that period I was writing books about the Gilded Age, reviewing art exhibitions for *Slate,* and teaching American literature at Mount Holyoke College. Twenty years earlier, beginning in the fall of 1977, I attended graduate school at Harvard; after receiving my doctorate in 1983, I worked for two years as an editorial assistant at the *New York Review of Books.* In America, where so many of our writers, from Benjamin Franklin to James Baldwin, have felt it necessary to give an account of their education, I may be forgiven for some stray remarks about mine. Three things in retrospect seem to have influenced the essays included here. One is the rise and partial demise of literary theory; another is the regional allegiance of so much American writing; and a third is the background disturbance of two wars—the aftershock of Vietnam and the more recent traumas of Iraq and the so-called "war on terror."

I entered graduate school during what seemed at the time a golden age of literary theory. To some it may still seem so; for others it was exposed, like so many golden ages in the past, as merely a gilded age. A great deal of intellectual energy was expended on such questions as whether prose is based on metonymy, or whether language has a life of its own beyond the intentions of individual writers, or whether literary language is different in kind from other uses of language. Harvard maintained, during those years, a self-congratulatory distance from developments in literary theory, which were centered at Yale. A wry bemusement, appropriate to prognostications for the Harvard-

Yale football game, was adopted vis-à-vis names like Paul de Man and Harold Bloom. I remember a social occasion when the president of the university told a group of literature professors that Jacques Derrida would never be hired to teach at Harvard. The announcement was met by applause.

The Harvard classrooms that seemed most vital to me were those in which literary theory was neither adopted whole hog (a few of which existed in an underground mode even at Harvard) nor rejected out of hand. Stanley Cavell, that fall of 1977, turned his seminar in aesthetics into an engaged but skeptical reading of Derrida's *Of Grammatology,* de Man's *Allegories of Reading,* and Bloom's *A Map of Misreading.* Beyond the exhilarating mood of the classroom (attended, as I remember, by regular visitors such as the philosopher and classicist Martha Nussbaum), there was an openness to figuring out precisely what these exotic texts might reveal in a poem by Stevens, say, or a paragraph by Rousseau. There was also an attempt to measure them against achievements already made in American literary criticism from Emerson and Thoreau to the New Critics and Northrop Frye.

That effort to ask how "theory" in its various guises might help to make sense of American writers and thinkers was also in play in Warner Berthoff's seminar on Emily Dickinson and Walt Whitman. When I came to write a doctoral thesis in comparative literature, I chose Dickinson's poetry as a rich field for putting together what I had taken from Cavell's seminar—especially questions about how writers address a world of other people—with Berthoff's questions about the distinctive contribution American writers make to world literature. The thesis became my first book, *Emily Dickinson and the Problem of Others* (1984).

Seamus Heaney's poetry workshops at Harvard gave me a different kind of distance on the academic squabbles of the day. Heaney had a deep commitment to poetic form and craft and an equally stirring sense of his own place in history, both the local history of Ireland and the larger history of the West. I had never known anyone with such palpable rootedness, with such a bedrock calm and certainty of having come from a particular place—this farm, this turn in the road, these trees. With Heaney's encouragement, I dug back to some of my own places: the

Quaker region in Indiana where I had grown up; the Piedmont of North Carolina, where my mother was from; and wartime Berlin, which my father, born into a German Jewish family, had escaped during the 1930s. I wrote and published poems in those years, but a kindred kind of archaeological imagination has, I believe, gone into the essays collected here.

The biggest surprise for me in going back to these essays is how regionally based they are, rooted in the two contrasting landscapes of New England and the South. Other ways of grouping the essays (poetry and prose, women and men, nineteenth century and twentieth) quickly yielded to regional divisions. When I began writing these essays, I was drawn to pockets of local earth in which I felt I had some stake. The first piece I wrote for the *New York Review of Books* was about Randall Jarrell, the poet and critic whose grave is in the Quaker graveyard at New Garden, just across the street from Guilford College, from which I, like my mother before me, had graduated and where my father had taught, and a five-minute walk from my parents' home in Greensboro, North Carolina. I have continued to write about the South and about southern writers, with essays on Faulkner, Allen Tate, Eudora Welty, Walker Percy, and James Agee.

Concurrently I have found occasion—or had the occasion suggested by editors (primarily Robert Silvers at the *New York Review of Books,* Leon Wieseltier at the *New Republic,* and James Campbell at the *Times Literary Supplement*)—to celebrate the achievements of the great generation of New England writers. The challenge for critics of my generation has been to find ways to dust off the layers of reverence and regard that have accumulated on the plaster busts of Emerson and Longfellow. My own impetus has come from the discipline of comparative literature. I was a latecomer to American literature, having begun my studies in French and German, and found it as rich and bizarre as anything I had read elsewhere.

But instead of insisting on some kind of American "exceptionalism"—the jingoist doctrine that American culture is a thing apart, and unique—I was drawn to the ways in which American writers participated in global networks of reciprocal creativity. The Asian imprint on Emerson's work is unmistakable, for example, and the rise of modern Zen Buddhism is inseparable from Emerson's influence on later Japanese thinkers. Longfellow is a bigger, richer writer if we think of him as a confluence of European and Asian imaginative tributaries rather than an individual talent immured in his Cambridge mansion on Brattle Street.

"The way we are living, timorous or bold, will have been our life," Heaney wrote in his elegy for Robert Lowell. I have called this book *American Audacity* as a clue to my own preferences in American literature. Probably every country asks of its artists a willingness to skate out on thin ice. But Americans seem particularly drawn to artists who display the quality that Emerson admired in Whitman, "the courage of treatment." We have our daredevils and our "safe men," as Bartleby's boss calls himself in Melville's dark tale, and one task of criticism is to tell them apart. It is difficult at this late date to recover Emerson's audacity, to separate, as I say in the opening essay, the Prometheus from the Polonius. And writers who once seemed to brave the elements—Dos Passos, for example, and Edna Millay—now seem, beneath their weather-beaten exteriors, a bit timid in their aesthetic choices. Others, Emily Dickinson and William Faulkner, seem all the more audacious as the years go by.

I had thought of subtitling this book "Northern Saints and Southern Sinners." The northern writers I have written about are by and large a moralizing bunch; latter-day Puritans, they are eager to set the world and their neighbors aright. The southerners, by contrast, seem more willing to concede human frailty. Sometimes this distinction plays out in political ways, between liberal and conservative tendencies, but then someone like Frost comes along who confounds geography and politics. Another way to put it is that the northerners often have a utopian streak while the southerners don't.

Anyone who approaches these two clusters of extraordinary writers, from New England and the South, must deal with the brute fact of war. The Civil War sometimes seems a war of New England intellectuals and southern generals. Lincoln famously remarked that Harriet Beecher Stowe's *Uncle Tom's Cabin* had caused the war. Many of our great books have been written in the periods "after the war," whether the postrevolutionary outpouring of "Young America" in the works of Melville and Hawthorne and Whitman, the post–Civil War narratives of Henry James and Edith Wharton, or the "lost generation" of Hemingway and Faulkner in the wake of World War I. But in some deep and still only partially explained way, the Civil War has remained the crucial war in the American imagination, outstripping the American Revolution, the two world wars, and Vietnam. It seems as though every literary season includes a harvest of historical novels set in the Civil War period, most recently E. L. Doctorow's *The March.* How can we account for the lingering emotional grip of the Civil War?

During the spring of 1882, Mark Twain traveled down the Mississippi River to refresh his memories of the American South. The trip helped him finish two of his greatest books: *Life on the Mississippi* and *Huckleberry Finn.* In chapter 45 of *Life on the Mississippi,* Twain compares how the Civil War is talked about in the North and South. "In the North one hears the war mentioned, in social conversation, once a month," he writes, "sometimes as often as once a week; but as a distinct subject for talk, it has long ago been relieved of duty." The reason, Twain maintains, is that so few northerners had direct experience of war.

> The case is very different in the South. There, every man you meet was in the war; and every lady you meet saw the war. The war is the great chief topic of conversation. The interest in it is vivid and constant; the interest in other topics is fleeting. Mention of the war will wake up a dull company and set their tongues going, when nearly any other topic would fail. In the South, the war is what A.D. is elsewhere: they date from it. All day long you hear things "placed" as having happened since the waw; or du'in' the waw; or befo' the waw; or right aftah the waw; or 'bout two years or five years or ten yeahs befo' the waw or aftah the waw. It shows how intimately every individual was visited, in his own person, by that tremendous episode. It gives the inexperienced stranger a better idea of what a vast and comprehensive calamity invasion is than he can ever get by reading books at the fireside.

It is possible that Twain draws too sharp a distinction between North and South. The war decimated a generation of young men on both sides. When one considers books written in the North, including Twain's own, the Civil War is rarely far from view. Stephen Crane was born too late for the war, but that didn't prevent him from writing *The Red Badge of Courage* (1895). The northerners Henry James, Henry Adams, and Herman Melville, as the historian C. Vann Woodward pointed out long ago, all wrote books in which a southern veteran of the war is the central conscience. And in our own time, the Civil War is increasingly seen as the opening salvo in a century-long battle for civil rights, lasting from the Emancipation Proclamation of 1863 to the Civil Rights Act of 1964 and beyond.

Writers competed to name the period of corruption and confusion that followed the Civil War. Henry James called it "The Awkward Age," while his friend Edith Wharton suggested "The Age of Innocence," despite the fact that no period in American history was less innocent. But it was Mark Twain himself who indelibly named the post–Civil War decades as "The Gilded Age." He meant to suggest that the great fortunes amassed and the great mansions erected during the era hardly amounted to a Golden Age, that fabled time of peace and prosperity that the Romans imagined in a time and place long ago and far away. Instead, it was merely gilded; scratch the veneer and you would find lead and misery.

I have published three books over the past fifteen years that deal with different aspects of the Gilded Age: *The Double Life of Stephen Crane* (1992), *Degas in New Orleans: Encounters in the Creole World of Kate Chopin and George Washington Cable* (1997), and *The Great Wave: Gilded Age Misfits, Japanese Eccentrics, and the Opening of Old Japan* (2003). In this Gilded Age trilogy I set out to broaden the borders of American literature. I tried to show, for example, that a single cultural realm connected New Orleans to France during much of the nineteenth century. Similarly, connections between New England and Japan were so intimate that the Reverend Phillips Brooks, the imposing minister of Trinity Church in Boston, once remarked that most of his parishioners were Buddhists.

In retrospect, I can see how imbued with war these books were. The case of Stephen Crane is clear enough; no American writer has been so engaged with the cultural memory of the Civil War for his own "second generation." It was a postwar crisis in the cotton economy that brought the impressionist painter Degas to visit his embattled family in New Orleans, some of whose members had adopted the cause of white supremacy. And it was in the wake of the spiritual malaise of the postwar period that many New Englanders sought solace and direction in the cultural traditions of "Old Japan."

In trying to define the generation of writers and critics to which I myself belong, I find that we, too, are a generation "after the war." Born in the 1950s, after World War II, we came of age after the Vietnam War and the turmoil of the 1960s. We were, in a sense, always latecomers. Even our intellectual formation carried a sense of late arrival and distance. The heady first wave of literary theory was already breaking when we arrived in graduate school during the late 1970s and early 1980s. Our intellectual inheritance, such as it was, was a new awareness of history.

If our teachers had schooled us in the techniques of close reading developed by the New Critics, it was the rise of varieties of historical analysis that marked our generation. Feminist criticism, New Historicism, and African-American studies gave fresh attention to the concrete lives of writers as both recorders of historical change and actors within it. We also reached back a couple of generations to such historically attuned critics and scholars as Edmund Wilson, Lionel Trilling, and Isaiah Berlin. My own taste for forgotten antiquarians such as Van Wyck Brooks and Constance Rourke reflects the same tendency. Some of our own best efforts betray this new historical awareness. And that historical awareness, in turn, served mainly to send us back to the wars.

Christopher Benfey<br>Amherst, Massachusetts<br>February 15, 2007

# Part I

# Northerners

# Emerson at Age Two Hundred

TWO-THIRDS OF THE WAY INTO KATE CHOPIN'S *The Awakening* (1900), the rebellious heroine Edna Pontellier finds herself alone in her mansion on Esplanade, her restrictive husband gone on a business trip and all the temptations of New Orleans beckoning at her door. Dressed only in her comfortable peignoir, she devours "a luscious tenderloin," downs plenty of red wine, and adds a marron glacé for dessert. Then she wanders into her library to curl up with a book. Will she choose Zola's *Nana* or some equally wayward fantasy by Maupassant or Gautier? *Mais non!* Edna—bold transgressor that she is—read "Emerson until she grew sleepy." But why Emerson? Is Edna—on the verge of a ruinous affair that will eventually drive her to suicide—experiencing a moment of remorse, to be shored up by the edifying Sage of Concord? Or is the apostle of impulse ("I would write on the lintels of the door-post, *Whim*") just the man to confirm her liberation from the suffocating constraints of marriage and motherhood?

Two hundred years after his birth in 1803, it remains unclear whether Emerson was the Prometheus of American literature or its Polonius. His status as fatherly advisor is at least secure. When Whitman was "simmering," Emerson brought him "to a boil." Thoreau's first entry in his great journal records a primal push from Emerson: "'What are you doing now?' he asked. 'Do you keep a journal?'—so I make my first entry today." Melville, Dickinson, Henry and William James—one sees the patriarch's provocation in all their works, the benevolent gift of "courage of treatment" (what Emerson most admired in Whitman's extravagant performances). But lost in such celebrations of Emerson's "legacy" is what to make of Emerson himself—his essays, his poems, his letters and journals—unencumbered by his brood. Does anyone, should anyone, read Emerson now, and if so, why and how?

If Emerson seemed scandalous to many of his contemporaries—for walking away from the pulpit after refusing to administer communion; for preaching a secular religion of self-reliance against all calls for social conformity; for dismissing formal education as an impediment to true learning ("Books are for the scholar's idle times")—the scandals that now dog his name have a late twentieth-century flavor. Today Emerson stands accused of going slow on abolition, responding in lukewarm fashion to the death of his young son ("I grieve that grief can teach me nothing"), writing tame poetry and muddled philosophy, and preaching a creed of self-reliance indistinguishable from American capitalism. If Emerson is the founding white male of American national literature, our younger scholars seem to think, then chipping away at his reputation strikes a blow at the foundation of American national identity.

In their different and complementary ways, two recent books on Emerson—timed to coincide with his bicentennial—seek to restore the firebrand, and liberate the liberator. Kenneth Sacks's subtle and fine-meshed *Understanding Emerson* examines the circumstances in which Emerson's first major public statement, his 1837 Phi Beta Kappa address at Harvard—popularly known as "The American Scholar"—took shape. Sacks, a historian at Brown University, shows how complicated the occasion was, and how easy it would have been, with a patriotic and flattering performance, for Emerson to fulfill the expectations of his audience and alma mater. Instead, Emerson heeded the hopes of young friends like Thoreau, and deliberately insulted almost everyone in the audience, criticizing the drill-based education on offer at Harvard and making a plea for the "self-trust" that he would later reformulate as self-reliance. "Breaking with the materialism in which he was raised," Sacks writes, "Emerson proposed an extreme vision of the intellectual who transcends all convention, including the institutions of one's own country, to speak the truth that emerges from within." Sacks gives a thrilling sense of what a thin-ice performance it was, and why Emerson was not asked back to Harvard for thirty years. The idea of the scholar as necessarily lonely and embattled became a watchword for Emerson. "To be great," he came to believe, "is to be misunderstood."

Emerson as embattled thinker is also central to Lawrence Buell's wide-ranging portrait, *Emerson,* which opens with a chapter on Emerson as "public intellectual"—"the first figure in U.S. history to achieve international standing and influence as a speaker and writer of comprehensive scope." Buell, a professor of American literature at Harvard, has written influential books on New England literary culture and on the fledgling field of ecological criticism. If he speaks as an insider here his paradoxical aim is to free Emerson from the Emersonians. Buell advances two major claims against the canonization—and consequent confinement—of Emerson within American literature. First, he argues (as does Sacks) that Emerson was far less the literary nationalist than he is usually portrayed. Oliver Wendell Holmes famously called "The American Scholar" "our intellectual Declaration of Independence," but the address conspicuously avoids national boosterism. Buell points out that even on such a patriotic occasion as the dedication of the monument for the Concord battlefield, in April 1836, Emerson dutifully raised the flag in the first stanza of his "Concord Hymn" ("By the rude bridge that arched the flood, / Their flag to April's breeze unfurled"), but by the second was already eliding friend and foe and sweeping the divisive bridge from sight:

> The foe long since in silence slept;
> Alike the conqueror silent sleeps;
> And time the ruined bridge has swept
> Down the dark stream which seaward creeps.

Buell's second major claim follows from Emerson's "international standing." He shows convincingly that Emerson's preferred reading was foreign writers, "the farther off the better." Not only was Emerson steeped in the scriptures of European romanticism—Goethe, de Stael, Coleridge, Carlyle—but he went farther afield to read and translate Indian sacred books and Persian poetry. "At the height of the Civil War," Buell notes, "we find him mentally moving back and forth from national crisis to Confucius, Vedanta, and the poetry of Sufi mysticism." Buell has gone deeply into Emerson's engagement with Asian literature and thought, and shows how Emerson's early excavations served as inspiration for such pioneering scholars as Max Müller (who dedicated his *Introduction to the Science of Religion* to Emerson) and Edwin Arnold. The first American translations of Buddhist scripture appeared in the *Dial* under Emerson's editorship. Poems like Emerson's wonderful "Brahma" ("If the red slayer think he slays, / Or if the slain think he is slain, / They know not well the subtle ways / I keep, and pass, and turn again"), a rough translation of a Vedic text, helped spread interest in Eastern philosophy among Boston "Brahmins" like William Sturgis Bigelow and Henry Adams, and fellow travelers like Lafcadio Hearn.

Not only Westerners in search of the eternal wisdom of the East turned to Emerson, but many conspicuous Easterners as well. Some of Buell's most interesting pages detail how such "experts" as D. T. Suzuki, "the most influential interpreter of Zen Buddhism in the west during the first half of the twentieth century," found inspiration in Emerson's writings. Late in his long life, Suzuki, whose first publication was his "Essay on Emerson" of 1896, recalled "the deep impressions made upon me while reading Emerson in my college days" in Japan, and how familiarity with Emerson meant "making acquaintance with myself." Buell notes that "some tenets of Suzuki's version of Zen seem strongly Emersonian" (for example, the idea that "the Buddha is your own mind"), but he stops short of making the obvious inference: that Emerson helped to invent our modern notion of Zen.

Emerson's fingerprints are visible on another early version of Zen not discussed by Buell, namely Kakuzo Okakura's cult classic of Zen aesthetics, *The Book of Tea* (1906). Okakura was a Japanese disciple of the Harvard-educated philosopher Ernest Fenollosa, one of the first wave of Western intellectuals invited to Japan and a passionate Emersonian. One reason that Okakura's book on the antimaterialist bases of Japanese aesthetics caught on with such taste-making Bostonians as Isabella Stewart Gardner, and with

Japan-friendly artists like Frank Lloyd Wright and Wallace Stevens, was that his ideas sounded so familiar—and in fact, so Emersonian. Okakura's eccentric tea masters embrace a bold new "conduct of life," countering the ways in which "slavish conformity to traditions and formulas fetters the expression of individuality."

If Buell's greatest achievement is to de-Americanize Emerson, restoring him to his cosmopolitan place in world literature, it is discouraging to find nearly fifty pages late in the book devoted to Emerson's line on "social thought and reform." Here, Buell gives too much scope to the concerns of what he calls "the American Studies movement," in which "*the* defining issue" is "the proper relation between scholarly and political work." What this entails for the inquisition of Emerson is "whether, when, and to what extent he actively furthered reform efforts, the underlying agenda being either defense of his efforts or criticism of his laggardliness"—in particular, with regard to slavery. The question is not whether Emerson was opposed or in favor of slavery—he was always firmly opposed—but whether his ardor matched that of Garrison or Wendell Phillips. The accusation of laggardliness comes in because only after 1844 or so did Emerson become—adopting the phrasing of the prosecution—an "activist."

Buell is disappointed that Emerson concluded his second series of essays not (as he once planned) with his essay on "Abolition" but rather with his caustic attack on the cant and self-righteousness of "New England Reformers." He accuses Emerson of "lamely backpedaling from poet-activist John Greenleaf Whittier's invitation to a liberty meeting on behalf of an abolitionist martyr jailed in Baltimore." There is something wrong with this facile contrast between the irreproachable "poet-activist" Whittier and the backpedaling Emerson, and it becomes clearer when we examine more closely Emerson's "lame" refusal. "I have not the sort of skill that is useful in meetings for debate," Emerson wrote Whittier, but "I delight to know that such meetings are holden." This isn't lame; it is Emerson's consistent response to occasions that called for him to speak as others spoke and think as others thought. Buell is quite right that "Emerson is too concerned to immunize his readers against groupthink to say much about social action."

It is probably true that early in his speaking career, when most of his money came from middle-class lyceum audiences, Emerson deliberately avoided the controversial subject of slavery and, as Kenneth Sacks suggests, "kept silent before a public he did not wish to alienate." But when he did publicly join in reform movements, he almost always regretted it, and not because it threatened his income. After writing a nationally published letter to President Van Buren protesting the federal removal of the Cherokee Nation across the Mississippi, Emerson lamented "a letter hated of me." As Sacks notes, Emerson felt he had "compromised his self-reliance" and vowed to withdraw from activism: "I will let the republic alone until the republic comes to me. I fully sympathise, be sure, with the sentiment I write, but I accept it rather from my friends than dictate it. It is not my impulse to say it & therefore my genius deserts me, no muse befriends, no music of thought or of word accompanies. Bah!"

If your measure of literary value is the rightness—judged by contemporary standards—of the opinions expressed therein, such things as genius and music will mean little to you. What finally goaded Emerson into abolitionist activism was violence against liberal northern printers. Freedom of expression had two meanings for him: its legal definition but also that freedom-granting genius he recognized in his own best work. Emerson's prose remains a marvel and a provocation, with each sentence detachable, quotable, yet set among other sentences so tightly that no light shines through. The sentences are like perfectly matched bricks, with none of the usual mortar—of "howevers" and "indeeds" and "nonethelesses"—slopped on to make them fit. Consider the "Piranesi-like" opening (as Buell nicely calls it) of Emerson's great essay "Experience":

> Where do we find ourselves? In a series of which we do not know the extremes, and believe that it has none. We wake and find ourselves on a stair; there are stairs below us, which we seem to have ascended; there are stairs above us, many a one, which go upward and out of sight. But the Genius which, according to the old belief, stands at the door by which we

> enter, and gives us the lethe to drink, that we may tell no tales, mixed the cup too strongly, and we cannot shake off the lethargy now at noonday. Sleep lingers all our lifetime about our eyes, as night hovers all day in the boughs of the fir-tree.

Buell's chapter "Emersonian Poetics" gets at some of the startling characteristics of Emerson's elastic prose: its refusal of systematic argument (Emerson once claimed that he did "not know what arguments mean, in reference to any expression of a thought"); its incomplete or fragmentary form; its "epigrammaticism" or "proverbialism." I think that Buell is right to relate Emerson's taste for gnomic aphorisms to his interest in the pithy concision of Persian poetry. "The characteristic structure of the aphorism," Buell writes, "itself implies at least two kinds of boundary crossing: a thrusting past banality to further reaches of insight, and an ongoing energy flow that reforms insight continuously in a transmissible form that invites perpetual continuation of the game."

What Robert Lowell called Emerson's "prose-haiku" has had more of an impact on American poets than Emerson's poetry. It was Emerson's prose that showed Whitman a way to loosen up the American poetic line. Robert Frost called Emerson's "Uriel" "the best Western poem yet"; but it was the Emersonian prose sentence, so close in its shifting rhythms to the ordinary speaking voice, that confirmed Frost's idea of intonational "sentence sounds" as the threads on which the words of poems should be strung. The very "ordinariness" of Emerson's phrasing and his explicit concern with our impoverished estate—"I embrace the common, I explore and sit at the feet of the familiar, the low"—have inspired the best writing, by Stanley Cavell, on Emerson as philosopher.

Buell devotes a scant five pages to Emerson's poetry, and while granting an appealing "awkwardness" to some of Emerson's knottier poems, he is mainly dismissive. Emerson "was no Emily Dickinson" and "never mastered the poetic line as he did the prose sentence." Perhaps, but I'd want to put in a word for such firmly constructed stanzas as this from "The World-Soul":

Cities of proud hotels,
Houses of rich and great,
Vice nestles in your chambers,
Beneath your roofs of slate.
It cannot conquer folly,
Time-and-space-conquering steam;
And the light-outspeeding telegraph
Bears nothing on its beam.

Emerson's favorite poetic music was the rune or riddle, captured in some of his translations from Hafiz and Saadi. Best of all, though, are his brief "mottoes," appended as self-quoting epigraphs to his essays, such as this bracing quatrain from "Self-Reliance":

Cast the bantling on the rocks,
Suckle him with the she-wolf's teat;
Wintered with the hawk and fox,
Power and speed be hands and feet.

Emerson's allure is no less enduring for being a bit mystical and elusive. The great German critic Ernst Robert Curtius, writing in 1924, compared Emerson's "stimulating influence" to the intoxicating "magic" of reading Balzac. For his committed readers, Emerson's work is like Edna Pontellier's red wine: "I will be drunk and down with wine, / Treasures we find in a ruined house," as Emerson translated a couplet of Hafiz. Both Emerson and Balzac, Curtius argued, wrote from the momentary intuition of the interconnectedness of everything. But while Balzac explores the sheer complexity of the human and spiritual world, Emerson is always cutting through the "variegated strands of his essays" to get at the "grandly simple." If this sounds too empyrean and detached from social causes, consider Camus's invocation of Emerson in 1957, the year he won the Nobel Prize. "Create dangerously," Camus challenged his fellow writers. And who was his model of "the creator's faith in himself"? Emerson, of course: "'A man's obedience to his own genius,' Emerson said magnificently, 'is faith in its purest form.'"

VOLUMES REVIEWED

*Understanding Emerson: "The American Scholar" and His Struggle for Self-Reliance*
By Kenneth S. Sacks
Princeton University Press, 2003

*Emerson*
By Lawrence Buell
Belknap Press of Harvard University Press, 2003

# Hawthorne's Smile

Nathaniel Hawthorne made Holgrave, the hero of his second major novel, *The House of the Seven Gables* (1851), a daguerreotypist. Descended from a Salem wizard burned at the stake, Holgrave pierces the dark secrets of the ancient house. "There is a wonderful insight in heaven's broad and simple sunshine," Holgrave remarks of his bewitching craft. "While we give it credit only for depicting the merest surface, it actually brings out the secret character with a truth that no painter would ever venture upon, even could he detect it." A chapter is titled "The Scowl and Smile"; Holgrave's photographs unmask the evil motives concealed beneath the "benign smile" of the crooked Judge Pyncheon, whose ill-gotten fortune is restored to its rightful owners. Hawthorne—"handsomer than Lord Byron," according to his sister-in-law Elizabeth Peabody—repeatedly subjected his own features to the secret-revealing medium. To Robert Lowell, scrutinizing one of the portraits (presumably Mathew Brady's of 1862), Hawthorne's face seems out of place among his august contemporaries—just as Hawthorne often seemed, by politics and temperament, out of place during his own lifetime:

> Look at the faces—
> Longfellow, Lowell, Holmes and Whittier!
> Study the grizzled silver of their beards.
> Hawthorne's picture,
> however, has a blond mustache
> and golden General Custer scalp.
> He looks like a Civil War officer.

He shines in the firelight.
His hard survivor's smile is touched with fire.

The celebration of his two hundredth birthday—he was born on July 4, 1804—is precisely the sort of occasion from which the "silence-loving and shade seeking" Hawthorne (in Henry James's phrase) would have shrunk. But a quick scan of the literary and political landscape reveals a Hawthorne firmly embedded in the American psyche.

During recent years we have had Paul Auster's "discovery," deep in the pages of Hawthorne's *American Notebooks,* of a hitherto unknown or at least ignored story of father and children called "Twenty Days with Julian & Little Bunny by Papa"; Andrei Codrescu's satirical novel *Wakefield,* inspired by a Hawthorne tale of the same name; the playwright Suzan-Lori Parks's *In the Blood,* in which a homeless African-American mother of five named Hester La Negrita, illiterate except for the letter *A,* steps in for Hester Prynne; the novelist Rick Moody's saturnine *The Black Veil: A Memoir with Digressions,* inspired by a Hawthorne tale with a possible connection to Moody's family; Barry Werth's *The Scarlet Professor,* a life of the Hawthorne scholar Newton Arvin, who was ostracized at Smith College when his homosexuality (his best-known lover was Truman Capote) came to light; and Brenda Wineapple's intimate critical biography *Hawthorne: A Life.* It is impossible to determine how many of these projects were hastened or delayed to coincide with Hawthorne's bicentennial. But such varied endeavours help to allay the fear enunciated twenty years ago, in Richard Brodhead's *The School of Hawthorne,* that "American literature's great survivor" might not "survive the next reorganization of American literary culture."

There are signs that Hawthorne's presence lies even deeper in contemporary American life. Two recent attempts to probe a supposed malignancy in American society have enlisted Hawthorne as guide. Philip Roth's *The Human Stain* seeks to make sense of an ascendant Puritanism on both the political right (the hounding of President Clinton in the Monica Lewinsky affair) and the left (the hounding of a dean for alleged racism and sexism on a college campus). The novel is saturated with Hawthorne—in its setting in the Berkshires (the narrator specifies in the third paragraph that "Hawthorne . . . in the 1860s, lived not many miles from my door"), in its quotations from Hawthorne on such matters as "the persecuting spirit" of American society, and in its overall theme—recalling both *The Scarlet Letter* and "The Birth-mark"—of imperfect humanity tangled in the wire mesh of Puritan perfectionism. Roth's narrator has selected his New England rural retreat as a way to get closer to Hawthorne:

> The trick is to find sustenance in (Hawthorne again) "the communications of a solitary mind with itself." The secret is to find sustenance in people like Hawthorne, in the wisdom of the brilliant deceased.

Hawthorne's brilliant wisdom is presumably what Leon R. Kass, professor of ethics at the University of Chicago and chairman of President Bush's Council on Bioethics, was after when he assigned "The Birth-mark" as required reading for the first meeting of the council in January 2002. (The story recounts a scientist's attempt to remove a tiny hand-shaped birthmark from his wife's face, the only blemish to her perfect beauty. The treatment—complicated by the unexpected depth of the mark—is successful, but the patient dies.) It is clear from Kass's summation of the discussion that he regarded the story as an unambiguous warning against meddling with human mortality, and hence, by extension, a cautionary tale regarding bioengineering, stem-cell research, and the like. The birthmark is "a sign of our finitude and limitation," Kass argues. "There is something in the culture at large and something in medicine today, however modestly practiced, that almost says, 'Look, we will never stop until we can deal with mortality as such.'" But one may draw a different moral from the story: that it warns against precisely those claims to moral purity that Kass and his council appeared to seek. Hawthorne seems, as always, poised between two extreme positions, his smiling equanimity unruffled.

One may wonder how Nathaniel Hawthorne, holed up in his third-floor bedroom in the port city of Salem, Massachusetts, managed to lay out so incisively the moral agenda of the young—as well as the now much older—nation. Among the most cosmopolitan of American cities at the time of Hawthorne's birth, Salem was also historically the most notoriously xenophobic; among its most strenuous witch hunters and floggers of Quakers were two direct ancestors of Hawthorne.

In "The Custom-House," his magnificent preface to *The Scarlet Letter,* Hawthorne evokes the punitive zeal of his "bearded, sable-cloaked, and steeple-crowned progenitor" William Hathorne (Hawthorne added the *w*). William's son, a judge, "inherited the persecuting spirit," according to Hawthorne, "and made himself so conspicuous in the martyrdom of the witches, that their blood may fairly be said to have left a stain upon him." (This is the passage that Roth quotes in relation to the "witch-hunt" of Bill Clinton in *The Human Stain.*)

Salem has often been enlisted to explain Hawthorne's isolation; it has less frequently been called upon to explain his sophistication. And yet, wherever we look in Hawthorne's early years, we see signs of a wider world. Salem at the time of his birth dominated the shipping trade in the Dutch East Indies, the Philippines, Mauritius, and both coasts of Africa.

In many parts of the world, as Samuel Eliot Morison remarks in *The Maritime History of Massachusetts,* Salem simply meant the United States. Hawthorne's father, a sea captain, died of yellow fever in Surinam when his son was not yet four. Hawthorne, his two sisters, and their mother moved in with her Salem relatives, a humiliating situation from which he found release only in his happy years at Bowdoin. There Hawthorne made the friendships of a lifetime, with Franklin Pierce and Horatio Bridge as well as, more distantly, Henry Wadsworth Longfellow. Pierce helped Hawthorne acquire those sinecures—in custom houses in Salem and Boston, and later as a consul in Liverpool—that supported him as a writer.

Hawthorne's admirers have sometimes been disappointed in his friendships. The Harvard scholar Elisa New, for example, laments that Hawthorne was "more comfortable among mediocrities than geniuses," preferring the company of the "potato-faced, shallow, loyal Franklin Pierce" to Melville and Longfellow.

This formulation implies that Hawthorne, cowed by his equals, found a cozy refuge among his underachieving Bowdoin classmates. But Franklin Pierce was president of the United States, and Hawthorne's other intimates—the naval officer Horatio Bridge and the publisher James T. Fields—were successful as "ambitious men of action," in Wineapple's phrase. What drew Hawthorne to Pierce, Fields, and Bridge was not their mediocrity but their worldliness.

It was Hawthorne's own tough practicality—his search for reliable living arrangements for himself and his fiancée, Sophia Peabody—and not his idealism that lured him in 1841 to join the utopian experiment of Brook Farm outside of Boston. Lacking high hopes for the venture, he was spared major disappointments; his novel based on the experience, *The Blithedale Romance* (1852), is notable for its sunny avoidance of satire. Elsewhere Hawthorne is pleasingly biting in his assessment of New England reformers; as Robert Lowell once remarked in an essay, "When Hawthorne stung, his style smiled." His superb "The Old Manse" (the preface to *Mosses from an Old Manse,* 1846) is laced with nasty asides toward his Concord neighbours, especially members of Emerson's circle: "Never was a poor little country village infested with such a variety of queer, strangely dressed, oddly behaved mortals, most of whom took upon themselves to be important agents of the world's destiny, yet were simply bores of a very intense water." In Brook Farm and then Concord, where he rented a house from Emerson, Hawthorne sought out men like Thoreau who—despite their oddity of dress or demeanor—knew how to bait a hook or survey an acre of land.

Hawthorne's campaign biography of Pierce, and his editing (and probable ghostwriting) of Bridge's naval adventures along the coast of Africa, gave him the illusion that he had stitched himself into the fabric of history. Men of stature regarded him as a trustworthy ally in spreading their fame. Commodore Matthew Perry—under whom Bridge had served—called on Hawthorne in Liverpool, during the winter of 1854, to beseech him to write the epic story of his triumphant voyage the previous year to open Japan to the West. "He was good enough to say that he had fixed upon me, in his own mind, for this office," Hawthorne wrote in his journal; "but that my public duties would of course prevent me from engaging in it. I spoke of Herman Melville." Perry, alas, did not want the disreputable author of *Typee* romancing Japan, and did the job himself.

Hawthorne did, in fact, play an indirect part in the opening of Japan, though he could not have known it. If Commodore Perry's gunboat diplomacy opened Japan to Western trade, it was the work of two Salem men of the next generation, the scientist Edward Sylvester Morse and the art historian Ernest Fenollosa, who contributed more than anyone else to the cultural discovery of Japan. Morse, a zoologist who became the world's expert on Japanese ceramics and architecture and was the longtime director of the Peabody-Essex Museum in Salem, arrived in Yokohama in 1877. He carried in his pocket, as a reminder to notice things, a journal entry from Hawthorne:

> Begin to write always before the impression of novelty has worn off from your mind, else you will be apt to think that the peculiarities which at first attracted you are not worth recording; yet these slight peculiarities are the very things that make the most vivid impression upon the reader. Think nothing too trifling to set down, so it be in the smallest degree characteristic. You will be surprised to find, on re-perusing your journal, what an importance and graphic power these little peculiarities assume.

Morse enlisted Fenollosa, a recent graduate of Harvard, to join him at Tokyo Imperial University and teach political science and Western philosophy. Fenollosa became enamored of Japanese art and literature instead; his papers and translations made their way to Ezra Pound, Fenollosa's literary executor. Oddly enough, the meaning of Japan for Fenollosa resided in a smile—the "quiet mysterious smile" of the Buddha and his followers—reminiscent, he thought, of the *Mona Lisa*.

An enigmatic smile is the distinguishing trait of two of Hawthorne's most enduring characters: the Reverend Mr. Hooper of "The Minister's Black Veil," and Wakefield. The minister's veil, donned one morning without explanation, so upsets his parishioners that no dinner invitation follows his sermon on secret sin:

> He returned, therefore, to the parsonage, and, at the moment of closing the door, was observed to look back upon the

> people, all of whom had their eyes fixed upon the minister. A sad smile gleamed faintly from beneath the black veil, and flickered about his mouth, glimmering as he disappeared.
>
> "How strange," said a lady, "that a simple black veil, such as any woman might wear on her bonnet, should become such a terrible thing on Mr. Hooper's face!"

When Hooper's fiancée asks for an explanation, she gets none, nothing but "that same, sad smile, which always appeared like a faint glimmering of light, proceeding from the obscurity beneath the veil."

Wakefield needs no fashion accessory to render his smile equally terrible. His wife detects nothing worse than a "harmless love of mystery" in Wakefield. When he takes leave of her one evening, Wakefield himself "has no suspicion of what is before him." He leaves for a few days and does not return for twenty years. At the moment of parting, Wakefield's wife registers his smile. As with the Cheshire Cat, it is all that survives his departure:

> After the door has closed behind him, she perceives it thrust partly open, and a vision of her husband's face, through the aperture, smiling on her, and gone in a moment. For the time, this little incident is dismissed without a thought. But, long afterwards, when she has been more years a widow than a wife, that smile recurs, and flickers across all her reminiscences of Wakefield's visage. In her many musings, she surrounds the original smile with a multitude of fantasies, which make it strange and awful; as, for example, if she imagines him in a coffin, that parting look is frozen on his pale features; or, if she dreams of him in Heaven, still his blessed spirit wears a quiet and crafty smile.

An awareness of photography hovers around this scene: the vision of the husband's face as seen "through the aperture" of the partly open door, and the parting look "frozen on his pale features."

Like all Hawthorne's best stories, "The Minister's Black Veil" and "Wakefield" leave an impression of incompleteness, of something not quite fully developed.

Rick Moody's *Black Veil* and Andrei Codrescu's *Wakefield* are attempts to extend them, with a bipolar divergence. Linking his own experience of depression to an exhaustive analysis of "The Minister's Black Veil," Moody gives us a relentlessly downbeat Hawthorne. The book ends with an anti-American diatribe: "To be an American, to be a citizen of the West, is to be a murderer. Don't kid yourself. Cover your face." An absurdist Hawthorne, derived from Borges's observation that "Wakefield" prefigures Kafka, finds expression in Codrescu's raucous road novel. Wakefield, exiled in an America of disposable architecture and computerization run amuck, leaves his home in New Orleans in search of his authentic self.

In thus dividing Hawthorne's equable smile into a ghastly scowl on the one hand and a manic grin on the other, these books unwittingly reproduce the split in the literary generations that immediately followed Hawthorne: William Dean Howells's Realist commitment to the "smiling aspects" of American life, on the one hand, and the harsh Naturalism of Frank Norris and Stephen Crane on the other. American writers, as Richard Brodhead has noted, aim to "complete" Hawthorne at their peril: "And when others go past where he left off, they show, however extraordinary their achievements, the reasons for his moderation."

Hawthorne's moderately conservative political views, a scandal to Abolitionist friends and family members who took turns trying to dislodge his Democratic Party convictions, remain a stumbling block to this day. Like certain contrarians of every era, he enjoyed shocking self-righteous sensibilities. He greeted the news of John Brown's execution—supposedly celebrated by Emerson as a day that "will make the gallows as glorious as the cross"—with the remark "Nobody was ever more justly hanged." He preferred almost any political arrangement to violence, and insisted on dedicating his sketches of British life collected in *Our Old Home* (1863) to the compromised Franklin Pierce, who had tried to forge a separate peace with Jefferson Davis. He wanted the North to win but he would have been just as happy to see the South leave the Union.

And yet, Hawthorne knew perfectly well that Pierce, whose views accorded with his own, was not a great president and that Lincoln, whose views he mostly deplored, most certainly was. Offered a chance in 1862 to travel to Washington to witness the war firsthand and meet the commander in chief, Hawthorne seized it. His pen-portrait of Lincoln in his last masterpiece, "Chiefly about War Matters," is as incisive as any photograph:

> He was dressed in a rusty black frock-coat and pantaloons, unbrushed, and worn so faithfully that the suit had adapted itself to the curves and angularities of his figure, and had grown to be an outer skin of the man. He had shabby slippers on his feet. His hair was black, still unmixed with gray, stiff, somewhat bushy, and had apparently been acquainted with neither brush nor comb that morning, after the disarrangement of the pillow . . . he has thick black eyebrows and an impending brow; his nose is large, and the lines about his mouth are very strongly defined.

As Lincoln entered the room to greet the Massachusetts delegation, Hawthorne noted the "comical twist of his face" and concluded: "I like this sallow, queer, sagacious visage, with the homely human sympathies that warmed it; and for my small share in the matter, would as lief have Uncle Abe for a ruler as any man whom it would have been practicable to put in his place."

Depressed by the war and suffering from an obscure illness—cancer, perhaps, or syphilis—Hawthorne increasingly sought refuge in a tower in Concord specially constructed to mimic his upstairs hideaway in Salem. Earlier he had lamented the tendency of political leaders "loudest to applaud the work of blood, latest to confess themselves miserably deceived." "Will the time ever come again, in America," Hawthorne now wondered, "when we may live half a score of years without once seeing the likeness of a soldier? . . . Not in this generation, I fear, nor in the next, nor till the Millennium." On May 19, 1864, Hawthorne died in his sleep during a meander through Maine and New Hampshire meant to cheer him up. Some have speculated that he hastened his death with poison administered by his own hand. A year later, the homely president whom Hawthorne had come to admire was also dead. Look at their faces—Hawthorne and Lincoln, the most illustrious victims of the American Civil War—and you will see what they had in common: the hard survivor's smile.

# Longfellow Lives Again

HENRY WADSWORTH LONGFELLOW, the most revered and reviled of all American poets, would have been two hundred years old in 2007. Perhaps the most that can be hoped is that his third century will be kinder to his reputation than his second. Longfellow was the most famous American writer of his age, and the most widely admired, but even before his death in 1882 he was mercilessly parodied and pilloried. Poe dismissed Longfellow's work as fit only for "negrophilic old ladies of the north," and repeatedly accused him of plagiarism. Margaret Fuller likened Longfellow's derivative poetry to "a tastefully arranged Museum" in which there were "flowers of all climes, and wild flowers of none." Literary nationalists like Emerson and Whitman, while less hostile to the genial Longfellow, thought there was something un-American in Longfellow's catholic tastes in literature and wine.

During the early years of the twentieth century, every modernist poet and critic seemed to take a ritual swipe at Longfellow, the symbolic corpse of what Santayana called the "genteel tradition." T. E. Lawrence told Robert Graves that Ezra Pound had "spent his life trying to live down a family scandal: he's Longfellow's grand-nephew." The once generous swatch of pages devoted to Longfellow in the anthologies shrank to a poem or two until, in 1950, F. O. Matthiessen announced in his *New Oxford Book of American Poetry* that it was time to "smash the plaster bust" of Longfellow's "dead reputation." Meanwhile, Longfellow's once-popular epics, with their Gitche Gumees and Minnehahas, were invoked for laughs around a thousand campfires.

Despite his plummeting reputation, Longfellow retained a

quietly loyal readership, especially among writers who aimed for the "common" or middlebrow reader. Robert Frost, the shape and substance of whose career owed more to Longfellow than to any other American poet, called his first book of poems "A Boy's Will," a phrase drawn without acknowledgment from Longfellow's retrospective poem "My Lost Youth," which was in turn derived from a Lapland lament in Herder's German translation from an earlier Latin version.

Willa Cather, aspiring like Frost to reach the common reader as well as the literary elite, movingly invoked Longfellow in the closing pages of her best novel, *The Professor's House.* Alienated from his materialistic family, and sensing the nearness of death, Professor St. Peter remembers the lines "of a translation from the Norse" (actually the Anglo-Saxon) that

> he used to read long ago in one of his mother's few books, a little two-volume Ticknor and Fields edition of Longfellow in blue and gold, that used to lie on the parlour table:
>
> For thee a house was built
> Ere thou wast born;
> For thee a mould was made
> Ere thou of woman camest.

Even here, however, the summoning of Longfellow is made to seem slightly embarrassing, requiring the proper old-fashioned setting on the previous generation's parlor table.

The last serious attempt to take a fresh look at Longfellow's work was Newton Arvin's discerning monograph of 1963, which arrived at precisely the wrong moment to salvage Longfellow's reputation. The dominant New Critics, with their commitment to ambiguity, tension, and the rest of the creed of complexity, were dumbfounded by Longfellow's straightforward sentiments; a poem of Longfellow's, read blind by a bright group of Cambridge undergraduates, elicited the most hostile response of all the specimens in I. A. Richards's *Practical Criticism.* (One student wrote that the poem, "In the Churchyard of Cambridge," seemed "written in a state of semi-somnolence by a man with St. Vitus's dance.") The practice of the leading American poets during the early 1960s, committed to free-verse explorations of the tortured psyche, could hardly be farther from Longfellow's sunny and measured confidence. Poets who maintained an interest in formalist experiments, such as Richard Wilbur and Howard Nemerov, salvaged a few poems from Longfellow's massive oeuvre, "The Fire of Drift-Wood" and "Snow-Flakes"—exquisite poems that, in their aching gesturing toward unnamed griefs, seem untypical of Longfellow's main achievement. Longfellow's harsh fate seemed to be that resuscitation could only follow complete and utter extinction

There are signs that the time has arrived. During the last twenty years, a quiet Longfellow revival seems to have gained momentum. In his book *New England Literary Culture* (1986), the Harvard scholar Lawrence Buell offered a fresh assessment of Longfellow's New England tragedies, and accorded them a central place in his 1988 Penguin Classics selection of Longfellow's poetry. Two years later, the poet J. D. McClatchy published his superb Library of America volume of Longfellow's poetry and prose, which includes a deft selection of Longfellow's translations. Even Longfellow's children have elicited new interest; Christine Guth's *Longfellow's Tattoos* (2004) is an excellent study of Longfellow's wayward, globetrotting eldest son, Charles, who was one of the first significant Western visitors to Japan.

And now we have Christoph Irmscher's friendly and readable *Longfellow Redux,* which seeks to introduce a cosmopolitan and democratically multicultural Longfellow for our time. Irmscher considers Longfellow's life and work under four headings: his relations with his readers; his views of authorship; travel as theme and practice; and literary translation. All four topics might be subsumed under the notion of Longfellow's sheer openness to others—other people, other languages, other countries. Irmscher is struck by Longfellow's "relentless availability" to his readers, both in the relatively undemanding nature of his published work and in his willingness to answer letters from strangers, as many as twenty a day, and receive visitors at his mansion on Brattle Street in Cambridge. Whittier was convinced that his friend Longfellow was "driven to death by these incessant demands." Whitman, by contrast, said of the letters piling up in Camden, "I practically never answer them." Irmscher concludes that Longfellow regarded writing as "less a privilege than a civic obligation."

Similarly, Longfellow regarded the author as a humble craftsman, creating possibly perishable objects for a ready market. "The Village Blacksmith," memorably parodied by Buster Keaton, relishes the daily rhythms of production: "Each morning sees some task begun, / Each evening sees it close;/ Something attempted, something done, / Has earned a night's repose." A more sustained expression is Longfellow's excellent long poem about pottery, "Kéramos" (1877), which Irmscher calls Longfellow's "last great poetic apotheosis of the values of craftsmanship." Longfellow circles the globe in the poem—from his native town of Portland, Maine, to Delft and Italy, and on to Japan—with vignettes for each pottery-making locale. In his stress on pottery as something handmade and handled, Longfellow, Irmscher argues, rejects the separate aesthetic realm of Keats's Grecian urn or the landscape-dominating jar on Wallace Stevens's Tennessee hill. Longfellow's real subject is "the strange kinship between people and the things they make and use." When pots are broken, they are discarded—"Behind us in our path we cast / The broken potsherds of the past, / And all are ground to dust at last"—an unsentimental view of the function of art that Longfellow accorded to poetry as well.

I wish that Irmscher had not tried to align this unsentimental view of literary production with Longfellow's family life in Cambridge. He wishes to persuade us that "for Longfellow, being an author meant being a father," and that "the walls of the poet's study" were "as permeable as the borders of the text"—permeable to intrusions by his five children, that is. It is good to learn that Longfellow made himself available to his children, most movingly after the horrible death of his second wife, Fanny, in 1861, after her dress caught fire and Longfellow sought, unsuccessfully, to douse the flames. It is even possible that Longfellow, ahead of his time, "imagined the family not as the playground of patriarchal power . . . but as a potentially egalitarian and dehierarchized space." But Irmscher's attempts to apply this vision to what he calls "literary paternity" are strained at best.

More interesting is Irmscher's discussion of Longfellow's best-known poem about fatherhood, "The Children's Hour," so influential in its time that Henry James thought it should be retitled "The Children's *Century*." While conceding that the poem, in its evocation of a father in his study besieged by his three daughters, "drips" with sentimentality, Irmscher thinks "the little text is less easy than it looks." (Charles Ives's haunting musical setting of the poem is further evidence of unsuspected depths.) Irmscher puts particular pressure on the seventh quatrain: "They almost devour me with kisses, / Their arms about me entwine, / Till I think of the Bishop of Bingen / In his Mouse-Tower on the Rhine!" The allusion is to the archbishop of Mainz, whose solution to a famine was to torch the barn in which he had assembled the poor townspeople. They get their revenge when an army of mice scales the walls of the tower on the Rhine where the bishop has taken refuge and devours him, and not with kisses. Irmscher plausibly suggests that Longfellow transforms the Mouse Tower of Bingen, besieged by "the patter of little feet," into a "Bluebeard-like fortress" in which the possessive father wishes to imprison his daughters. In discerning a violent subtext to the poem, Irmscher stops short of aligning it with "the tradition behind Goya's gruesome painting *Saturn Devouring His Child*." Nevertheless, he is surely right to discern a darker strain in a poem in which we least expect to find it.

No one has gone more deeply and sympathetically into Longfellow's work as a translator. Irmscher concedes Fuller's assessment of Longfellow's lack of originality, and tries to convert it into a virtue. "I contend that Longfellow was fully aware of the mediated, irrepressibly allusive nature of his literary work." Irmscher reminds us that Longfellow was the first professor of modern languages at Harvard, a field that barely existed, and the first to teach a class on *Faust*. Longfellow assembled and published his own foreign dictionaries and anthologies of world poetry; no one was more of a bridge "between the past and the present, Europe and America, the world of poetry and the man or woman on the street."

After Fanny's death in 1861, Longfellow assumed the task of translating the entire *Divine Comedy,* meeting regularly with his "Dante Club" to try out individual cantos. The time was ripe for translation, as Van Wyck Brooks noted long ago, with Bayard Taylor working on his version of *Faust* and T. W. Higginson translating Epictetus. Irmscher, carefully comparing the original Italian with Longfellow's successive drafts, makes a spirited defense of Longfellow's archaisms and involutions. Longfellow didn't subscribe to the modern aim of literary translators to create a plausible English poem. Instead, he anticipated Walter Benjamin's conviction that a translation should reflect the imprint and irreducible strangeness of the original. The results, especially where Longfellow sought to preserve the sound of the original, can seem daunting to a modern reader: "Upon this journey, whence thou givest him vaunt, / Things did he hear, which the occasion were / Both of his victor and the papal mantle."

Irmscher has fun with *The Song of Hiawatha,* Longfellow's "experiment in literary bilingualism" of 1855, noting that the poem sometimes "reads like a draft of a translation abandoned halfway through." The poem was almost immediately parodied, of course, most memorably perhaps in Lewis Carroll's "Hiawatha Photographing": "From his shoulder Hiawatha / Took the camera of rosewood, / Made of sliding, folding rosewood; / Neatly put it all together. / In its case it lay compactly, / Folded into nearly nothing." There is more to say about Longfellow and photography. Julia Margaret Cameron's great photograph of Longfellow, taken in England in 1868, captures our lasting image of Longfellow as long-haired and bearded Victorian sage, his hand and profile, as Irmscher notes, pointing in opposite directions. Longfellow's face, singed in the fire that killed his wife, couldn't tolerate a razor. Another photograph, shot in the Rockies, inspired his beautiful sonnet commemorating her death: "There is a mountain in the distant West / That, sun-defying, in its deep ravines / Displays a cross of snow upon its side. / Such is the cross I wear upon my breast, / These eighteen years, through all the changing scenes, / And seasons, changeless since the day she died."

VOLUME REVIEWED

*Longfellow Redux*
By Christoph Irmscher
University of Illinois Press, 2006

# The Mystery of Emily Dickinson

TO PREPARE A NEW EDITION of a poet's work, a scholar may spend years in the archives, weeding out the "corruptions" planted by previous editors and scribes, only to see his own decisions denounced by the next generation of editors. In his poem "The Scholars," W. B. Yeats saw a comic contrast between the passionate poet and the painstaking editor:

> Old, learned, respectable bald heads
> Edit and annotate the lines
> That young men, tossing on their beds,
> Rhymed out in love's despair.

For a century now, however, the editing of Emily Dickinson's poetry has been entangled with human passions, sex, and blindered partiality, as though the editors were (and sometimes they were) the despairing lovers tossing on their beds. Despite impressive scholarly attempts, by Thomas Johnson in 1955 and now by Ralph Franklin, to resolve disputes and provide a text based on widely shared principles, there are already indications that the squabbles initiated a hundred years ago will continue, and perhaps even intensify, in the wake of Franklin's careful work. This unsettled situation arises from several factors, including Dickinson's own fraught relations with publishers; the strange fate of her manuscripts after her death; current critical views of her work; and, finally, the very nature of her poetry.

1.

Audacity marked Emily Dickinson's career from the beginning—if "career" is the right word for her improbable persistence in the face of patronizing advice and general incomprehension. She was born in 1830, the middle child of three. Her privileged childhood as a lawyer's daughter in Amherst, Massachusetts, gave her the time and literary education, as well as the confidence, to try her hand at writing verse. Her father, she noted affectionately, was "too busy with his Briefs—to notice what we do—He buys me many Books—but begs me not to read them—because he fears they joggle the Mind." After a solid course of study at the private Amherst Academy, she spent a year at the Mount Holyoke Female Seminary a few miles away in South Hadley. Though she found the religious rigor of the founder Mary Lyon's regimen somewhat oppressive, she enjoyed her fellow students, who were not as "rough & uncultivated" as she snobbishly expected. In her letters home we can already see her imaginative way of making national events her own. "Wont you please tell me when you answer my letter who the candidate for President is?" she wrote her brother Austin in the fall of 1847, when she was sixteen.

> I have been trying to find out ever since I came here & have not yet succeeded. . . . Has the Mexican war terminated yet & how? Are we beat? Do you know of any nation about to besiege South Hadley? If so, do inform me of it, for I would be glad of a chance to escape, if we are to be stormed. I suppose Miss Lyon would furnish us all with daggers & order us to fight for our lives, in case such perils should befall us.

The "mind-joggling" intellectual debates of her time, such as revivalism versus the inroads of modern science, elicited a similarly wry and idiosyncratic response from her, as in this early verse epigram:

> "Faith" is a fine invention
> When Gentlemen can *see*—
> But *Microscopes* are prudent
> In an Emergency.

During her twenties, as she settled into her life in her family's capacious and conspicuous house on Main Street (hardly the frontier outpost suggested by its nickname "The Homestead"), Dickinson was part of a lively circle of friends with literary tastes that included Susan Gilbert, her future sister-in-law. At times, Dickinson seemed as infatuated with Susan as her brother, Austin, was. "I love you as dearly, Susie, as when love first began, on the step at the front door," she wrote in 1855. When Susan and Austin, who were married the following year, moved next door into the Italianate villa known as the Evergreens, the circle became even tighter. Dickinson wove snatches of verse and even complete poems into her lyrical correspondence with Susan, such as her birthday greeting for 1858, which begins:

> One Sister have I in our house—
> And one, a hedge away.
> There's only one recorded,
> But both belong to me.

Such "letter-poems," as Susan called them, gave Dickinson a chance to try out poetic strategies without committing herself to an audience beyond the trusted recipient.

Emily Dickinson turned thirty in 1860. She had never formally submitted poems for publication, though Susan—turning, as she later put it, "love to larceny"—had sent some of Dickinson's verses to friends like Samuel Bowles, the dashing editor of the local *Springfield Daily Republican.* On March 1, 1862, the following poem by Dickinson appeared in the *Republican:*

> Safe in their alabaster chambers,
> Untouched by morning,
> And untouched by noon,
> Sleep the meek members of the Resurrection,
> Rafter of satin, and roof of stone.
>
> Light laughs the breeze
> In her castle above them,
> Babbles the bee in a stolid ear,
> Pipe the sweet birds in ignorant cadence:
> Ah! What sagacity perished here!

Susan criticized the second stanza of this now famous poem, and Dickinson sent her an alternative, with the note, "Perhaps this verse would please you better—Sue." In the new ending, Dickinson substituted planetary and political cycles for the birds and bees, amplifying the contrast between the noisy life above and the dead asleep in their tombs.

> Grand go the Years—in the Crescent—above them—
> Worlds scoop their Arcs—
> And Firmaments—row—
> Diadems—drop—and Doges—surrender—
> Soundless as dots—on a Disc of snow—

Susan liked this ending even less.[1] Perhaps to emphasize the Resurrection, which is all but obliterated in those alliterative dots and discs, the devout Susan advised Dickinson to cut her losses and treat the first stanza as a complete poem. "Strange things always go alone," Susan told her sententiously, "as there is only one Gabriel and one Sun."

Emboldened by the publication of the poem, and frustrated with Susan's response, Dickinson was ready to aim for a wider and more sophisticated audience. In April 1862, six weeks after the appearance of "Safe in their Alabaster Chambers," she enclosed it (with the ending Susan liked least) and three others in a letter to Thomas Wentworth Higginson, a well-known man of letters from Boston. Higginson, a kindly man with "bird-lidded eyes" and "inalienable muttonchop whiskers" (Edmund Wilson's description), had written a column in the *Atlantic* offering advice to young contributors. "Are you too deeply occupied," she wrote Higginson, "to say if my Verse is alive? The Mind is so near itself—it cannot see, distinctly—and I have none to ask."

It was at this juncture that Dickinson's courage as a poet was confirmed, for Higginson was not encouraging. A conventional poet and nature writer himself, he dutifully pointed out her departures from those conventions. We don't know exactly what he said (his letters, like most others sent to Dickinson, were destroyed at her request after her death), but her follow-up letters quoted some of his strictures. She thanked him, twice, for his "surgery," but didn't change a thing in her poems. She magisterially deflected the words that must have hurt:

> You think my gait "spasmodic"—I am in danger—Sir—
> You think me "uncontrolled"—I have no Tribunal.

And to his most sweeping piece of advice, she is even more imperious: "I smile when you suggest that I delay 'to publish'—that being foreign to my thought, as Firmament to Fin." She is like Coriolanus (one of her favorites among Shakespeare's characters), who, when exiled from Rome, retorts, "I banish you!"

It is difficult to separate the defiance from the defensiveness in Dickinson's letters to Higginson. The wonder is that with so little encouragement, she had the inner strength and ambition to keep at her task, and the confidence to know that her eccentricities of language—"spasmodic," "uncontrolled," "wayward"—were her strengths. She had no use for the conventional verse Higginson admired, and advised him of her resolution to "never consciously touch a paint, mixed by another person." She knew that her own poems, if they were beautiful, had a new kind of beauty: "Myself the only Kangaroo among the Beauty." In this regard she resembles Whitman, though she told Higginson, who evidently saw the resemblance, "I never read his Book—but was told that he was disgraceful."

Rather than feeling discouraged, Dickinson seems to have taken provocation from her correspondence with Higginson. The following year, 1863, was her most productive (and not, as Ralph Franklin points out, 1862, as had previously been thought); she wrote or arrived at finished versions of nearly three hundred poems during that year alone. Though ten of her poems were published, none at her own instigation, during her lifetime, she was never seriously tempted by publication again. She did keep an orderly record of hundreds and hundreds of her poems, however, making sure at the same time that many more were in the hands of trusted friends.

2.

A week after Dickinson's death in 1886 from kidney failure, her sister Lavinia discovered in the Dickinson house a locked chest that held forty hand-sewn albums of Dickinson's poems in manuscript, as well as many more poems neatly copied on loose sheets. Determined to get these "7 hundred wonderful poems" published, and with no literary expertise herself, Lavinia approached the two potential editors least likely to agree on anything. First she asked her sister-in-law, Susan Dickinson, an obvious choice, since Susan, an amateur poet and occasional journalist, had received more poems from Emily—some 250—than anyone else. When Susan dawdled at the considerable task of choosing among the more than a thousand poems at her disposal, Lavinia asked her to return the albums. In a decision that showed perhaps as much hostility as impatience, Lavinia turned in early 1888 to Mabel Loomis Todd, wife of an astronomy professor at Amherst College. Mabel Todd, whom her biographer Polly Longsworth describes in an entry in the *Emily Dickinson Encyclopedia* as "a pretty, vivacious woman with limpid brown eyes and bewitching mouth," had been Austin Dickinson's not very secret mistress for several years.[2] While Mabel had corresponded with Emily Dickinson, and received poems from her, they had never met face to face—a concession, apparently, to propriety.

Working in conjunction with Thomas Wentworth Higginson, who was now free to perform the surgery that Dickinson had resisted, Mabel produced three popular volumes of Dickinson's poetry from 1890 to 1896. Higginson and Todd have been much criticized for regularizing the rhyme schemes, punctuation, and capitalization of Dickinson's manuscripts, rendering her work more palatable to turn-of-the-century taste. (Faced with Dickinson's line "I wish I were a Hay," for example, Higginson switched "a" to "the," since "everybody would say that *hay* is a collective noun requiring the definite article.")

Even in their cleaned-up versions, the poems were regarded as boldly innovative in language and subject. The approximate rhymes still grated for traditionalists; "'Alcohol' does not rhyme to 'pearl,'" as one English reviewer complained of the now familiar poem "I taste a liquor never brewed." When anomalous or experimental poems by other poets appeared during the 1890s, they were often compared to Dickinson. The ironic, free-verse parables in Stephen Crane's *Black Riders,* perhaps the most original American poetic production of the 1890s, displayed for one critic an "audacity of . . . conception, suggesting a mind not without kinship to Emily Dickinson's." And Alice James, the brilliant sister of William and Henry James, noted with patriotic pleasure that British critics were deaf to Dickinson's peculiarly American excellence. "It is reassuring to hear the British pronouncement that Emily Dickinson is fifth-rate," she reflected in January 1892, "they have such a capacity for missing quality; the robust evades them equally with the subtle."

Mabel Todd, who had published stories and travel sketches in prominent magazines, was an effective publicist for Dickinson's poems, attracting the attention of William Dean Howells (who welcomed this "distinctive addition to the literature of the world") among others. But whatever gratitude she had earned from the Dickinsons was shattered when Austin Dickinson died in 1895, leaving a strip of land to his mistress in his will. Lavinia was outraged, and sued Todd successfully for the recovery of the land. The rift between Mabel and Susan, each of whom possessed a substantial collection of manuscript material, was eventually bequeathed to their daughters. From 1914 to 1945 more poems and letters appeared in dueling editions edited by Martha Dickinson Bianchi and Millicent Todd Bingham. With Bingham's publication of *Bolts of Melody* in 1945, nearly all Dickinson's poems had appeared in print, with various degrees of editorial intervention. It fell to Thomas Johnson, a noted scholar of early American poetry enlisted by the Harvard University Press, to make order among these many editions.

Johnson's three-volume variorum edition of 1955, and the publication of Dickinson's letters three years later, marked a watershed in the public response to Dickinson. Readers had a fresh sense of Dickinson's idiosyncratic poetic practice—her pervasive use, for example, of dashes, and of unexpectedly capitalized words. Her best-known poem at the time, "Because I could not stop for Death," gained a stanza previously excised by Todd and Higginson. And Johnson's edition recorded the alternative words—sometimes placed at the bottom of the page, sometimes between the lines, and sometimes floating in the margins—that Dickinson marked on her later manuscripts, as her interest in publication waned. There was a general feeling that here at last was the "real" Dickinson, the poems as she had written them. Readers skeptical of her achievement were now persuaded. "Did I really make snide remarks about Emily Dickinson?" Elizabeth Bishop wrote Robert Lowell in 1956. "I like, or at least admire, her a great deal more now—probably because of that good new edition, really. I spent another stretch absorbed in that, and think . . . that she's about the best we have."

But there were problems with the Johnson edition, and they increased over time. Forced to work from photostats of many of the poems, Johnson made errors of transcription. Manuscripts unknown to him, generally variants of already familiar poems, continued to surface. And scholarly debates about the dating and the arrangement of poems on the page proliferated. For some time it has been evident that a new edition of Dickinson's poems was needed. Ralph Franklin, director of the Beinecke Rare Book and Manuscript Library at Yale, and the author of a searching monograph, *The Editing of Emily Dickinson* (1967), seemed the obvious choice for the job. Franklin's edition is more an updating and correction of Johnson's edition than an overturning of it, and some of the changes will merely cause inconvenience. Since Franklin has redated many of the poems, Johnson's numbers—until now the accepted way of identifying Dickinson's untitled poems—are now obsolete.

But Franklin has made startling discoveries through the whole corpus of poems, now numbering 1,789 to Johnson's 1,775, which will help silence the cynical view that this new edition is Harvard University's way of retaining the lucrative copyright on Dickinson's work into the next millennium. He includes seventeen poems not in the Johnson edition. Many of these are short passages of verse, couplets and triplets, set apart from the prose of Dickinson's letters, like this typical example from the early 1860s:

No Rose, yet felt myself a'bloom,
No Bird—yet rode in Ether—

Franklin's research has led him to conclude that certain texts previously published as separate poems are in fact fragments of other poems. (The final poem in Johnson's edition, which begins with the words "The earth has many keys," is now identified as the ending from an earlier draft of the well-known and much-anthologized poem about a cricket, "Further in Summer than the Birds," which ends, in Johnson, "Antiquest felt at Noon / When August burning low / Arise this spectral Canticle / Repose to typify / Remit as yet no Grace / No Furrow on the Glow / Yet a Druidic Difference / Enhances Nature now.") Other poems, previously thought to be parts of the same poem, are now separated. And five texts treated as poems by Johnson, such as the rhythmic letter to Austin that is the second poem in the Johnson edition ("There is another sky, ever serene and fair, and there is another sunshine, though it be darkness there") are excluded by Franklin, since they are not arranged as verse in Dickinson's manuscript. While conceding that "there is no definite boundary between prose and poetry in Dickinson's letters," Franklin provides enough information in his annotations to make his decisions clear.

Those who argue that the absence of a "definite" boundary means there is no boundary at all will not be satisfied with this new edition. But I think there will be wide agreement regarding most of Franklin's editorial decisions. He states his principles clearly and does not conceal his uncertainties (about the dating of individual poems, for example). He is deeply respectful of Dickinson's writing practices, following her often erratic spelling and, "within the capacity of standard type," her capitalization and punctuation. His textual apparatus is informative without being intrusive, and includes such useful information as where Dickinson broke her lines on her manuscript sheets, as well as any other information—pinned attachments, tears in the paper, and the like—that might have a bearing on interpretation. All scholars and readers of Dickinson are in his debt.

## 3.

As part of the preliminary work for his edition of the poems, Ralph Franklin brought out in 1981 a facsimile edition of Dickinson's hand-sewn albums, or "fascicles" (as Mabel Todd called them), entitled *The Manuscript Books of Emily Dickinson.* The fascicles had been unbound during the 1890s, and Franklin reconstituted the order of the poems, which required the most painstaking analysis of paper type, handwriting, holes, and folds. The publication of the poems in facsimile has inspired, somewhat surprisingly, some of the most influential criticism on Dickinson's work of the past two decades. Critics have debated whether Dickinson's ordering of the poems in the fascicles suggested a structure of meaning as well as convenience, and whether her handwriting was deliberately expressive. Since Franklin has done more to publicize the fascicles than anyone else, it is surprising that he himself has found no evidence for treating the fascicles as "careful constructs governed by theme, imagery, narrative and dramatic movement, or similar principle."

Franklin has made some discoveries since the publication of the "manuscript books," however, and a couple of these seem to me to suggest that some of the poems have at least some thematic order. Consider for example the following lines, first published in 1891, then as Poem 18 in the Johnson edition:

> The Gentian weaves her fringes—
> The Maple's loom is red—
> My departing blossoms
> Obviate parade.
>
> A brief, but patient illness—
> An hour to prepare—
> And one below, this morning
> Is where the angels are—
> It was a short procession,
> The Bobolink was there—
> An aged Bee addressed us—
> And then we knelt in prayer—
> We trust that she was willing—

We ask that we may be—
Summer—Sister—Seraph!
Let us go with thee!

In the name of the Bee—
And of the Butterfly—
And of the Breeze—Amen!

In his new edition of the poems, Franklin announces, astonishingly, that "The Gentian weaves her fringes" is not one poem but three. He bases this discovery on a hitherto unnoticed principle of division. "On earlier sheets [of the fascicles], which contain poems of more than one stanza, ED drew lines of separation where poem breaks needed to be distinguished from stanza breaks. On this final sheet, she did not draw lines, leaving only a blank space between poems, for here the distinction was unnecessary: every poem, regardless of length or form, was copied as a single stanza." On the sheet with the "Gentian" poem, according to Franklin, "Dickinson appears to have been cleaning up, taking in various pieces lying at hand, including small ones such as 'In the name of the bee.'" I think that Franklin is right, and a couple of other examples of such fascicle pages—heretofore treated as single poems and now separated—are even more convincing.

And yet how tempting it is to read the three stanzas appended to "The Gentian" as somehow related. The speaking flower of the first stanza says that her departing blossoms "Obviate parade," but in the second stanza "a short procession" is arranged anyway. And what better words for that aged bee to intone than "In the name of the Bee—/ And of the Butterfly—/ And of the Breeze—Amen!"? If the three stanzas aren't part of the same poem, could they make up a poetic sequence? It is easy enough to imagine Dickinson "taking in various pieces lying at hand" and arranging them in an order that makes more sense than, say, these three stanzas in reverse, starting with "In the name of the Bee."

Do such local linkings of poems mean that the fascicles in general are poetic sequences? Not at all. Just as a poet preparing a book for publication may associate certain lyrics with others, while at the same time leaving other poems more or less on their own, Dickinson probably had no grand principles of organization for her manuscript books. Twenty-five years of avid searching, and several books, have brought no convincing structural schemes to light. Those inclined to find patterns in the fascicles will continue to find them; those disinclined won't.

The wide availability of Dickinson's texts in facsimile has sparked a related debate about the possible expressive intent of Dickinson's handwriting. Martha Nell Smith, a ubiquitous and influential feminist scholar of Dickinson's work, asks us in her book *Rowing in Eden* (1992) to notice the "wide-mouthed *W*" in the first stanza of Dickinson's popular love poem "Wild nights," contributing in her view to the "breathless sexuality" of the poem:

> Wild nights—Wild nights!
> Were I with thee
> Wild nights should be
> Our luxury!

Critics like Smith treat Dickinson as a calligrapher, as much a visual artist as a verbal one. They believe that Dickinson's run-over lines are themselves expressive, and do not—as Johnson and Franklin believe—simply mean that she ran out of space on her often narrow sheets and scraps of paper. So Smith insists that the final stanza of "Wild Nights" is made up of five lines instead of four:

> Rowing in Eden—
> Ah! The Sea!
> Might I but Moor—
> Tonight—
> In Thee!

The word "Moor" almost reaches the right-hand margin of the manuscript sheet, and "Tonight," the run-over word, is pretty long. But Smith argues that to print the poem as Franklin does, as a four-line stanza (with the third line as "Might I but moor—tonight—"), eliminates Dickinson's "unconventional lineation" as well as the "passionate pause, consonant with the poem's sensual suggestions." Of course, it is possible to read the poem in this "breathless" way. But Smith's treatment of "Tonight" as a "passionate pause" vulgarizes, to my ear, a poem that is wittily aware of its own excesses. And what exactly would a closed-mouth *W* look like?

There can be no serious doubt that Dickinson played with her handwriting. She adjusted it to the bizarre shapes of the scraps of envelopes and stationery on which she often drafted poems, curled around watermarks and printed headings, and employed bold strokes like "the stunning flourish" that, as Smith notes, "crosses both T's in 'Tonight.'" Whether such characteristics, hardly foreign to the manuscripts of other poets, should be treated as essential to understanding the meaning of the poems is another question altogether. John Hollander and others have argued that Dickinson, had she allowed her poems to be printed, would have yielded to editorial regularizing. (She did not complain, for example, about how "Safe in their Alabaster Chambers" was printed, with her dashes and capitalizations eliminated, in the Springfield newspaper.)

Martha Nell Smith, in her contribution to a new collection of essays called *The Emily Dickinson Handbook,* takes the extreme position that Dickinson, at least in the later fascicles with their frequently unresolved word choices, was not writing "with the printed page in mind." In Smith's view, Dickinson was deliberately inviting her future readers to "pick and choose" among the variant wordings of her apparently unfinished manuscripts. Smith adopts a liberationist rhetoric in her effort to "free" Dickinson from editors' attempts to "fix" and "finish" her manuscripts by "translating" them into print. She shares the view of the poet and Dickinson scholar Susan Howe that there is something typically male about these editorial practices. ("It takes a woman," Howe has written, "to see clearly the condescending tone of these male editors when they talk about their work on the texts.")

Smith wants a Dickinson "*un*bound and liberated from the fixed patternings that books cannot eschew." In an interesting combination of pre-Gutenberg aesthetics and postmodern technology, she claims that the best manner of publishing Dickinson is to reproduce her handwriting electronically. "Computer technologies that will enable distribution of facsimiles across the World Wide Web and on CD-ROM . . . create even more possibilities for thorough critical interrogations of the material evidence left by the poet at work." The Internet, according to Smith, "encourages pliant and accommodating principles of judgment" and "readers' free play."

Smith, Howe, and their supporters, who have now formed the Dickinson Editing Collective, deserve credit for raising questions about Dickinson's writing practices. But their some-assembly-required procedures, where the reader is invited to "coauthor" Dickinson's poems, are not how most readers expect to encounter poetry. (If you don't like the opening lines of "I measure every Grief I meet / With narrow, probing, eyes," just click the mouse and substitute Dickinson's alternative, "Analytic eyes.") The end result of such technological innovations will be to make a poet already regarded as eccentric seem even more so.

4.

Martha Nell Smith wants to undo the "fixity and finality" of the poems as printed by Johnson and others. You might think that she would be drawn to a similarly open-ended view of Dickinson's psychology. But precisely where we could expect to find fluidity, in a passionately imaginative unmarried woman's relations with men and women, Smith identifies a coded landscape with a single key. In a bold argument aired in the *New York Times* Sunday magazine,[3] Smith claims that Dickinson and her sister-in-law, Susan, were lovers, hence the subtitle of her edition, jointly edited with Ellen Louise Hart, of "Emily Dickinson's Intimate Letters" to Sue. The letters, Smith told the *Times,* are "powerful witness to a lesbian passion." Smith and Hart argue that Dickinson's "ongoing passion" survived "the unavoidable shift in Susan's availability once she undertakes her wifely duties" in her marriage with Austin Dickinson in 1856.

The biographical assertions of Smith and Hart can be seen as the latest in a long history of Dickinson biography to identify Dickinson's elusive lover. The initial impetus for this search came, oddly enough, from Susan Dickinson herself (as Marietta Messmer points out in the *Handbook*), followed by her daughter Martha Dickinson Bianchi's fingering of the Reverend Charles Wadsworth. The definitive statement about all such efforts to pin down Dickinson's affections comes from Elizabeth Bishop, in her review of Rebecca Patterson's *The Riddle of Emily Dickinson,* which appeared in the *New Republic* in 1952. Patterson, like Smith and Hart, thought the "riddle" of Dickinson's life and work could be solved by attention to her love affairs with women—first, according to Patterson, with Susan, and then with another friend, Kate Anthon. "That her thesis is partially true," wrote Bishop, "might have occurred to any reader of Emily Dickinson's poetry—occurred on one page to be contradicted on the next, that is."

No one has ever denied that Emily Dickinson wrote passionate letters to Susan before and after Susan's marriage. "Oh Susie," she writes on a stormy night in 1852, "I would nestle close to your warm heart, and never hear the wind blow, or the storm beat, again. Is there any room there for me, or shall I wander away all homeless and alone? Thank you for loving me, darling." Carroll Smith-Rosenberg, in her influential work on what she calls "the female world of love and ritual," demonstrated how common such gushing rhetoric was among women friends in nineteenth-century America. But Smith and Hart are out to show that "Emily and Susan's relationship surpasses in depth, passion, and continuity the stereotype of the 'intimate exchange' between women friends of the period."

Smith and Hart make much of the fact that Dickinson's letters to Susan were selectively mutilated after her death. Susan's name was erased from some of the poems Dickinson sent to her, and affectionate passages in the letters were crossed out or excised. In *Rowing in Eden,* Smith argued that "the censorship of Dickinson's papers at the end of the century suggests that her passionate friendship with Sue was not simply innocent." In *Open Me Carefully,* Smith and Hart do not claim that the mutilation of Dickinson's letters, which they ascribe to Mabel Todd, was a nervous cover-up of a lesbian relationship. Instead, they argue that Todd was trying "to hide Susan's central role in Dickinson's writing process," and to "suppress any trace of Susan as Emily's primary audience." For Todd and Higginson, "the most marketable image of Dickinson the poet was that of the eccentric, reclusive, asexual woman in white." Smith and Hart want to substitute a passionate Dickinson whose literary relationship with her sister-in-law was "collaborative," and whose correspondence with Sue alludes "to unkempt appearance, shared cups of coffee, and private interludes, which Susan's daughter Martha described as taking place in the back hallway of the Homestead."

The evidence for literary collaboration in those back hallways is slight and unconvincing. "Susan was the only reader at whose behest Emily changed a poem," writes Smith in her entry on Susan in *An Emily Dickinson Encyclopedia.*[4] The wording suggests that there might have been more than one poem changed. But some unfinished drafts included in *Open Me Carefully* as evidence of collaboration were in fact, according to Ralph Franklin, sent to Susan after Dickinson's death. Susan's remarks on the one poem she is known to have discussed with Dickinson, "Safe in their Alabaster Chambers," were high-handed and wrongheaded, and Dickinson wisely ignored them. Susan's obituary for Dickinson, reproduced in *Open Me Carefully,* strikes a condescending note, praising Dickinson's poems for "their simplicity and homeliness" and their lack of any identifiable "creed." Dickinson, "hardly knowing the names of dogmas, . . . walked this life with the gentleness and reverence of old saints." For Susan, Dickinson was an innocent child of nature, to be praised in a tired and sentimental sequence of comparisons as "a part of the high March sky, the summer day and bird-call."

5.

Dickinson's erotic life is one of the many unknown things about her, and she evidently preferred to keep it so. We don't know what she looked like as an adult (the lone daguerreotype shows her as a seventeen-year-old); what audience, if any, her poetry was intended for; why she gradually withdrew from society. She assiduously guarded her privacy, and spoke, to Higginson and others, in a deliberately riddling way, shrugging off his questions ("You ask of my Companions Hills—Sir—and the Sundown"). "All men say 'What' to me," she told him, "but I thought it a fashion." As a consequence of her reticence, it has been easy for her many and diverse admirers to invent their own private Emily: Emily the fierce feminist; Emily the pliant lover; Emily the "voice of war"; Emily the prophet of modernism; Emily the guardian of old New England; and so on. But it is the reticence itself that tells us most about Emily Dickinson.

The overwhelming impression conveyed in Dickinson's letters to Susan Dickinson and to her other correspondents is of someone who couldn't stand—who had a visceral shudder in the presence of—the flatulent rhetoric of church and state around her. I don't believe that her feelings toward Susan were modified by Susan's "availability" after her marriage to Austin. I think they cooled when Dickinson discovered that Susan was conventional in her language and in her religious views, and that Susan tolerated her and enjoyed her poems as one might enjoy the quirky writings of a child.

Susan was not equipped to understand that Dickinson's genius lay in her brittleness of language, and her refusal to indulge in the dead metaphors and sentimental nature worship that studded Susan's prose. Dickinson was out to purge her own language of deadness. This is what she meant when she asked Higginson whether her verse was "alive." This is what she was trying to explain when she told him that she shunned men and women "because they talk of Hallowed things, aloud—and embarrass my Dog." This is why people constantly disappointed her, including Higginson, who remarked after an intense visit with Dickinson in 1870 that "she often thought me tired." With Higginson, with Susan, and others, infatuation yielded to a friendly formality, as Dickinson increasingly preferred the company of children, animals, and people of her father's more restrained generation.

Already in her teenage year at Mount Holyoke Dickinson had shown her intellectual honesty in her refusal to count herself among the "saved." Hollow religious language disgusted her: "He preached upon 'Breadth' till it argued him narrow . . . The Truth never flaunted a Sign—/ Simplicity fled from his counterfeit presence / As Gold the Pyrites would shun." Dickinson was immune to the war fever around her as well. Scholars have combed her verse and prose for mention of the Civil War, which coincided with her greatest outpouring of verse. But her inspiration during those years seems to have been resistance to high rhetoric. A reference to bells tolling here and to bullets there has been adduced to show her awareness of the war. (As though she could have been oblivious to it!) But Edmund Wilson may well be right in claiming that she never referred to the Civil War in her poetry. Her father's commitment to the Whig values of compromise—he had served a term in Congress and campaigned for Zachary Taylor and Henry Clay—may have tempered her response. While Julia Ward Howe was writing her saber-rattling "Battle Hymn of the Republic," and Whitman his "Drum-Taps," Dickinson was quietly demolishing myths of heroic pomposity:

> Finding is the first Act
> The second, loss,
> Third, Expedition for the "Golden Fleece"
>
> Fourth, no Discovery—
> Fifth, no Crew—
> Finally, no Golden Fleece—
> Jason, sham, too—

Dickinson's language, oblique and sharply objective, can be seen as one response to the degraded verbiage of the Civil War era, and the Gilded Age pieties that followed. This is one explanation for her special appeal to such poets and translators of her work as Paul Celan (discussed in an essay in *The Emily Dickinson Handbook* by Kerstin Behnke) and Eugenio Montale.[5] In these poets we find a kindred prosody of obliquity and harsh specificity in the face of the degradation of the Italian language under Mussolini and the German language under the Nazis. That the leading German-language poet of the post-Nazi era and the leading Italian poet of this century looked to Emily Dickinson should invite us to read her in this way, as a voice raised against the pompous posturing of both sides. She once mentioned to Higginson her adamant resolution to "never try to lift the words which I cannot hold." She never did. In its modesty and majesty, it could serve as her epitaph.

NOTES

1. Dickinson eventually wrote two more endings for the poem. For a useful analysis of Dickinson's departures from poetic conventions in this and other poems, see Elizabeth A. Petrino, *Emily Dickinson and Her Contemporaries: Women's Verse in America, 1820–1885* (Hanover, N.H.: University Press of New England, 1998). In a chapter entitled "'Alabaster Chambers': Dickinson, Epitaphs, and the Culture of Mourning," Petrino argues that Dickinson's poems about the dead are "closer to the acerbic wit of the Puritan graveyards than to the mawkishness of the nineteenth-century elegy."

2. Jane Donahue Eberwein, ed., *An Emily Dickinson Encyclopedia* (Westport, Conn.: Greenwood Press, 1998), 289.

3. November 29, 1998.

4. See Eberwein, *An Emily Dickinson Encyclopedia,* 78.

5. Montale's versions of Dickinson are included in *Emily Dickinson: Tutte le Poesie,* edited by Marisa Bulgheroni (Milan: Mondadori, 1997). Celan's eight translations date from 1961.

VOLUMES REVIEWED

*The Poems of Emily Dickinson: Variorum Edition*
Edited by R.W. Franklin
3 vols.
Belknap Press of Harvard University Press, 1998

*Open Me Carefully: Emily Dickinson's Intimate Letters to Susan Huntington Dickinson*
Edited by Ellen Louise Hart and Martha Nell Smith
Paris Press, 1998

*The Emily Dickinson Handbook*
Edited by Gudrun Grabher, Roland Hagenbüchle, and Cristanne Miller
University of Massachusetts Press, 1998

## The Convert

FOR MOST AMERICANS, the name Emma Lazarus is likely to recall at best a brief injunction associated with the Statue of Liberty: "Give me your tired, your poor, / Your huddled masses yearning to breathe free." Frédéric-Auguste Bartholdi's statue *Liberty Enlightening the World* was a gift from the people of France, meant to serve as a monument to a hundred years of friendship between the two nations conceived in *Liberté*. If the statue was free, the considerable costs associated with its installation were not. Congress agreed to pay for erecting and maintaining it, but balked at paying for the pedestal. Various schemes were launched to raise funds, amid widespread ridicule. Montague Marks, an art critic who later married Lazarus's younger sister Agnes, compared the torch to "an immense double tooth which has just been extracted from some unfortunate mastodon." Friends of the architect Richard Morris Hunt, who had designed the pedestal for the statue for Bedloe's Island (renamed Liberty Island in 1956), decided in May 1883 to organize a benefit exhibition. Emma Lazarus, a close friend of several of the artists involved, was asked by the writer Constance Cary Harrison to write a poem for the catalog.

Lazarus was reluctant at first to write anything "to order." Besides, she was not particularly fond of France or French society. "Take away the Louvre & the pictures & the statues," she wrote of Paris, "& I should never wish to see it again." She had just returned from her first trip abroad, where she had sought to raise funds for a completely different cause: the plight of Russian Jews recently arrived in New York City. It was only when she saw a way to link her concern for Russian refugees with the colossal statue destined for New York Harbor that she managed to fulfill the commission. Borrowing some of the rhymes and key words from Shelley's "Ozymandias," she wrote a sonnet with the title "The New Colossus." The poem dramatically recast the meaning of Bartholdi's statue, which Lazarus viewed not as a symbol of *amitié* between nations but as an invitation to refugees from the Old World to find sanctuary in the New:

> Here at our sea-washed, sunset gates shall stand
> A mighty woman with a torch, whose flame
> Is the imprisoned lightning, and her name
> Mother of Exiles. From her beacon-hand
> Glows world-wide welcome.

There is an irony here, and the scholar and poet Esther Schor, in her lively, short, and deftly argued biography, is quick to note it. For Emma Lazarus could hardly be considered an immigrant herself. She was at least a fourth-generation American, with as much claim to native descent as any Mayflower descendant. Her refugee status, if one could call it that, dated from 1492, when the Jews were expelled from Spain and Portugal. Some of these made their way to South America and then, in 1654, to New Amsterdam; their descendants were the "elite Sephardim" of the city that became New York.

1.

Emma Lazarus was born in 1849 into a large, secular, and very rich family. They lived in a brownstone on Fourteenth Street near Union Square and spent summers in Newport, where the family had ancestral ties, making annual visits to Saratoga and other fashionable resorts for the "upper ten thousand" of the richest families in New York. Little beyond luxury is known of Emma Lazarus's life until the age of fourteen, when she began, at the height of the Civil War, to write poetry. Her father, Moses Lazarus, made his fortune in refining sugar; his dependence on raw materials from the South may have influenced his attitude toward the war. When the exclusive Republican Union Club refrained from expelling Judah P. Benjamin, secretary of state for the Confederacy and a Jewish sugar planter from Louisiana, Moses Lazarus did not join members who left the club in protest to found the Union League Club. Schor notes that Lazarus maintained a business partnership into the 1880s with another plantation owner from Louisiana named Bradish Johnston who was known for abusive treatment of his slaves before the war. While there is no evidence that Moses Lazarus was a "copperhead," an active supporter of the Confederacy, there is no indication that he cared greatly which side won the war.

Perhaps it is not surprising, then, that when Moses Lazarus's fourth daughter, Emma, began writing poems at a precocious rate of two or three a day, she had little to say about the national cataclysm. Her poetry of the early 1860s, as Schor notes, was "impervious to the war" until Lee's surrender, when she wrote a poem that might be mistaken for one of Emily Dickinson's abstract and oblique responses to the war:

> More hearts will break than gladden when
> The bitter struggle's past;
> The giant form of Victory must
> A giant's shadow cast.

Lazarus was more drawn to the drama of John Wilkes Booth's flight from Ford's Theatre than to Lincoln's death. She wrote a narrative ballad, reminiscent of Whittier, in which she treated Booth as though he were a hunted slave ("I've wandered all night in this deadly air, / Till, sick'ning, I drop with pain and despair"). Two weeks later, she wrote a poem in the voice of Booth's grieving mother. An accomplished poem on the theme of national reconciliation called "Heroes" begins in "rich Virginian woods," where "the scarlet creeper reddens over graves."

Proud of his precocious daughter, Moses Lazarus published her book *Poems and Translations, Written Between the Ages of Fourteen and Sixteen* in 1866; dedicated "To My Father," it was reissued by a commercial press the following year. On the strength of this volume, the young poet was introduced to Emerson as a potential guide. The meeting took place at the Madison Avenue home of the lawyer-aesthete Samuel Gray Ward, the former editor of the *Dial,* close friend of Margaret Fuller, and brother of Julia Ward Howe. Emma Lazarus was eighteen, Emerson sixty-five. Based on a photograph of the time, Schor describes Lazarus's "large features" as "adrift between handsome and homely," but she seems quite beautiful to me and probably seemed so to Emerson as well.

Emerson and "Miss Emma" (as he called her) adopted the coy Abelard-and-Heloise banter with which Emily Dickinson engaged her own literary adviser, Thomas Wentworth Higginson. "I would like to be appointed your professor," Emerson wrote her, "you being required to attend the whole term." She in turn begged him to "guide & correct" her. When the corrections came they were mild enough at first; "I observe that my poet gains in skill as the poems multiply," Emerson wrote, with light irony on the verb "multiply." He praised "Heroes," suggesting only that she cut some archaisms and rephrase a few lines, but he questioned her prolific output. "You permit feeble lines & feeble words," he wrote of one poem; of another, on Thoreau, he commented wryly, "I do not think it cost you any day-dawn or midnight oil." "Their correspondence," Schor notes, "is astonishing and painful, from its opening notes of audacity (hers) and rapturous enthusiasm (his) to the progressive, mutual irritation that develops as Emerson's misgivings become too obvious—and too exasperating—to mask."

Schor suspects that Emerson harbored "a tacit unease" with Emma Lazarus's "Jewish ethnicity." She needs to advance more evidence for the claim. The subject never came up in Emerson's correspondence with Lazarus, and the pattern of their relationship—from initial intimacy to "mutual irritation"—is congruent with Emerson's relations with other passionate literary women, most conspicuously Margaret Fuller. When he failed to include any of Lazarus's poems in an anthology called *Parnassus,* she wrote a blistering, bridge-burning letter accusing him of hypocrisy. She quoted his encouraging words to her about specific poems, and declared: "I frankly confess I never could have imagined that they were not sufficiently emphatic for your favorite poems." She closed her brief as a lawyer might, demanding "a reply at your earliest convenience." I doubt that Emerson regarded this letter, as Schor suggests, as "an epitome of her shameless self-assertion." It seems more likely that Emerson felt troubled and sorry—sorry that he had, as Lazarus feared, overpraised her youthful efforts and graded her more for progress than achievement.

2.

During the summer of 1872, while vacationing in Newport, Lazarus found a substitute for Emerson. Astonishingly, it was the same man that Emily Dickinson had chosen for herself a decade earlier. Colonel Thomas Wentworth Higginson, recovering in Newport from a wound received during the Civil War when he commanded a black regiment in South Carolina and Florida, was something of a specialist in encouraging young women writers. Helen Hunt Jackson, Rose Terry Cooke, and Harriet Prescott Spofford had all served informal apprenticeships under Higginson's benevolent regime; his relations with Dickinson had been less successful, as he tried in vain to "correct" what he perceived to be her "spasmodic" excesses.

Higginson was a snob and Lazarus's social status appealed to him. "She is a Jewess," he wrote to his sisters;

> they are very rich and in fashionable society in New York, and she has never seen an author till lately, though she has corresponded with Emerson. It is curious to see how mentally famished a person may be in the very best society.

Schor discerns a "parallel pathos" in Higginson's relations with Lazarus and Dickinson, noting "the urgency with which each woman poet approached an older, male mentor to confirm her claim to poethood."

Higginson introduced Lazarus to his own circle of artists and scientists in Newport: the painter John La Farge and the architect Richard Morris Hunt (who later designed the pedestal for the

Statue of Liberty); the astronomer Maria Mitchell; the actress Charlotte Cushman and her companion, the sculptress Emma Stebbins. Higginson generously shopped around Lazarus's poems, something he never did for Dickinson until after her death, but he gave her a more important gift when he introduced her to Richard Watson Gilder, an editor at *Scribner*'s magazine.[1] Gilder and his wife, the painter Helena deKay, became Lazarus's closest friends and, as Schor notes, "the focus of her social and intellectual life." Lazarus's self-revealing letters to deKay, which first came to light in 1980, are Schor's major source for the last ten years of Lazarus's life. Schor suspects, plausibly enough, that Lazarus's undated and unpublished sonnet "Assurance," which also first became known in 1980, reveals her feelings about deKay, a beautiful and talented woman with whom Winslow Homer, among others, had fallen in love before her. It begins:

> Last night I slept, & when I woke her kiss
> Still floated on my lips. For we had strayed
> Together in my dream, through some dim glade,
> Where the shy moonbeams scarce dared light our bliss.

Whatever the precise nature of Emma Lazarus's feelings about Helena, it was with her brother Charles, an influential art critic and minor poet, that Lazarus formed a more conventional companionship, and apparently entertained hopes of marriage. He was an anti-Semite and a cad who seemed amused when Emma stumbled upon an unsavory relationship (the precise nature of which Schor doesn't reveal) that he maintained in secret. Charles deKay reviewed Lazarus's poems after her death, using the occasion to attack Jews for being "too much engrossed in mercantile and professional work to give time to literature." Of deKay's anti-Semitism there can be no doubt, but Schor is on shakier ground when she discerns a kindred undercurrent of prejudice in Lazarus's brief friendship with the artist Maria Oakey, a close friend and studio-mate of Helena deKay.

According to Schor, Lazarus "found Maria captivating, and when Maria turned on her for courting commercial success, she reeled." Schor doesn't quote Oakey's qualms directly, noting only that her "charge of writing poetry for 'vulgar' commerce gave off a whiff of anti-Semitism." Again, as with Emerson's "tacit unease," Schor needs to offer more evidence. Maria Oakey was a tough and fiercely independent woman artist who had studied in France and at Cooper Union. It seems entirely possible that Oakey really did sense something meretricious in Lazarus's well-documented craving for approval and publication. Oakey herself struggled with the lure of commercial success. She later recalled how Oscar Wilde, during his tour of the United States in 1882, had lavishly praised her design for a theater curtain. "Why don't you go into decoration and wipe them all out?" Wilde asked Oakey. She responded, "Because I must paint pictures or die."[2] It is unfortunate that Lazarus and Oakey, who became engaged to the painter Thomas Dewing soon after their acquaintance began, had so little time together. Among other things, they might have discussed the perils of seeking artistic advice, for Oakey had recently broken off an affair with her own mentor, John La Farge, who retaliated by blackballing her candidacy for the Society of American Artists.[3]

Lazarus's intimacy with the Gilder circle invites a wider analysis than Schor is able to offer in the confines of a brisk biographical account. The Gilders and Charles deKay were at the center of the Aesthetic Movement in America, a vague program elevating "beauty" over the claims of utility and moralizing promoted by Wilde and others. The aims of the American aesthetes seemed at times contradictory; they favored both a more international sophistication in the arts as well as a distinctively American artistic expression. It is interesting to learn from Schor's book that in June 1879, Charles deKay invited Lazarus to visit the Greenwich Village studio of the maverick painter Albert Pinkham Ryder. DeKay wrote the first major article on Ryder's work, seeking to portray him as a sort of American impressionist. Writing of Ryder's *Spring,* the painting he specifically wished Lazarus to see, he conceded that Ryder might seem "deficient in knowledge of the figure," but that "he is an impressionist in so far as he strives for the 'feeling' of a figure."[4]

The occasion suggests a possible answer to a riddle concerning Ryder's work. Ryder painted several pictures inspired by poems of the German Romantic poet Heinrich Heine. It has been suggested that he "may have been introduced to the work of Heine through [Charles] deKay, who translated Heine's family letters."[5] Emma Lazarus, however, was one of the best-known translators of Heine of her time. Heine was among the poets she translated as a child, and in 1881 she published *Poems and Ballads of Heinrich Heine,* with an excellent literary essay, her first, as introduction. Schor observes that "she turned to the very poems in which Heine, a cultured, assimilated Jew who had accepted a baptism he later recanted, had struggled painfully to render his Jewish predicament."

3.

Emma Lazarus's own "Jewish predicament" is at the heart of her poetic achievement. As early as 1867, at the age of eighteen, she had written an impressive poem titled "In the Jewish Synagogue at Newport," which all readers recognized as a response to Longfellow's dignified and respectful poem about the Jewish cemetery there. "Closed are the portals of their Synagogue," Longfellow had written, ending his poem with a lament that "the dead nations [shall] never rise again." In a tribute to Longfellow after his death in 1882, Lazarus wrote sharply that "Jewish readers will not be so willing to accept the concluding stanzas of the poem."[6]

Her own poem, however, is less a corrective to Longfellow than a mild extension of his theme. It is true that her synagogue is open, but only to "mournful echoes through the empty hall." Longfellow evoked "the narrow streets and lanes obscure" of the "Ghetto and Judenstrass" of European cities; Lazarus, aiming for a longer historical view, adopts an exotic and hackneyed imagery of "tropic bloom" and "luxury's barbaric pomp." Schor tries hard to see this as an improvement: "Whereas Longfellow deemed the Jews exceptional, Emma Lazarus allows them a normal existence in an oriental homeland." But John Hollander is more accurate when he writes, in his discerning selection of Lazarus's poetry, that her poem "might easily have been written by a Gentile poet with a bit of knowledge of post-bibilical Jewish history."

In retrospect, however, "In the Jewish Synagogue at Newport" can be taken, as Schor remarks, as "the first sign of Emma Lazarus's willingness—her eagerness—to cross the gulf between her own assimilated, modern American life and the ancient tradition of Judaism and its people." This imaginative "crossing" was complete by the late 1870s, and with it came a corresponding growth in lyric power, as Lazarus became perhaps the most accomplished American writer of sonnets between the generations of Longfellow and Robert Frost. In "1492," that "two-faced year" of both Columbus and the expulsion of the Jews, Lazarus wrote of the gap between the promise of modern civilization and the suffering of Jews in exile:

> Hounded from sea to sea, from state to state,
> The West refused them, and the East abhorred.
> No anchorage the known world could afford.

A bittersweet melancholy suffuses her understated sonnet "Long Island Sound," where a seemingly random list of observations carries an unexpected emotional freight, and perhaps a hint of alienation:

> The quiet fishing-smacks, the Eastern cove,
> The semi-circle of its dark, green grove.
> The luminous grasses, and the merry sun
> In the grave sky; the sparkle far and wide,
> Laughter of unseen children, cheerful chirp
> Of crickets, and low lisp of rippling tide,
> Light summer clouds fantastical as sleep
> Changing unnoted while I gazed thereon.
> And these fair sounds and sights I made my own.

Sonnets were not the only form in which Lazarus excelled. While not "the first instance of a prose poem written in English," as Schor claims, Lazarus's remarkable "Little Poems in Prose," the title borrowed from Baudelaire, ranged with visionary power across centuries of Jewish experience.[7] In the pivotal fourth section of the poem, titled "The Test," she contrasted an idealized figure of the poet, "who plucked from his bosom the quivering heart and fashioned it into a lyre," with a caricature of the modern urban Jew: "And suddenly I heard a burst of mocking laughter, and turning, I beheld the shuffling gait, the ignominious features, the sordid mask of the son of the Ghetto."

4.

More than a third of Schor's book is devoted to the years from 1880 to 1883, when Lazarus, fully mature as a poet, also emerged as the leading American advocate for three causes: the repatriation of Jews in a homeland of their own; vocational training for Jewish immigrants; and suppression of anti-Semitism. Schor convincingly links Lazarus's conversion (not to Jewish faith but to Jewish activism) to three events: the Seligman scandal in Saratoga during the summer of 1877; the pogroms that followed the assassination of Czar Alexander II in 1881, when Jews were widely blamed for the crime; and the subsequent arrival in New York of Russian Jewish refugees by the thousands.

The Seligman incident, while not quite the American equivalent of the Dreyfus case, nonetheless galvanized public opinion concerning anti-Semitism. Joseph Seligman, a rich banker from New York, had stayed at the Grand Union Hotel in Saratoga for ten years when, in June 1877, he was told by the manager that "no Israelites shall be permitted in future to stop at this hotel." When Seligman called for a boycott of the Grand Union and other hotels under Henry Hilton's ownership, Hilton drew a distinction between newly arrived German-Jewish immigrants like Seligman and Sephardic "families like the Hendricks and Nathans" who "are welcome everywhere." Since Emma Lazarus was related to both the Hendricks and Nathans, and her family continued to visit Saratoga until at least 1880, it would have been easy for her to ignore the Seligman scandal. Instead, as Schor notes, Lazarus "chose the moment when many American Jews minimized, sidestepped, or finessed their identity to declare herself as a Jew." In her ironically titled "Epistle to the Hebrews," which she began as a weekly column for the *American Hebrew* in November 1882, she arrived at her often quoted formulation, "Until we are all free, none of us is free."

During the early spring of 1882, Lazarus visited Ward's Island at the northern end of the East River, where vacant buildings served as a makeshift shelter for overflow refugees from the shelters at Castle Garden in lower Manhattan. She was both appalled at the conditions and inspired by the people she saw there. In an article in the *New York Times* called "Among the Russian Jews," aimed at a primarily Gentile audience, she noted that "the coarser features of the Jewish type are singularly lacking among these refugees." They were, for the most part, well educated, "emancipated in religious matters," and free of "national as well as religious prejudice." At the same time, she realized that the United States could not serve as the refuge for the entire Jewish Diaspora. In 1883, she founded the Society for the Colonisation and Improvement of Eastern European Jews. As "the first American to make the case for a homeland in Palestine," eight years before the word *Zionism* was coined, Lazarus was following the lead of several British philo-Semites, including George Eliot, whose novel *Daniel Deronda* had a decisive influence on her evolving views.

A recurrent word in Lazarus's writing on behalf of Jewish refugees during the early 1880s is *practical.* She advocated artisanal and industrial training for immigrants, arguing that Jews at all levels of society "should be brought up to consider their education incomplete until it has supplied them with the art of using their hands and earning their livelihood in at least a single branch of productive industry." She was directly involved in the founding of the Hebrew Technical Institute in November 1883. Schor is probably right to relate these activities to Lazarus's interest in William Morris's community of craftsmen, which she visited in England in 1884. But a model closer to home, unmentioned by Schor, is Booker T. Washington's dedication to industrial training as a means of "uplift" for freed slaves. The Hampton Institute, which Washington attended, and the Tuskegee Institute that he founded were better models for the Hebrew Technical Institute than Morris's neomedieval community.

During the late spring and summer of 1883, Lazarus made her first trip to Europe, partly to raise funds for her various causes but also to meet Morris, Edward Burne-Jones, Robert Browning, Edmund Gosse, and other artists and writers she admired. It was on her return from this trip that she wrote her sonnet "The New Colossus." The poem appeared in the catalog of the exhibition organized to raise money for the Statue of Liberty's pedestal, and it was widely mentioned in the press; but it was not read at the dedication of the Statue of Liberty in the fall of 1886. Instead, the organizers reasserted the theme of French-American friendship, and, as Schor notes, "the only immigrants invoked were those 'illustrious descendants of the French nobility who crossed the Atlantic 100 years ago' in aid of the American Revolution." It was only in 1903, through the combined efforts of Lazarus's family and friends, including the Gilders, that a plaque with Lazarus's nearly forgotten poem was attached to the pedestal. Just two weeks earlier, in a grim coincidence noted by Schor, fifty Jews were killed and hundreds injured in a pogrom in the Russian city of Kishinev. During World War II, thanks to the efforts of the Slovenian immigrant Louis Adamic, the poem was invoked again, for exiles from Hitler's Europe, to interpret the meaning of the statue as Lazarus's "Mother of Exiles." This time the interpretation prevailed.

All this was too late for Emma Lazarus, however. During the fall of 1884 she observed the first symptoms of the cancer that would kill her three years later at the age of thirty-eight. Like a doomed heiress from a novel of Henry James, she sailed again for Europe in April 1885, determined to travel to Italy. She met James himself in Paris—"He looked well—but no longer young"—when he was caring for his own gravely ill sister, Alice. Lazarus reached Rome in January and was dazzled by her first glimpse of the Colosseum. "I do not know myself at all," she wrote Helena deKay.

> To me, it is so overpoweringly beautiful, strange & significant, that from the very first instant I was crushed by it, & have continued to feel the spell of it all, more & more profoundly with each hour of my stay.

But like Daisy Miller in the moonlit Colosseum, she knew that she was doomed. On her return to New York she prepared a final manuscript version of her selected poems, giving "The New Colossus" pride of place, and died on November 19, 1887. She had survived Colonel Higginson's other precocious protégé, Emily Dickinson, by a little over a year, and would have to wait considerably longer for anything like the public recognition that her remarkable achievements deserved.

NOTES

1. Gilder's editor in chief at *Scribner's* was Josiah Gilbert Holland, one of Emily Dickinson's closest friends. We can wonder whether Dickinson's name was ever mentioned in conversations Lazarus had with Higginson or Gilder.

2. See Erica E. Hirshler, *A Studio of Her Own: Women Artists in Boston, 1870–1940* (Boston: Museum of Fine Arts, 2001), 73.

3. See Hirshler, *Studio of Her Own,* 37 and 162.

4. Charles deKay, quoted in Elizabeth Broun, *Albert Pinkham Ryder* (Washington, D.C.: Smithsonian Institution Press/National Museum of American Art, 1989), 37. Ryder's *Spring* (Toledo Museum of Art) is reproduced on p. 38. The Whitney Museum of American Art owns a mirror commissioned by Charles deKay for his mother, with panels painted by Ryder portraying Helena deKay Gilder and other members of the family. See Doreen Burke et al., *In Pursuit of Beauty: Americans and the Aesthetic Movement* (New York: Rizzoli/Metropolitan Museum of Art, 1986), 310–11.

5. Broun, *Albert Pinkham Ryder,* 249.

6. Lazarus, "Henry Wadsworth Longfellow," *American Hebrew,* April 14, 1882, reprinted in Morris U. Schappes, *Emma Lazarus: Selections from her Poetry and Prose* (New York: Emma Lazarus Federation of Jewish Women's Clubs, 1967), 99.

7. See Emerson's manuscript poem "Woods, A Prose Sonnet" in David Lehman, *Great American Prose Poems: From Poe to the Present* (Scribner, 2003). Lehman also includes the first section, "The Exodus (August 3, 1492)," of Lazarus's "Little Poems in Prose."

VOLUMES REVIEWED

*Emma Lazarus*
By Esther Schor
Nextbook/Schocken, 2006

*Selected Poems*
By Emma Lazarus
Edited by John Hollander
Library of America, 2005

# Dark Darker Darkest

Robert Frost's poetry is full of actions taken on obscure impulse. A man reins in his horse on "the darkest evening of the year" to watch the woods fill up with snow. Why does he interrupt his journey? "The woods are lovely, dark and deep." Another man hesitates where "two roads diverged in a yellow wood" and takes "the one less traveled by." These poems are so familiar that it is almost painful to quote them. Others less well known are no less driven by impulse. "Into My Own," the sonnet that opens Frost's first book of poems, evokes a distant prospect of "dark trees": "I should not be withheld but that some day / Into their vastness I should steal away." Every true poem, Frost wrote in "The Figure a Poem Makes," the lovely little manifesto that served as the preface to his *Collected Poems* of 1939, is the child of impulse: "It begins in delight, it inclines to the impulse, it assumes direction with the first line laid down, it runs a course of lucky events, and ends in a clarification of life—not necessarily a great clarification, such as sects and cults are founded on, but in a momentary stay against confusion."

In the summer of 1912, following his own impulse to "steal away," Frost abandoned a life of raising chickens and teaching school in small towns on the outskirts of Boston, and took his family to England, with little money and no real prospects for making more. The Frosts had four children; two others died in infancy. Elinor, Frost's high school sweetheart turned long-suffering wife, acquiesced in this impulsive scheme as she did in so many others; besides, she confessed to a wish to "live under thatch." Frost at thirty-eight soon had enough poems to fill two books and part of a third, though no publisher, and a terrific theory of how those poems had gotten written. The poems were of two main kinds. In the first group were short lyrics of an extraordinarily high level of craftsmanship. In the second were longer poems, stories really, that could be as harrowing ("Home Burial" or "A Servant to Servants") as a Hemingway short story, or ruminative and wry like an extended joke allowed to go off the tracks.

The theory, which looms large in *The Notebooks of Robert Frost*—seven hundred pages of wisdom and prophecy, raving and rant, expertly edited and annotated by Robert Faggen—involved what Frost called "sentence-sounds," primal patterns of intonation and impulse that, in Frost's view, precede and underlie the words of a conversation or a good poem. Birds have their song; humans have their sentence sounds. "So many and no more belong to the human throat, just as so many runs and quavers belong to the throat of the cat-bird, so many to the chickadee." The job of the poet was to collect them and identify them, like an ornithologist in the outback, and then to set memorable words to the sounds.

England was good to Frost. He quickly found a publisher for the poems and a friend, the writer Edward Thomas, who was as excited about the theory as he was. The shorter poems were gathered in *A Boy's Will,* the title borrowed without acknowledgment—since everyone knew its provenance anyway—from a poem called "My Lost Youth" by Longfellow, who had in turn borrowed the phrase from Herder's translation of a Lapland lament: "Knabenwille ist Windeswille," or "A boy's will is the wind's will." Something like Longfellow's spectacular success with the common reader was what Frost in England already had in mind for himself. As he wrote to his friend and former pupil John Bartlett in 1913, "There is a kind of success called 'of esteem' and it butters no parsnips. It means a success with the critical few who are supposed to know. But really to arrive where I can stand on my legs as a poet and nothing else I must get outside that circle to the general reader who buys books in their thousands. . . . I want to reach out, and would if it were a thing I could do by taking thought." The last phrase is peculiar, and characteristic of Frost; "by taking thought" sounds like it means "deliberately," but it also probably means "without sacrificing thought," hence without "dumbing down," as well. That January, Frost had met Ezra Pound, "my quasi-friend," who represented the "critical few who are supposed to know." Pound told Frost he'd better adopt free verse or he would let Frost "perish by neglect." Pound liked the poems, though, and wrote an admiring review of *A Boy's Will* when it appeared in April.

The longer poems became Frost's second and greatest book of poems, *North of Boston,* a title he took from the real-estate ads in the Boston newspapers. Frost's working title had been "Farm Servants and Other People." In its array of lonely eccentrics and troubled couples, *North of Boston* bears a slight resemblance to Sherwood Anderson's *Winesburg, Ohio,* which Frost admired, and Edgar Lee Masters's *Spoon River Anthology.* But a better analogy might be with such talk-heavy stories of Hemingway's as "Hills Like White Elephants" or "The Sea Change," where a conflict between two speakers is gradually revealed in language by turns figurative and emotionally raw. The bereaved mother in "Home Burial" lashes out at her husband after he has dug the grave for their dead baby:

> I can repeat the very words you were saying,
> "Three foggy mornings and one rainy day
> Will rot the best birch fence a man can build."
> Think of it, talk like that at such a time!
> What had how long it takes a birch to rot
> To do with what was in the darkened parlor.

It's not really a question, and Frost doesn't use a question mark. But the father stands for poetry here, for metaphorical language, while the literal-minded mother (who isn't, as Frost might say, "at home in the metaphor") refuses to take a hint.

The biggest surprise in *The Notebooks of Robert Frost,* sixty years of private notebook jottings in preparation for poems and prose, is the spectacular profusion of epigrams, aphorisms, and what Frost called "dark sayings." Frost once wrote, in relation to Emerson: "I don't like obscurity and obfuscation, but I do like dark sayings I must leave the clearing of to time." He remarks in an early notebook entry, "It is best to be flattered . . . when your simile passes for a folk saying from a locality." Certain phrases recur many times in these notebooks, as Frost worries them into final shape: "Great thoughts grave thoughts" or (later used as the title for a poem) "Happiness makes up in height for what it lacks in length." Another saying, repeated at least a dozen times in the course of the notebooks, consists of three stark words, "dark darker darkest"—a sort of ominous refrain for the whole. Faggen calls Frost's notebooks—which are neither diaries nor journals but rather workbooks or outlets for thinking—"a chaotic laboratory in which many of his inventions went through constant experimentation and trial." While the notebooks "embrace a wide variety of forms," Faggen notes, "fragmentary notations and suggestively epigrammatic meditations predominate."

In an undated notebook entry, Frost marks his intention to "round up a lot of wise saying[s] such as I suspect we have from the Spartans such as Good fences make good neighbors." *North of Boston* opens with two men arguing about the merit of building walls to separate their property, even as they repair the stone wall that divides cows on one side from apple trees on the other. The poem begins oddly and grandiloquently, like a preacher or a blowhard politician: "Something there is that doesn't love a wall." The line from the poem that everyone knows best (it was quoted in congressional debates about the merits of building a wall along the border with Mexico) is the saying "Good fences make good neighbors."

The proverb is itself a little wall of words that the speaker of the poem, in his wheedling and deliberately annoying fashion, is trying to undermine. "*Why* do they make good neighbors?" he asks, sounding the patient schoolteacher's note, while looking down on his farmer-neighbor as though he's a cloddish student.

> I see him there
> Bringing a stone grasped firmly by the top
> In each hand, like an old-stone savage armed.
> He moves in darkness as it seems to me,
> Not of woods only and the shade of trees.
> He will not go behind his father's saying,

> And he likes having thought of it so well
> He says again, "Good fences make good neighbors."

"Mending Wall" is typical of several of Frost's finest poems in the way it builds itself on two opposing "sayings" held in momentary equilibrium: in this case the "dark" saying of the laconic farmer and the apparently more enlightened position of the undermining speaker: "Something there is that doesn't love a wall."

A similar opposition of sayings lies at the emotional heart of Frost's wonderful poem "The Death of the Hired Man," first published in the *New Republic* in 1915, in which a man and wife gently debate the merits of providing shelter for an old man who was an unreliable worker in his prime and is useless now. "Warren," the wife says, "he has come home to die: / You needn't be afraid he'll leave you this time." Competing definitions of home follow. First the husband:

> Home is the place where, when you have to go there,
> They have to take you in.

And then the wife:

> I should have called it
> Something you somehow haven't to deserve.

A whole intellectual, political, and emotional terrain is covered in that simple opposition: justice versus mercy; welfare versus charity; male (in Frost's mind, at least) versus female. In the notebooks, Frost writes that the "most beautiful thing in the world is conflicting interests where both are good." Frost wanted his reader to hesitate between the two definitions of home, and not be too quick to adopt the woman's as superior. As he told an audience at Haverford College in 1937: "The thing about that, the danger, is that you shall make the man too hard. That spoils it." Not spoiling it, in Frost's view, depended on hearing the "sentence-sounds" accurately.

It sometimes seems that every American poet after Poe has had to work up a theory in the light of which his or her poems are to be read. Many of the notations in the *Notebooks* concern the theory of poetry that Frost had formulated by the time of his English sojourn. Frost's theory about what he was up to in his poems is more consistently interesting than the self-justifications to be found in the prose writings of Pound ("Make it new") or Williams ("No ideas but in things"), Marianne Moore or Wallace Stevens. "I give you a new definition of a sentence," Frost wrote Bartlett in early 1914, parodying Jesus' new commandment. "A sentence is a sound in itself on which other sounds called words are strung. You may string words together without a sentence-sound to string them on just as you may tie clothes together by the sleeves and stretch them without a clothes line between two trees, but—it is bad for the clothes." Frost imagined that it would be possible that these sentence-sounds "could be collected in a book though I don't at present see on what system they would be catalogued." He offered some examples of such verbal gestures: "Put it there, old man! (Offering your hand)"; "I ain't a going hurt you, so you needn't be scared."

Frost was interested in the relation between language and action, in how we do things with words. We know from the notebooks that Frost thought of calling one of his Norton Lectures at Harvard in 1936 "Poetry as Performance (Feat of Words)." Though the text of those lectures is lost, we can get some sense from the notebooks of what Frost was after. We find him resisting the idea of words as mere description, existing in a separate sphere from deeds. "It is the common way to think of the sentence as saying something," he wrote. "It must do something as well." The words accompanying a handshake were one example; blessings and curses were another. "I was always in favor of the solid curse as one of the most beautiful figures," he wrote in his essay on Emerson. "We were warned against it in school for its sameness. It depends for variety on the tones of saying it and the situations." Frost's poems often turn on such "feats of words," such as the spell in "Mending Wall" or the curse and the husband's closing threat ("I'll follow and bring you back by force. I *will*") in "Home Burial."

Frost's theory of sentence-sounds might profitably be compared to what came to be known as "ordinary language" philosophy, first developed during the 1930s, and finding its fullest expression in the work of the Oxford philosopher J. L. Austin. Austin's *How to Do Things with Words* (based on lectures given at Harvard in 1955) is concerned with precisely the kind of situations, where sentences actually do something, that interested Frost. Austin called these sentences—utterances such as marriage vows and christenings and challenges to duels—"performatives." Like Frost, Austin was impatient with the jargon of experts and sedentary theorists, preferring to do what he called "field work" in the ways people actually talked. "When we examine what we should say when, what words we should use in what situations, we are looking again not *merely* at words (or 'meanings,' whatever they may be) but also at the realities we use the words to talk about."

Ordinary language was best for the purpose, Austin claimed, since "our common stock of words embodies all the distinctions men have found worth drawing, and the connections they have found worth marking, in the lifetimes of many generations." Such formulations, in Austin's view, were likely to be "more subtle, at least in all ordinary and reasonably practical matters, than any that you or I are likely to think up in our arm-chairs of an afternoon—the most favored alternative method." In a famous paper published in 1957, Austin proposed "excuses" as an "admirable topic" for fieldwork, since "we can discuss at least clumsiness, or absence of mind, or inconsiderateness, even spontaneousness, without remembering what Kant thought." While Austin's theory of "speech acts" has had a significant impact on literary theory, through the work of Stanley Cavell and Jacques Derrida among others, Frost's suggestive ideas about the relation between ordinary language and sentence-sounds await their full application.

Edward Thomas, the close friend Frost made in England, was so excited by Frost's theory of sentence-sounds that he wanted to write a book about its implications for literary criticism. Frost's injunctions offered a way to preserve musicality in verse without adopting the notion that "the music of words," as in Swinburne and Tennyson, was "a matter of harmonized vowels and consonants." In the notebooks, Frost refers to the latter as "death by jingle." At Frost's instigation, Thomas, who made a living by writing literary journalism and hack biographies, took up writing poetry himself, with extraordinary results. In poems like "Rain" ("Blessed are the dead that the rain rains upon") and "The Owl" and "Thaw," Thomas gave a heartbreaking and wholly original turn to Frost's ways with a flexible sentence strung across the grid of meter.

Frost had many occasions for grief in his life—a sister and daughter committed to insane asylums, a son who committed suicide. "Life is punishment," he wrote in a stark notebook entry. "All we can contribute to it is gracefulness in taking the punishment." But Edward Thomas's death in France in the spring of 1917, killed on Easter Monday by a German shell, was a terrible blow: "I hadn't a plan for the future that didn't include him." Recently, Robert Stilling, a graduate student at the University of Virginia, discovered an unpublished poem, written in Frost's hand in a friend's copy of *North of Boston,* called "War Thoughts at Home." The poem, published in *Virginia Quarterly Review,* begins with a deft description of blue jays fighting "On the back side of the house / Where it wears no paint to the weather," and then shifts to the wife's thoughts of her absent husband, who is in "a winter camp / Where soldiers for France are made." Glyn Maxwell, while admiring the beginning of the poem, has made a persuasive case for why the poem, with its parallel of bird rage and human war, doesn't quite come off. Since the poem "might be about the Thomases," Maxwell suggests, Frost, while "forcing . . . the underbrush" in that line about the winter camp, is finally too tactful to invade the woman's private thoughts.

Frost thought his theory of sentence-sounds had implications for classroom teaching, a profession he had abandoned not because of ineptitude but because he was so good at it, so consumed by it, that it took away from the energies he thought were better spent on poems. After his return to the United States in 1915, he was offered a job by Alexander Meiklejohn, the new and progressive young president of Amherst College. Thus began a long and sometimes difficult association with the college that continued until Frost's death in 1963. Frost was a dazzling and irreverent teacher, and you can get a feel for what he sounded like in his brilliant set of aphorisms, first worked up in the *Notebooks,* titled "Poetry and School." "We go to college to be given one more chance to learn to read in case we haven't learned in High School," he wrote. He didn't like most of what passed for teaching at Amherst, a ritual exchange of "progressive" views on this and that. Exasperated by the results, he wrote in the notebooks that "going to school is a game like running the gauntlet in which the object is to see if you can get through without being hurt too much by the books in the hands of the teachers." Sounding a theme in the notebooks he often expressed elsewhere, Frost wrote: "Half our conversation is no more than voting—signifying our adherence to some well known idea in the field. What's the good of it?"

Frost's politics followed from his poetics. You might say his party affiliation was Heraclitean: "The strength of a man is in the extremity of the opposites he can hold together by force." He viewed social arrangements as a clash of opposing views held in the best of times in momentary balance—"a momentary stay against confusion." It is notoriously difficult to pin Frost down to a political position on either right or left. Though the dating of the notebook entries is conjectural at best, Frost's fullest forays into political thinking seem, predictably, to come from the 1930s. Here, in his embrace of a populist individualism and his distaste for anything smacking of progress ("Leave progress to take care of itself," he wrote), he often sounds like a fellow traveler of the Southern Agrarians of the post-depression era—John Crowe Ransom, Allen Tate, and Robert Penn Warren.

One of the revelations of Jay Parini's recent biography of Frost was how close Frost felt to this group of reactionary writers, telling Warren on one occasion that he considered himself "a Yankee Agrarian." Frost's own Harvard-educated Yankee father had been a Southern sympathizer as a teenager during the Civil War and had named his son Robert Lee Frost after his hero. But Frost, unlike the Southern Agrarians, had no residual indignation against the breakup of the southern plantations or the so-called "southern way of life." Small farms in New England were his vision of the good, the difficult, the hard-bitten life. He thought that industrialism and socialism were a threat to what he called "the agricultural end of our system." He worried that "abolishing the capitalist would mean abolishing the farmer included." He hated big government because he liked small farms, not because Lincoln had freed the slaves.

"Radicalism is young folly," Frost wrote in a characteristic notebook entry. "Conservatism is old stupidity." And yet, conservatives were not wrong to sense that on many fronts they had an ally in Frost. "The only things I ever wished were different were the moon and goodness," he wrote. He wished the moon weren't single, but didn't specify how goodness might be altered. Frost didn't like the way the New Deal legislated charity, suspecting that Eleanor Roosevelt had hoodwinked her husband into such an unmanly scheme: "Mercy to the weak is handicapping the strong." He distrusted any government built around "the poor the unpretentious the ineffectual and the whipped." He had a Nietzschean distaste for the New Testament as a "poor man's book," preferring what he took to be the hardheaded wisdom of the Old Testament prophets, "who can manage to bear it that there must be good and bad losers."

Frost resisted anything that smacked of utopian thinking or utopian schemes for improving society. "Country people are never Utopian," he wrote. Over and over, we find him writing in the notebooks, in various guises, "Civilization is the opposite of Utopia." "Utopia is a recourse of the tribe in emaciation," he proclaimed. "Civilization is an exuberance of peace and plenty. It is beautifully dangerous in its capacity for self destruction." He confessed, "I hate the poor don't you Yes and I hate the rich. I hate them both as such." He speculated in the privacy of these notebooks that maybe slavery wasn't such a bad thing, as long as race was left out of it. "The mistake of the south," he wrote, "was in not enslaving of their own race." And wasn't welfare, he asked, with its exchange of money for good behavior, a form of slavery anyway? "Let us not gag at words."

Such views, even in the sanitized form in which they entered Frost's public poems (such as "Two Tramps in Mud-Time") and speeches, were of course abhorrent to many readers during the 1930s. But they came from a view of human existence best expressed in that mantra of "dark darker darkest," which Frost glossed in a characteristic fragment (lightly edited here, with variants and excisions deleted):

> Here where we are life wells up as a strong spring perpetually piling water on water with the dancing high lights upon it. But it flows away on all sides as into a marsh of its own making. It flows away into poverty into insanity into crime. Now like all other great things poverty has its bad side and so has insanity and so has crime. The good side must not be lost sight of. Poverty inspires ambition. Poverty has done so much good in the world I should be the last to want to see it abolished entirely. Only insanity can lift ability into genius. Crime is that smoldering defiance of law that at times bursts forth enobled into rebellion and revolution. But there is a bad side to all three poverty insanity and crime and this a dark truth and it is undeniably a dark truth.
>
> But dark as it is there is darker still. For we haven't enough to us to govern life and keep it from its worst manifestations. We haven't fingers and toes enough to tend to all the stops. Life is always breaking at too many points at once. Government is concerned to reduce the badness but it must fail to get rid of it. There is a residue of extreme sorrow that nothing can be done about and over it poetry lingers to brood with sympathy. I have heard poetry charged with having a vested interest in sorrow.
>
> Dark darker darkest. Dark as it is that there are these sorrows and darker still that we can do so little to be rid of them the darkest is still to come. The darkest is that perhaps we ought not to want to get rid of them. They be the fulfillment of exertion. What life craves most is signs of life. A cat can entertain itself only briefly with a block of wood. It can deceive itself longer with a spool or a ball. But give it a mouse for consummation. Response response. The certainty of a source outside of self—original response whether love or hate or fear.

In this extraordinary passage, one can see Frost moving toward an ethical position beyond good and evil, where a vitalist commitment to life itself comes before all other claims. His position seems almost pre-Socratic: measure in all things, a clash of opposites, and ceaseless flux. Frost's pessimism can itself be vivifying. In his preface to E. A. Robinson's "King Jasper," Frost wrote memorably: "Give us immedicable woes—woes that nothing can be done for—woes flat and final."

"Original response" was a phrase Frost used in his poem "The Most of It," in which a lonely man longing for community of some kind finds an ambiguous answer in a great buck lunging into the water. In the passage just quoted, by contrast, there is an unmistakable embrace of cruelty in that line about the cat: "But give it a mouse for consummation." What exactly is the equivalent human "entertainment" envisioned here? John F. Kennedy was not wrong in enlisting Frost in the great fight against collectivism. "The separation is as important as the connection," he wrote repeatedly. "True in a poem and true in society." But on other points of a democratic or Democratic agenda—poverty, civil rights, peace—Frost was at best a quixotic ally. At worst, he could be callous, small-minded, paranoid, and cruel. Imagine Frost murmuring at the White House, as he does in these notebooks, that "of course poverty has its bad side just the same as war has." Of course.

Perhaps what is most striking in Frost's long-running success as traveling bard, culminating in his windswept recital of his jingoistic sonnet "The Gift Outright" at Kennedy's inauguration, is the image he managed to maintain of the avuncular old patriot barding about. "One ordeal of Mark Twain," he wrote in the Robinson preface, "was the constant fear that his occluded seriousness would be overlooked." One task of modern criticism of Frost—in the work of Richard Poirier, William H. Pritchard, Jay Parini, and others—has been to make sure that Frost's own occluded seriousness is never lost sight of.

In September 1946, Lionel Trilling attended one of Frost's performances at Kenyon College and was appalled by what he saw. Frost was seventy-two at the time, and had long since perfected his routine: "he makes himself the buffoon—goes into a trance of aged childishness—he is the child who is rebelling against all the serious people who are trying to organize him—take away his will and individuality." While conceding that Frost's speech was "full of brilliantly shrewd things," Trilling couldn't help cringing at "the horror of the old man—fine looking old man—having to dance and clown to escape (also for his supper)."

It was largely in recoil against an audience that could do this to Frost—"that deadly intimacy, that throwing away of dignity"—that Trilling, in his famous eighty-fifth-birthday tribute to Frost in 1959, took pains to distinguish what he called "my Frost" from "the Frost I seem to perceive existing in the minds of so many of his admirers." Trilling confessed that, as a man of the city, he had only recently overcome a "resistance" to Frost's country-based work. The Frost Trilling had discovered "is not the Frost who reassures us by his affirmations of old virtues, simplicities, pieties, and ways of feeling: anything but." According to Trilling, "The universe that he conceives is a terrifying universe." Trilling challenged the audience to read "Neither Out Far Nor In Deep," which he called "the most perfect poem of our time," and "see if you are warmed by anything in it except the energy with which emptiness is perceived." He concluded: "I regard Robert Frost as a terrifying poet."

Trilling wasn't the first critic to suggest a darker side of Frost, but the occasion was a very public one, and Frost was visibly shaken when he tried to recite some poems after dinner. Trilling, who left the party early, wrote Frost to apologize if he had hurt his feelings. "Not distressed at all," Frost replied. "Just a little taken aback or thrown back on myself by being so closely examined so close by. . . . You made my birthday party a surprise party. I should like nothing better than to do a thing like that myself—to depart from the Rotarian norm in a Rotarian situation." In Trilling's performance and its aftermath, what Frost savored wasn't the revelation of his true dark self, but rather, as always in Frost, the clash of two sides, two sayings, in momentary equilibrium. "You weren't there to sing 'Happy Birthday, dear Robert,' and I don't mind being made controversial," he told Trilling. "No sweeter music can come to my ears than the clash of arms over my dead body when I am down."

VOLUME REVIEWED

*The Notebooks of Robert Frost*
Edited by Robert Faggen
Belknap Press of Harvard University Press, 2006

# Flawed Perfection

EDNA MILLAY GOT HER VIVID AND aristocratic-sounding middle name from the hospital in New York City that saved her Uncle Charlie's life. Drunk on the New Orleans waterfront, Charles Buzzell boarded a ship while it was loading grain and fell asleep on a bale of cotton in the hold. He woke to find himself pinned below deck, out of earshot and unable to move. After ten days without food or water, he saw a bright light expanding suddenly in the black hull, "& I could see through the ship as though it was made of clear glass." Found and rushed to St. Vincent's, he was convinced forever after that he had entered the spirit world and been reborn. He began to appear at the Globe Museum on the Bowery as "The Adventurer and Evangelist Chas. A. Buzzell, The New Orleans Stowaway." Six days after his miraculous rebirth, Edna St. Vincent Millay—nicknamed "Vincent" almost immediately—was born on Washington's birthday, February 22, 1892, in Camden, Maine.

Millay's parents were so badly matched that, as her mother Cora wryly remarked, "Any crank on Eugenics would have said we were perfectly mated for the propagation of a family." Henry Millay liked to fish, play poker, and drink. When his industrious wife complained about his inability to hold a job, he beat her. Cora finally kicked him out in 1900, when Edna turned eight, and raised her three daughters—one blonde, one brunette, and one (Edna, the eldest) redhead—alone. A hairdresser and self-taught nurse, she found occasional work in neighboring towns, often leaving the girls to their own devices.

Under their mother's tutelage, all the girls played the piano and wrote poetry and acted. Cora Millay had a bohemian strain intertwined with aristocratic pretensions, a sometimes unattractive combination she passed on to her eldest daughter. When a *New Yorker* profile in 1925 harped on Edna Millay's humble beginnings, her mother sent in a haughty correction: "Certain Millays owned houses and lands—but that was long ago." Still, as Cora remarked with equal pride in an interview, "The hardships that bound the children together made them stronger, and banded them together in self-defense against the world. . . . I let the girls realize their poverty." That use of "realize" is nicely turned; in her best poetry it can be said that Edna Millay realized—acknowledged even as she made something real and lasting from—her poverty.

Edna Millay's childhood is a story of precocious virtuosity. She excelled at everything, was always the leading lady in the school play, the class poet (except once, when her classmates, tired of her queenly ways, voted for the class dullard instead), the star. Music and poetry were her refuge from the daily grind of keeping house in ever more modest rented rooms along the rocky Maine coast. Nancy Milford, in the moving opening section of her painstaking and sympathetic biography, cites a poignant memory of Millay searching for a chord on the organ, and asking her exhausted mother for help.

> We did not have the notes of it, it was something she knew by heart. I called her to help me with the chord, and she came in. She had been doing washing, and her hands, as she placed them upon the keys were very pink, and steam rose from them. Her plain gold wedding ring shone very clean and bright, and there were little bubbles on it which the soap suds had left, pink, and yellow, and pale green. When she had gone and I was sure that she would not hear me, I laid my cheek softly down upon the cool keys and wept. For it had come into my mind with dreadful violence as she bent above me and placed her fingers upon the keys . . . that my mother could die; and I wanted to save her from that, for I knew she would not like it; and I knew that I could not.

Poetry also came from Cora—"Mother gave me poetry," Millay wrote. Her discovery of the physical thrill of poetry was a perfect match for Emily Dickinson's famous statement, "If I feel physically as if the top of my head were taken off, I know *that* is poetry." Millay said of her own first encounter with poetry: "I know that it knocked the wind clear out of me, and left me giddy and almost actively sick . . . when, on opening at random my mother's gargantuan copy of Shakespeare, I read the passage from Romeo and Juliet about the 'dateless bargain' and Death keeping Juliet as beautiful as she was in life, to be his 'paramour.'" She began writing poems early, and perhaps too early learned to meet perfectly the editorial expectations of the popular children's magazine *St. Nicholas.* By the time she was eighteen, the cutoff age for submissions, she had won every poetry contest *St. Nicholas* offered. The awareness that poetry was a matter of prizes and editors as much as a giddy and gut-wrenching experience set her on the path of a big career—but one sometimes wishes that her eyes weren't always so firmly locked on the prize.

By her twentieth birthday, in 1912, she had written the first half of a masterpiece, the claustrophobic "Renascence," which recalls in its hammering tetrameters both her hemmed-in Maine childhood landscape and her Uncle Charlie's below-deck ordeal:

> All I could see from where I stood
> Was three long mountains and a wood;
> I turned and looked another way,
> And saw three islands in a bay.
> So with my eyes I traced the line
> Of the horizon, thin and fine,
> Straight around till I was come
> Back to where I'd started from;
> And all I saw from where I stood
> Was three long mountains and a wood.

Two hundred lines or so detail this circular feeling of boundedness. "The sky, I thought, is not so grand; / I 'most could touch it with my hand! / And reaching up my hand to try, / I screamed, to feel it touch the sky."

What saves the poem from bathos is a verbal dexterity and self-mocking wit never far from light verse, as well as such Tin Pan Alley tricks as placing the reached-for rhyme first. The ending of the poem perfectly skirts the edge between grandiosity and a nimble tread:

> The world stands out on either side
> No wider than the heart is wide;
> Above the world is stretched the sky,—
> No higher than the soul is high.
> The heart can push the sea and land
> Farther away on either hand;
> The soul can split the sky in two,
> And let the face of god shine through.
> But East and West will pinch the heart
> That can not keep them pushed apart;
> And he whose soul is flat—the sky
> Will cave in on him by and by.

Those last four lines, with the skittish dash and the culminating throwaway "by and by," could hardly be improved upon.

"Renascence," the title poem of Millay's first book (1912), was in the running for a big prize given by *The Lyric Year.* The much-publicized indignation of critics such as Louis Untermeyer, protesting Millay's honorable mention, was worth more to her reputation than winning. The poem and the controversy also brought Millay a more discerning audience and more powerful patrons than her childhood submissions to *St. Nicholas.* The wealthy Caroline Dow, dean of the YWCA Training School in New York City, heard her recite "Renascence" at a party and offered to pay her way through Vassar, which Millay entered, four years older than her classmates, in 1913. It was at Vassar that the Millay legend can truly be said to begin. A diminutive five foot one and never weighing more than a hundred pounds, she stood out with her flame-red hair, waist-length as a child but pinned up at Vassar, her complementary green eyes, her trained voice, and her sexual swagger that combined a New Woman androgyny with an aristocratic remove.

The ostensible subject of Daniel Mark Epstein's breezy and carelessly written book—on one page he manages to include the clichés "from the moment he laid eyes on her," "would not take no for an answer," and "went toe to toe with"—is Millay's "lovers and love poems"; Vassar gives him his first cast of characters. Epstein is fascinated by Millay's "megawatt libido" and her "harem of sex-starved Vassar girls eager for same-sex experiments right there on campus." Calling Millay "the Sappho of North Hall," he quotes liberally from love letters sent to her: "I think of you when I brush my teeth because I use the same kind of toothpaste that you do—I think of you when I bathe—for obvious reasons." Shifting gears from the prurient to the therapeutic, Epstein ascribes the "element of androgyny" in Millay's temperament and erotic life to her poetic ambition, "the cultivation of a multitude of rich voices from a profound and androgynous emotional center. If the male in her was not so firmly in touch with the female, she could never have written so insightfully of men and women in love."

This getting-in-touch-with-her-male-side stuff misses the transgressive excitement of Millay's Vassar. Millay's tastes at this time encompassed both athletic women—she described one of her lovers as "another hockey hero, cheerleader, rides horseback a lot, very boyish, not tall, but *all* muscle"—and effeminate men. While indulging in "both serial and simultaneous sexual relations with Katharine Tilt, Catherine Filene, Isobel Simpson, and Elaine Ralli" (Epstein's list), she also maintained an off-campus affair with an international man of mystery called Arthur Hooley. Unknown to previous biographers, Hooley was a man of disguises and aliases, shifting identities and addresses. Epstein thinks Hooley had "something to hide" and suggests, credibly, that this something was homosexuality. He only let her touch him in the dark: "There in the darkness he would let her have her way with him," Epstein writes, "and he might use her in the way he would use a wicked little schoolboy who would not do as he had been told." "Might" marks the speculation in this passage.

From Vassar where her legend lived on, to be apotheosized some think in the lesbian Lakey character in Mary McCarthy's *The Group,* Millay graduated to the world of Greenwich Village bohemia. The most eloquent witness of this period of her life is Edmund Wilson, who saw a performance of her antiwar play *Aria da Capo* early in 1920, and met her at a postperformance party downtown.

> She was dressed in some bright batik, and her face lit up with a flush that seemed to burn also in the bronze reflections of her not yet bobbed reddish hair. She was one of those women whose features are not perfect and who in their moments of dimness may not seem even pretty, but who, excited by the blood or the spirit, become almost supernaturally beautiful. She was small, but her figure was full, though she did not appear plump. She had a lovely and very long throat that gave her the look of a muse, and her reading of her poetry was thrilling.

Wilson was twenty-five at the time, and had never slept with a woman. Like many of Millay's lovers before and after, Wilson thought he was seducing her until he felt the hook in his mouth. Wilson's friend and colleague at *Vanity Fair,* the poet John Peale Bishop, swallowed the bait as well. In one scene played for comedy in both biographies, Bishop and Wilson joined Millay in bed, and divided her body at the waist between them—"with a polite exchange of pleasantries about which had the better share," Wilson (who chose below the waist) recalled. Epstein, half-jokingly, suggests such scenes might have been the source of Millay's Jazz Age quatrain "My candle burns at both ends."

In his poignant and clear-eyed "Epilogue, 1952," which concludes *The Shores of Light,* Wilson tells how their friendship survived Millay's refusal of his marriage proposal. Milford, who insists on calling him Edmund Wilson, Jr., has found things in his diary not included in the memoir. For example, when Wilson told Millay, "By the time we're fifty years old, we'll be two of the most interesting people in the United States," she replied, "You behave as if you were fifty already." His mature presence, though, was calming and restorative during a period when Millay was drinking heavily and going through lovers with apparent desperation. In a body of poetry in which almost no particular people are identifiable, Millay's "Portrait" is a gentle gesture of thanks to

Wilson for hours spent in his company seriously discussing literature:

> I could not ever nor can I to this day
> Acquaint you with the triumph and sweet rest
> These hours have brought to me and always bring,—
> Rapture, coloured like the wild bird's neck and wing,
> Comfort, softer than the feathers of its breast.

Greenwich Village during the twenties was leftist, of course, and Millay moved weightlessly among the "Reds" circles of Max Eastman and John Reed. In the summer of 1927, she wrote a once-famous poem in protest of the execution of Sacco and Vanzetti, "Justice Denied in Massachusetts," and managed to get herself arrested at a picket line at the Boston State House. The five-stanza poem, which employs like *The Waste Land* symbolist evocations of a blighted harvest, appeared in the *New York World* on August 22 and created a sensation.

> What from the splendid dead
> We have inherited—
> Furrows sweet to the grain, and the weed subdued—
> See now the slug and the mildew plunder.
> Evil does overwhelm
> The larkspur and the corn;
> We have seen them go under.

Despite the occasion and the *parti pris,* Edna Millay's deepest instincts were hardly populist; as a propagandist, here and in the saber-rattling poems she wrote during the early years of World War II against American neutrality, she is always too much the poised and self-righteous performer. Aristocratic and apolitical, she hated the Nazis because they were vulgar and invaded civilized countries. A Cinderella who had, at least in wish, left the ashes and her two less lucky sisters far behind her, she loved expensive gowns (ever present in her poems and her closets), champagne, English accents, and English men. "She seemed sometimes rather British than American," Edmund Wilson wrote, "in her quick way of talking to people as well as in her reading of her poems." As a child she fantasized about having a black mammy. Late in life she owned an estate in Columbia County, New York, and—it is the major discovery of Epstein's book—a stable of racehorses in Maryland that consumed the cash she made on her diva-like tours. (To warm up her voice she would recite the winners of the Kentucky Derby from 1875 onward.) Her marriage to a Dutch sugar importer named Eugen Boissevain, whom a close friend described as behaving "like a cruise director," gave her during the final decades of her life the stability and European air she required.

The narrative of those years, in Milford's detailed and forgiving treatment, has a ghoulish fascination, as Millay killed herself slowly and then, in a headlong pitch downstairs, once and for all. Three accidents marred her years with Boissevain. There was, first of all, her chance encounter in Chicago with a twenty-one-year-old poet called George Dillon, with whom she fell desperately in love. Their affair—with her in the driver's seat and him, timid and passive and probably gay, curled up in back—gave her material for the fifty-two sonnets of *Fatal Interview,* which many consider her finest work. Its mock-Elizabethan pastiches show a kind of perverse genius. I would challenge poets and English professors not familiar with Millay to name the century of lines like these: "Nay, learned doctor, these fine leeches fresh / From the pond's edge my cause cannot remove: / Alas, the sick disorder in my flesh / Is deeper than your skill, is very love."

In 1936 she lost the manuscripts of two books in a hotel fire in Florida. A couple of years later she was thrown from a moving car, suffering a back injury that was treated with large doses of morphine. By 1940 she was holed up in the upstairs rooms of Steepletop, her upstate estate, dosing herself heavily with morphine, alcohol, and cigarettes. On New Year's Eve, she filled out a medical chart in her notebook. The first two entries are unexceptional: "Awoke 7:30, after untroubled night. Pain less than previous day. 7:35—Urinated—no difficulty or distress." And then:

> 7:40—3/8 gr. M.S. [morphine] hypodermically, self-administered in left upper arm + profuse bleeding, almost instantly quenched.

7:45–8—smoked cigarette (Egyptian) (mouth burns from excessive smoking)
8:15—thirsty—went to ice-box for glass of water, but no water there. Take glass of beer instead which do not want. Headache, lassitude and feeling of discomfort & stuffiness from constipation.
8:20—cigarette (Egyptian)
9:00—"
9:30—Gin Rickey (cigarette)
11:15 Gin Rickey
12:15—Martini (4 cigarettes)
12:45—1/4 grain M.S. & cigarette
1.—pain bad & also in lumbar region. No relief from M.S.

This deadpan record of five hours of torment is worthy of William Burroughs, or Baudelaire.

The final chapters of Milford's book read like one of Willa Cather's bitter portraits of gifted women in decline. Indeed, Eugen Boissevain's male-nurse ministrations to Millay bear an eerie resemblance to Oswald's well-meaning but ultimately unbearable care for Myra in *My Mortal Enemy*. During the early morning of October 19, 1950, unable to sleep, she smoked a few cigarettes and took another Seconal, wandered from her bedroom to the top of the dark staircase, pitched forward and fell down the stairs to the landing, breaking her neck. Her head rested on a notebook with the draft of a poem in pencil. She had drawn a ring around the last three lines:

> I will control myself, or go inside.
> I will not flaw perfection with my grief.
> Handsome, this day: no matter who has died.

It all makes one wonder what went so hideously wrong for the golden girl of the early twenties. Milford and Epstein look to family dynamics, especially between Millay and her smothering mother and Millay and her competitive and resentful sisters. (An interesting aspect of Milford's book is the interpolated conversations between her and the "authorizer" of her official biography, Norma Millay.) Both biographers are kind to Boissevain, neither suspecting that he might have gotten some satisfaction from watching his brilliant and independent wife turn into the helpless prisoner of his care. Drug addiction, alcoholism, expensive tastes and expensive horses—of course, these all took their toll. But what of the poetry that, after all, must be the reason why we take an interest in Edna Millay in the first place? The aristocracy of poets was, as she well knew, the true aristocracy—and where in its ranks does she stand?

First of all, it must be admitted that Edna Millay's reputation as a writer of poems is not sufficiently inflated today to suffer puncture. Judgments from the past don't help much. In 1923, she became the first woman to win the Pulitzer Prize for poetry—true, but four years later the prize went to the utterly forgotten Leonora Speyer. Millay's books sold hundreds of thousands of copies, but so did James Whitcomb Riley's. Thomas Hardy said there were "two great things in the United States": the poetry of Edna St. Vincent Millay and skyscrapers. An arresting opinion, surely, but it was also a clever way for Hardy to register his disdain for the modernists, placing Millay above Eliot and Pound, while seeming at the same time to embrace the modernity of the New York skyline. And besides, English readers liked the Englishness of Millay's poetry, which confirmed their prejudice—Frost and Eliot benefited from it as well—that British poetry and poetic diction constituted the mainstream of poetry in English.

No one doubts Millay's extraordinary skill as a poet, what Hart Crane once called her "equipment," which, in his view, was "bound to succeed to the appreciative applause of a fairly large audience."[1] But it was that applause, as essential to her dependent solace as alcohol or morphine, that closed off the full exploration of her powers as a poet. Of the two biographers, Daniel Epstein makes the greatest claims for her poetry, asserting again and again that she is the great love poet of the century, "America's foremost love poet." But Millay's love poems are among her most meretricious. The sonnet from which he takes his title, "What lips my lips have kissed," includes such unbearable bits as this: "And in my heart there stirs a quiet pain / For unremembered lads that not again / Will turn to me at midnight with a cry."

Epstein claims, absurdly, that T. S. Eliot, Marianne Moore,

Robert Frost, and Wallace Stevens "together did not produce three love poems comparable to Millay's 'Pity me not because the light of day.'" Leaving aside Eliot's "The Love Song of J. Alfred Prufrock," which is surely some kind of love poem, Frost wrote incomparable love sonnets, including "Putting in the Seed," "The Silken Tent," and "Never Again Would Bird's Song Be the Same." It seems needlessly cruel to place these great sonnets, with their verbal panache and delicate specificity, alongside Millay's. It is undeniable that, as Epstein claims, "Millay's lovers were flesh-and-blood men and women." But it isn't true at all that "her sonnets preserve them in vivid detail." Those unremembered lads are right out of Housman, another English admirer of her poetry. Edmund Wilson is right that "when she came to write about her lovers, she gave them so little individuality that it was usually, in any given case, impossible to tell which man she was writing about."

Millay published hundreds of sonnets, and these, with rare exceptions, leave the impression of demands finely met—she wins the prize. There's a revealing passage in one of Millay's reports on a poet who had applied for a Guggenheim.

> He writes nothing but sonnets. He has become so skilled in this form that he writes sonnets easily and naturally; his emotion is accustomed to being penned in this stall, and enters it willingly.

The same, alas, could be said of Millay herself. The exceptions are those poems in which she seems unruly in the stall. The early "Bluebeard" remains a wonderful poem, in which the secret of the pirate's castle is not his murdered wives, to whose number each disobediently curious wife is added, but a little room he'd reserved for himself:

> This door you might not open, and you did;
> So enter now, and see for what slight thing
> You are betrayed. . . . Here is no treasure hid,
> No cauldron, no clear crystal mirroring
> The sought-for Truth, no heads of women slain
> For greed like yours, no writhings of distress;
> But only what you see. . . . Look yet again:

An empty room, cobwebbed and comfortless.
Yet this alone out of my life I kept
Unto myself, lest any know me quite;
And you did so profane me when you crept
Unto the threshold of this room tonight
That I must never more behold your face.
This now is yours. I seek another place.

The penultimate line too closely echoes Keats's "love and fame" sonnet, and I wish the last sentence was less grandiloquent, less like the closing of Tennyson's "Ulysses." (Frost would have found something closer to the speaking voice: "I'll find another place"?) Still, the poem is terrific in both conception and execution, and it confirms Edmund Wilson's claim that Millay's great subject was not love but loneliness.

If we want to find a Millay for our times, it can't be the Greenwich Village gamine who burned her candle at both ends. We need to find, instead, those poems that register what Wilson thought was deepest in her character, "something austere and even grim." Lyrics like "Eel-Grass" and "Scrub" and "The Return" ("Earth does not understand her child,/ Who from the loud gregarious town / Returns, depleted and defiled, / To the still woods, to fling him down") express this austerity. So, in a different key, does her fine "Ballad of the Harp-Weaver," which I once heard Mabel Mercer recite at Carnegie Hall with unnerving effect. One of her deepest soundings of this desolate region is the neglected sequence (unmentioned by Milford or Epstein) *Sonnets from an Ungrafted Tree,* each sonnet of which has a fourteenth line extended to fourteen syllables. Here is the last part of the eleventh sonnet, when the speaker finds after the snow has melted an apron frozen on the ground:

An apron long ago in such a night
Blown down and buried in the deepening drift,
To lie till April thawed it back to sight,
Forgotten, quaint and novel as a gift—
It struck her, as she pulled and pried and tore,
That here was spring, and the whole year to be
lived through once more.

That final line, in its heavy-hearted clarity and "realized" poverty, is worth any number of mock-Elizabethan sonnets strung together in *Fatal Interview*.

NOTE

1. Hart Crane, *Complete Poems and Selected Letters*, edited by Langdon Hammer (New York: Library of America, 2006), 255.

VOLUMES REVIEWED

*What Lips My Lips Have Kissed: The Loves and Love Poems of Edna St. Vincent Millay*
By Daniel Mark Epstein
Henry Holt, 2001

*Savage Beauty: The Life of Edna St. Vincent Millay*
By Nancy Milford
Random House, 2001

# Deserters

WHATEVER GERTRUDE STEIN MEANT when she called Ernest Hemingway and his expatriate entourage a lost generation—lost to whom or to what?—it is now clear that some of the young Americans born around 1895 were more lost than others. Stein may have seen limited promise, at least when measured against her own unimpeachable genius or her friend Picasso's, in this band of ambitious refugees from the American Midwest and South. They had learned what they knew of art and life in the brothels and museums of Paris, and in dragging corpses from the battlefields of Italy. Stein herself, with her cubist décor and her mannered prose, schooled them in what one of their number, John Dos Passos, called "a certain esperanto of the arts that has 'modern' for its trademark." A century later, with their popularity and prestige undiminished, it is hard to feel sorry for such perennially found writers as Hemingway, Fitzgerald, and Faulkner, even as other writers of the Great War (such as Claude McKay, author of *Home to Harlem*) have been retrieved from oblivion. No lostness to complain of here when the British lost Wilfred Owen, Edward Thomas, and Gaudier-Brzeska, and the French lost Charles Péguy and Alain-Fournier. Actually, the previous generation (Stein's own) has more pathos if less real war, with the burnout and early passing of Frank Norris, Jack London, and Stephen Crane.

Not every luminous name of the *entre deux guerres* has retained its gloss. Recent salvaging efforts applied to the reputations of Edna Millay and Sinclair Lewis yielded mixed results. Now it is John Dos Passos's turn, and we have about three thousand pages of prose, courtesy of the Library of America, to help us make up our minds. The adjective *neglected* has dogged Dos Passos's reputation almost from the beginning—a peculiar form of recognition. From about 1925 to 1936, no American writer seemed more promising or more "serious" than Dos Passos, but by 1951 the critic Arthur Mizener could remark that Dos Passos had "very nearly achieved the rank of a neglected novelist." This eclipse was partly the result of World War II, which made such "committed" writing of the thirties as Dos Passos's masterpiece, the trilogy of novels gathered under the immodest title *U.S.A.,* seem—except in France, where Sartre called Dos Passos "the greatest writer of our time"—somehow beside the point. Dos Passos's sharp swing to the political right after the war, when he supported Joseph McCarthy and later Barry Goldwater, disgusted critics on the left without inspiring conservatives to read his preconversion works.

When the Library of America reprinted *U.S.A.* in 1996, it seemed a dutiful homage to a classic that no one but graduate students reads anymore. The unexpected commercial success of that volume has inspired two sequels: a clutch of early novels, including the durable *Manhattan Transfer* (1925), and a miscellany of travel writing, journalism, letters, poems, and diaries. It remains to be seen whether these well-intentioned, well-annotated, and reverential volumes will bring Dos Passos back to life or bury him once and for all.

Whatever the quality of his work, Dos Passos's conflict-ridden life has an enduring fascination. He was born John Roderigo Madison in a Chicago hotel in 1896, the bastard son of a prominent New York corporate lawyer and his mistress, both of whom were married to others. His father, John Randolph Dos Passos, was the son of a Portuguese cobbler, but this exotic lineage did not prevent him from publishing in 1903 a political treatise entitled *The Anglo-Saxon Century and the Unification of the English–Speaking People.* After what he called a "hotel childhood" wandering with his mother through the fashionable capitals of Europe and learning French before English, John Madison had a formal education in line with his father's WASP ideals. At Choate, he was teased as a wimp with a foreign accent. At Harvard, from 1912 to 1916, he majored in English, found like-minded artsy friends such as E. E. Cummings, wrote poems for the *Advocate,* and was deeply impressed by the modernist Armory Show of 1913. His parents meanwhile had married, having shed their respective spouses, and John Madison became John Roderigo Dos Passos, Jr.

Soon after his Harvard graduation, Dos Passos traveled to Madrid—the first of many sojourns in Spain—to study architecture and Spanish, and made a lasting friendship with Jose Robles, a student at the time and later a leader of the Spanish Republic as well as Dos Passos's Spanish translator. His mother died in 1915, his father in 1917, and Dos Passos returned to the United States, where he was promptly cheated by an aunt from a large share of his inheritance. Then he joined other Harvard men in the gentlemanly Norton-Haries volunteer ambulance unit, serving in Italy and Alsace, meeting—inevitably—Hemingway, and returning to Madrid, already a kind of second home, at the end of 1919 to write in Goya's homeland of the disasters of war.

The Library of America volume of travel books and other writings includes letters and diaries from these years, and most of the material is embarrassing. Extended passages sound like outtakes from Kipling and Lafcadio Hearn, two of Dos Passos's favorite writers, interrupted by free verse that reads like a parody but isn't:

> Today,
> As if a gritty stinking sponge
> Had smeared the slate of my pale memories,
> I stand aghast in a grey world,
> Waiting . . .

The ellipsis marks are Dos Passos's own. A few pages later, "The stream of sensation flows by—I suck it up like a sponge." Dos Passos in 1917 was himself a sponge for vague but violent political sentiments, mediated through maudlin bonhomie: "all young men are frightfully decent. If we only governed the world instead of the swag-bellied old fogies in frock-coats that do! oh what a God-damned mess they have made of organized society, the bankers and brokers and meat-packers—and business men. Better any tyranny then theirs. Down with the middle-aged!" He dreamed of drastic remedies: "My only refuge from the deepest depression is in dreams of vengeful guillotines."

Dos Passos collaborated with some Harvard buddies on a sprawling novel, a chunk of which was published in England in 1920 as *One Man's Initiation—1917.* The offensive bits that Dos Passos was obliged by his editors to cut might have spiced up a drab book; this "novel" is really a set of impressionistic sketches concerning an American aesthete named Martin Howe who joins the army and at first is exhilarated to be in France. Disillusion with the bureaucratic military soon follows, and in a set scene that feels like a radio play Howe listens to a group of Frenchman—including a Catholic and a socialist—debate solutions to the mire of the modern world before all are killed. *Three Soldiers* (1921), which Dos Passos worked on in Madrid, is a much better war novel with similar themes: the mechanistic bureaucracy of the military against the free spirits of the young men caught in its gears. Already aiming for the panoramic reach of his later fiction, Dos Passos chooses three representative men from different regions of the United States—the West, the Midwest, and the East—but the clear hero is John Andrews, an aspiring Harvard-educated composer who deserts the army in rural France to work on a symphonic poem entitled *Body and Soul of John Brown.* Andrews is clearly a stand-in for Dos Passos; he finds musical inspiration in reading "the gorgeously modulated sentences" of Flaubert's *Tentation de Saint Antoine.* When he is betrayed by his French girlfriend and the military police come to pick him up, he leaves the sheets on his writing table: "First one sheet, then another, blew off the table, until the floor was littered with them."

*Three Soldiers* is too slackly constructed, and too predictable in its narrative unfolding, to stand comparison with Hemingway's *A Farewell to Arms* or with Cummings's war novel, *The Enormous Room.* We know right away that the obstreperous Hoosier Chrisfield will get his revenge on the bullying sergeant, that Andrews will desert the military machine for the cultural playground of Paris. A better comparison might be with Willa Cather's Pulitzer Prize–winning, sporadically engaging, but now forgotten *One of Ours* (1922), which also has a sensitive musician as sacrificial lamb. Like Dos Passos's aesthete-heroes, Cather's

Claude Wheeler (who has left his frigid wife in Nebraska) is more comfortable in sensual France than back home. That Cather's central figures, Claude and his close friend David, are meant to be gay is pretty clear by the end of the book; when both are killed, Cather suggests that they would have committed suicide in modern macho America if they had survived the war. Martin Howe considers putting a bullet through his head at the end of *One Man's Initiation,* and suicide as an escape from the regimentation of both military and civilian life is a recurrent theme in *Three Soldiers.*

Cather and Dos Passos seem to agree that the United States of the twenties is no place for sensitive men. Jimmy Herf, in *Manhattan Transfer* (1925), is another of these, but he is a much richer character than anyone in the war novels. The novel itself is extraordinary in its ambitious sweep, an attempt to portray all of New York City in its kaleidoscopic interconnectedness. A hundred characters—I'm guessing—are accorded short, fragmentary chapters that hurtle forward, linked by proximity in time or place or theme. A fire engine (a recurring motif) heard through the window in one chapter puts out a fire in which a character dies in the next and a man declares his fiery passion for a woman in the one that follows.

Dos Passos is particularly eager to capture the visual shock of New York City, which he called "the city of scrambled alphabets" and "the city of gilt letter signs." From the time of the Armory Show, Dos Passos had been interested in modern art. For a time he thought of being a painter, and he exhibited and published his own drawings and paintings, some of which are included in these volumes. In 1923, while working on *Manhattan Transfer,* he had shown his Fauve-ish paintings in New York and admired the newspaper headlines that his friend the artist Gerald Murphy designed as a backdrop for Cole Porter's ballet *Within the Quota.* In *Manhattan Transfer,* Dos Passos's characters are always reading newspapers, or coming across newspapers abandoned in the streets, or glimpsing headlines on the run ("ADMITS KILLING CRIPPLED MOTHER"), or—in the case of Jimmy Herf—writing for them. The modernist thrill of juxtaposing bits of newsprint in different fonts, exploited by Picasso and Murphy, became for Dos Passos a central technique in the "newsreel" sections of *U.S.A.*

Dos Passos tried other ways to give visual immediacy to *Manhattan Transfer,* for example by filtering all his visual descriptions through the operations of light. Sometimes he achieves effects that recall, perhaps intentionally, the so-called Ashcan School of American realist painters: "Outside the lemoncolored dawn was drenching the empty streets, dripping from cornices, from the rails of fire escapes, from the rims of ashcans, shattering the blocks of shadow between buildings." At others, he aims for a spangled, hothouse manner more reminiscent of Bonnard's bathroom beauties than Picasso: "The bathroom door opened; a stream of sunlight reflected out of a pierglass cut the murky hall in half, out of it came a head of hair like copper wire, bluedark eyes in a brittlewhite eggshaped face. Then the hair was brown down the hall above a slim back in a tangerine-colored slip, nonchalant pink heels standing up out of the bathslippers at every step."

Despite the rich array of figures—businessmen and theater producers and actors and drunkards and prostitutes—the reader's attention is brought back to the newspaper reporter Jimmy Herf, who arrives in New York as a baby with his mother on July 4, and Ellen Oglethorpe, the aspiring actress with copper-colored hair and nymphomaniac tendencies (Millay seems a model) wearing the tangerine slip. They are briefly married, but the marriage is only happy while they travel in France. The novel ends as Dos Passos's novels always end, with desertion. Herf walks out of his newspaper job at the Pulitzer building and leaves New York on foot. He hitches a ride on a furniture truck. "How fur ye goin?" the driver asks. "I dunno," says Herf. "Pretty far."

We may wonder what made American urban life, with its undeniable modernist charms, so unbearable for John Dos Passos. Partly, he seems to have recoiled from the sheer toughness of the city, its clubby atmosphere of male competitiveness. Jimmy Herf, bullied as a child for being a "girlboy" and a crybaby, is clearly another stand-in for Dos Passos himself. A gay actor who is trying to get straightened out by psychoanalysis tells Herf he always thought Herf was gay. Dos Passos's friends seem to have had the same suspicions about Dos Passos. Edmund Wilson in *The Twenties* tells of a conversation between Dos Passos and Cummings during a trip to Spain they took together.

> When we got to a town, Cummings said, I'd want to go out to the square or somewhere to see if I could find something [he meant a girl]. Dos would never go with me—he'd say, "I'll just stay here in the hotel, I think." One day I said to him. "Dos: don't you ever think about women?" No. "Don't you ever dream about sex?" No. What I went through with that man! He'd wake me up in the night groaning and throwing himself around in his sleep. I'd say, "What's the matter, Dos?" He'd say, "Why, I thought there were some beautiful wild swans flying overhead."

Dos Passos's on-again, off-again engagement with Crystal Ross, beginning in 1922, and cut off in 1926 when she married another man, must have reinforced his friends' suspicions. Still, Dos Passos was happily married to Katharine Smith, a childhood friend of Hemingway's, for almost twenty years, from 1929 until her death in a car accident in 1947; he remarried two years later.

Dos Passos spent much of his life in a feverish search—a hotel adulthood to match his hotel childhood—for a good place in the sun where art and life could flourish. He discovered Spain earlier than Hemingway, and his Spain is a more nuanced cultural terrain that Hemingway's romp of trout streams and bullfights. The reasons for the affinity may be partly ancestral: Dos Passos's grandfather had come from Portugal, and in his engaging travel book *Rosinante to the Road Again* (1922) Dos Passos archly portrays himself as Telemachus in search of his father. What Dos Passos found in Spain was partly what northern travelers have always found there: "Nights of dancing and guitar—playing at vintage-time, *fiestas* of the Virgin, where older, realer gods were worshipped than Jehovah and the dolorous Mother of the pale Christ, the *toros,* blood and embroidered silks aflame in the sunlight, words whispered through barred windows at night, long days of travel on stony roads in the mountains." It is, in Dos Passos's view, an agrarian and communal world to oppose to the competitive industrialism of the United States. When Spanish peasants greeted him with a glass of wine or a slice of watermelon, Dos Passos suggested that in America "these same people would come out after us with shotguns loaded with rock salt." Despite his leftist convictions, Dos Passos's nostalgia for an agrarian society close to the land—"the walking, consciously or not, of the way beaten by generations of men who had tilled and loved and lain in the cherishing sun"—isn't that far from the inchoate longings of such southern conservative contemporaries as Faulkner and Allen Tate.

The freshest, least forced writing in these new Library of America volumes is in a few pages from the Rosinante sketches and in the exceptional *Orient Express* (1927), a "travel book" only in the sense in which Graham Greene and Ryzard Kapuscinski and Naipaul write travel books. The book has an elegiac feel, nostalgic for both an earlier world of heroic travel and an earlier world of civilized human behavior. In a vivid chapter on the French writer Blaise Cendrars, entitled "Homer of the Trans-Siberian," Dos Passos recalls a childhood visit to the Paris world's exposition of 1900, where the Trans-Siberian train was on display, "virtual travel" almost a century before the Internet: "That stationary trans-Siberian where the panorama unrolled Asia every hour was the last vestige of the Homeric age of railroading." Dos Passos plunges the reader into the contrastingly unheroic modern world of 1921–22, when "there's an American bar in Baghdad and the Grand Lama of Thibet listens in on Paul Whiteman ragging the Blue Danube and the caterpillar Citroens chug up and down the dusty streets of Timbuctoo."

The heart of the book is a journey through the brutalized Middle East following the Great War. The pages on rat-infested Baghdad have a gloomy contemporary poignancy, and Dos Passos's camel trek across the desert to Damascus (arranged with the help of British officials like Gertrude Bell, who were carving up Arabia with maps and rulers) is continually arresting. Lying in his crimson tent the first night out gave him "the feeling of being a worm in a fuchsia flower. . . . At last here was an end of colonies and whisky and soda and the *Strand* and canned goods and the American Bar on Tigris bank and the soldier-littered rail-scarred dumping grounds of the West."

It is easy to make too much of Dos Passos's politics, by according his novels more sophistication about the class struggle than they in fact display. He is more interested in cultural producers like actors and artists and newspapermen than he is in factory workers or captains of industry. Though he once bragged that "everyday I become more red," Dos Passos, as Daniel Aaron remarks in *Writers on the Left,* was "an observer rather than a joiner." He did not fight in the Spanish Civil War, never joined the Communist Party, never helped organize a strike. Like Edna Millay, he was never farther to the left than during the Sacco and Vanzetti case of 1927, and like her he wrote bad poetry inspired by it: "They are dead now / The black automatons have won. / They are burned up utterly / their flesh has passed into the air of Massachusetts." Such ponderous lines owe as much to T. S. Eliot as to Karl Marx.

It is also easy to make too little of Dos Passos's politics, by explaining his hatred of organized society as an Oedipal conflict with his wealthy corporate father, resolved when Dos Passos recovered in court, soon after World War II, some of the money due him from his inheritance. Edmund Wilson thought Dos Passos was perfectly consistent in his shift from left to right since his real enemy was liberalism. This too is overly simple. What Dos Passos treasured was what he called in *Rosinante* "the strong anarchistic reliance on the individual man." One of his revolutionary ideas, conveyed to Theodore Dreiser in 1937, was to instill something of the spirit of the New England town meeting into American politics. His deepest political moorings were in the turn-of-the-century populism of Eugene Debs and Thorstein Veblen, who are accorded two of the most eloquent and deeply felt biographical tributes in *U.S.A.* His dream of a good society, as outlined in the Veblen sketch, sounds like a stump speech by Albert Gore: "a new matteroffact commonsense society dominated by the needs of the men and women who did the work and the incrediby vast possibilities of peace and plenty offered by the progress of technology."

During the Spanish Civil War, a particularly excruciating period for him, Dos Passos supported the Republic and sympathized with Communist factions until he learned that his old friend Jose Robles, an official in the Republican government, had been secretly shot by Communists on a bogus charge of spying. One of the most moving pieces of writing in these volumes is a letter to the *New Republic,* dated July 19, 1939, in which Dos Passos lays out the facts of the shameful execution as he knows them. Hemingway, playing hard man to Dos Passos's scruples, had looked into the execution and concluded that since Robles was shot as a spy, he must have been a spy. Dos Passos's measured response kept his fury in bounds: "Anyone who knew Spaniards of any stripe before the civil war will remember that they tended to carry personal independence in talk and manners to the extreme. It is only too likely that Robles, like many others who were conscious of their own sincerity of purpose, laid himself open to a frame-up . . . pushed to the point of execution because Russian secret agents felt that Robles knew too much about the relations between the Spanish war ministry and the Kremlin." Conversations with George Orwell and others solidified Dos Passos's sense that "personal independence" and Soviet-style Communism were antithetical; he wrote a friend in 1937 that "Anglo-Saxon democracy is the best political method of which we have any . . . I have come to believe that the CP is fundamentally opposed to our democracy."

I am not alone in wishing that this personal voice of Dos Passos, lyrical and skeptical at once, were more audible in his best fiction. There is a depersonalized deterministic grimness in *Manhattan Transfer* and *U.S.A.* that is only alleviated by the momentary flashes of Jimmy Herf's insight and by the "camera eye" sections of *U.S.A.,* when Dos Passos allows himself brief stretches of autobiographical musings. Otherwise, it is the relentless momentum of modern society that Dos Passos is after, and the equally relentless suppression of his own authorial voice. This suppression provoked equal and opposite responses from two formidable midcentury critics. For Jean-Paul Sartre, who once chastised François Mauriac for using an omniscient narrator ("Only God is omniscient, and God is not a novelist"), Dos Passos seemed the novelist of the future, who had successfully purged every authorial presence from his work, including the shaping power of narrative. "There is no narrative," wrote Sartre, "but rather the jerky unreeling of a rough and uneven memory, which sums up a period of several years in a few words only to dwell languidly over a minute fact. . . . For Dos Passos, narrating means adding. This accounts for the slack air of his style."

The British critic F. R. Leavis criticized Dos Passos for exactly the same reason, the absence of a palpable personal voice, even while recognizing the fundamental seriousness of Dos Passos's intentions: "The shortcomings of the work both as art and propaganda are related to a certain insufficiency in it when it is considered as an expression of personality (which on any theory a work of art must in some sense be." I can see Sartre's point, but as a reader I side with Leavis. If Dos Passos's development as a writer, at least up to *U.S.A.,* was among other things a steady suppression of his own lyrical and authorial voice, we may as readers find some paradoxical pleasure in reading backward in his work, and listening for those moments—especially in his travel writing and in the nonfiction sections of *U.S.A.*—when his own voice most comes through.

"I never dared be radical when young," wrote Robert Frost, "for fear it would make me conservative when old." Was Dos Passos an American George Orwell, converted from youthful fantasies by the hard facts of twentieth-century total war? It is tempting to think so. Both men in their youth were made to feel uneasy in elite schools, and tried to feel at home among the down and out. Both labored hard as novelists but found their most compelling voices as essayists and satirists. For both, the Spanish Civil War was a turning point, or rather a point of no return. Both are most moving as poets of cold-eyed disillusionment. In an essay in the *New York Review of Books* (September 25, 2003), Timothy Garton Ash speculated on what Orwell's fate might have been had he lived beyond age forty-five ("an iconoclastic left-wing voice on the *New Statesman*? a curmudgeonly old cold warrior" on the CIA-funded *Encounter*?), and concluded that "only his early death allowed everyone to beatify him in their own way."

With Dos Passos, who lived until 1970, the question is the opposite: Had he died in 1939, with his most movingly disillusioned works—the pages on the Spanish Civil War and the biographical sections of *U.S.A.*—complete, would he now be revered by left and right, like Orwell, as a clear-eyed man in a time of propagandists? The two men met only once, in a hotel in Barcelona in 1937, where Orwell was recovering from a gunshot wound through his neck. Understandably they did not talk long, but Dos Passos, as Townsend Ludington notes in his biography of Dos Passos, "remembered his sense of relief to be conversing with an honest man at last." "There's a certain majesty in innocence in the face of death," Dos Passos wrote in *Journeys between Wars*. "This man Orwell referred without overemphasis to things we both knew to be true. . . . Perhaps he was still a little afraid of how much he knew."

VOLUMES REVIEWED

*Novels, 1920–1925*
By John Dos Passos
Library of America, 2003

*Travel Books and Other Writings, 1916–1941*
By John Dos Passos
Library of America, 2003

## Covering Her Century

WHATEVER ELSE SHE WAS—novelist, travel writer, celebrity wife, socialite—Martha Gellhorn was one of the greatest American war correspondents of her generation or any other. Through almost four decades, she covered in succession the Spanish Civil War, World War II, Vietnam, the Arab-Israeli conflict, the civil wars in El Salvador and Nicaragua, along with related skirmishes and horrors from Helsinki to Hong Kong. She was in Barcelona in November 1938—"perfect bombing weather," she noted dryly—as Franco's planes closed in. She was at Dachau when news came of the German surrender. Descended from German Jews herself, Gellhorn found Dachau "the most suitable place in Europe to hear the news of victory." In 1994, four years before her death at age eighty-nine, Gellhorn was in Brazil, writing about violent deaths of street children there. Fearless, attentive, with a quick eye for the heartbreaking detail, she had the perfect temperament for the war reporter. "I never found my own private disorderly place in the world except in the general chaos of war," she wrote to a friend in 1960, when she and the twentieth century still had plenty of war to go.

Gellhorn's distinctive voice fused two major strands of American reportage: the WPA-inspired documentation of the suffering of ordinary folk during the depression; and the hard-boiled, ironic take on war of American reporters from Stephen Crane to Ernest Hemingway. Gellhorn's four years of marriage to Hemingway, during the initial phase of his long decline, bolstered her fame while diminishing—at least among his legions of admirers—her status as a writer. He told anyone who would listen what a bitch and a phony she was. She resented being reduced to "a footnote in history, a passing reference in others' books and letters," while maintaining a dignified public silence. Now that we have a generous selection of her letters, assembled by her authorized biographer, Caroline Moorehead, we can piece together her account of the marriage. She left him because he was a crybaby and got in the way of her work.

Like so many nomads of her lost generation, Martha Gellhorn was a child of the Midwest who wanted out. She was born in St. Louis in 1908. Her father, son of a Breslau merchant, was a gynecologist and obstetrician who specialized in syphilis; her mother, a St. Louis native, campaigned for women's suffrage. Both were half Jewish. Dismayed by the educational options for their three children, they helped to found a progressive school in St. Louis named for the nature writer John Burroughs. Martha went from Burroughs to Bryn Mawr, didn't like it, and left to become a cub reporter for a newspaper in Albany, covered women's clubs for six months, didn't like it, and headed for Europe with two suitcases, a typewriter, and seventy-five dollars.

Gellhorn's first brush with love was pure Henry James. In 1930, floating among odd jobs in Paris, she met a sophisticated, charming, and married journalist named Bertrand de Jouvenel. Half-Jewish like Gellhorn, Jouvenel drifted during the 1930s between anti-liberal positions on the left and right; and after the war he emerged as a significant political theorist, best known for works such as *On Power,* which analyzed the growth of the modern state as a threat to individual liberty. Bertrand was twenty-six when he met Gellhorn; ten years earlier he had been seduced by his stepmother, the writer Colette. Gellhorn could read all about it in the novel *Chéri.* Bertrand and Martha considered themselves married, but St. Louis, where they sought refuge, didn't agree. Neither did Jouvenel's wife, who refused a divorce. In 1931, the *St. Louis Post-Dispatch* agreed to fund her travels through the Southwest, as recorded in a series of letters to Stanley Pennell, her English teacher at the Burroughs school and later the author of the superb Gettysburg novel *The History of Rose Hanks.* She wrote to Jouvenel from the highway in California, where her platinum-colored Dodge, bought for twenty-five dollars, had broken down:

"I've repaid ardor with impatience and sponged your assurance with icy water . . . forget me—I'm a shit face; and make yourself realize again what you knew before I came. I'll write from Carmel."

The affair, like the Dodge, limped on for another three years—through faked orgasms, two abortions, and, in 1933, an encounter with Colette herself. "What impressed me," Gellhorn wrote, "was to come in and find her writing on a book, with such steady, bored persistence—so little flame and fireworks—but just the determined weariness of one adding up accounts. . . . What wouldn't I give for that will and discipline." Gellhorn was writing a novel herself, published as *What Mad Pursuit,* about a young American woman reporter who has affairs and becomes disillusioned. The book caught the attention of Harry Hopkins in the Roosevelt administration, who was assembling a team of young reporters to fan out across the depression-ravaged country and document the lives of ordinary people—the impulse that gave rise to Dorothea Lange's photographs, John Steinbeck's *The Grapes of Wrath,* and, best of all, the collaboration of James Agee and Walker Evans in *Let Us Now Praise Famous Men.*

Two episodes stand out from Gellhorn's modest contribution to this worthy effort: she made up a story about a lynching in the South and published it as fact, and she encouraged laborers in North Carolina to break factory windows in protest against their working conditions. Eleanor Roosevelt, a college friend of Gellhorn's mother, admired the lynching article, and Martha explained, giddily and lamely, that she was "getting a little mixed-up around now and apparently I am a very realistic writer (or liar), because everyone assumed I'd been an eye-witness to a lynching whereas I just made it up." Her fake story dogged her for the rest of her life; her incitement to riot got her fired by Hopkins. *The Trouble I've Seen,* Gellhorn's collection of what Moorehead gingerly calls "semi-fictional stories about the Depression," appeared in 1936 to admiring reviews. Eleanor Roosevelt praised it in her column, "My Day": "I cannot tell you how Martha Gellhorn, young, pretty, college graduate, good home, more or less Junior League background, with a touch of exquisite Paris clothes and 'esprit' thrown in, can write as she does. She has an understanding of many people, and many situations, and she can make them live for us."

Gellhorn's father died on Christmas Day, 1935, and she and her mother spent the following Christmas together at Key West. One night, they walked into a bar named Sloppy Joe's where "a large, dirty man in untidy somewhat soiled white shorts and shirt" just happened to be sitting. She was twenty-eight. Hemingway was thirty-seven and—like most of the men in Gellhorn's life—married. Of course, the encounter can't have been completely by chance. It was hardly a secret that Hemingway hung out in Key West in the winter and liked to drink. And Gellhorn, along with half her generation, had already adopted Hemingway's creed as her own. "I take my code out of Hemingway," she had written to Stanley Pennell while still at Bryn Mawr. "Do you remember *A Farewell to Arms*? The hero talks to the woman; she is worried about something; and he says: 'You're brave. Nothing ever happens to the brave.' Which is somehow enough—a whole philosophy—a banner—a song—and a love. And something to fill up time—busily, passionately."

One of the oddest things about being Ernest Hemingway must have been the uncanny sense that so many of the people he met had stepped out of the pages of his own books. Gellhorn modeled herself on Hemingway's heroes, however, not his women. When he told her that he was going to Spain to write about the civil war, Gellhorn decided that she was going, too. When she arrived in Madrid in the spring of 1937, Hemingway, surrounded by his admiring entourage of fellow journalists and prostitutes, greeted her with the condescending words: "I knew you'd get here, daughter, because I fixed it so you could." She checked into the Hotel Florida, where Hemingway had two rooms on the quiet side away from the shelling. Hemingway locked her in her room the first night because he didn't what her to be mistaken, as he wittily explained, for a "whore de combat." Gellhorn was furious. "I should have known at that moment what doom was," she remarked. The moment is emblematic of the seven bumpy years that followed. He wanted her home where he could find her, waiting and adoring; she wanted the life he had.

According to Gellhorn, Hemingway was a "ghastly lover—wham bam thank you maam, or maybe just wham bam."

Gellhorn's dispatches from Spain established one of her great themes as a war reporter, the intrusion of horror into ordinary life.

> It seemed a little crazy to be living in a hotel, like a hotel in Des Moines or New Orleans, with a lobby and wicker chairs in the lounge, and signs on the door of your room telling you that they would press your clothes immediately and that meals served privately cost ten percent more, and meantime it was like a trench when they lay down an artillery barrage. The whole place trembled to the explosion of the shells.
>
> The concierge was in the lobby and he said, apologetically, "I regret this, Mademoiselle. It is not pleasant. I can guarantee you that the bombing in November was worse."[1]

The war, as she saw it, pitted the relentless machinery of Franco's forces and his Fascist allies against the merely human resistance of the brave Loyalists. She told Eleanor Roosevelt of watching for fifty minutes "twelve black German planes, flying in a perfect circle, not varying their position, flying and bombing and diving to machine gun: and they were working on one company of Government soldiers, who had no planes or anti-aircraft to protect them but who were standing there, holding up the advance so as to permit an orderly retreat."

Gellhorn followed Hemingway back to Cuba in February 1939 where he was writing *For Whom the Bell Tolls* and expected her to keep house. Instead, much to his annoyance, she flew to Helsinki to cover the Russo-Finnish conflict, which confirmed her David-and-Goliath view of war. "I promise you," she wrote Hemingway, "that I have never yet seen the innocent and unarmed other than hunted and destroyed." She also promised him, in a half-joking document titled "Guaranty," that she would "never brutalize my present and future husband in any way whatsoever" and that she recognized "that a very fine and sensitive writer cannot be left alone for two months and sixteen days." By September 1940 she was complaining that "E wants me for himself, altogether," and that "E's book has been an agony, like having children without interruption for months and months." She married him a month later, in Cheyenne, Wyoming, with roast moose for dinner.

Gellhorn and Hemingway honeymooned, if you could call it that, in Hong Kong, after *Collier's* hired her to cover the "Chinese army in action"—in retreat, more accurately, from the occupying Japanese forces. The journey gave Gellhorn one of the liveliest chapters in *Travels with Myself and Another,* her 1978 memoir of what she called her "horror journeys." She referred to Hemingway as U.C., for "Unwilling Companion"; as he hung out in the hotel bar in Hong Kong, she explored the opium dens, the brothels, the mahjong parlors and sweatshops, all overrun with refugees. She expected Hemingway to share her horror:

> When finally I visited a dank ill-lit basement factory where small children carved ivory balls within balls, a favorite tourist trinket, I could not bear to see any more. I had a mild fit of hysterics.
>
> "They look about ten years old," I shouted at U.C. "It takes three months to make one of those damned things, I think it's eight balls within balls. They'll be blind before they're twenty. And that little girl with her tortoise. We're all living on slave labor! The people are half starved! I want to get out, I can't stand this place!"
>
> U.C. considered me thoughtfully. "The trouble with you, M., is that you think everybody is exactly like you. What you can't stand, they can't stand. What's hell for you has to be hell for them. How do you know what they feel about their lives?"

Their diverging temperaments could hardly be clearer: Gellhorn's utopian indignation versus Hemingway's stoical acceptance.

The slow unraveling of the marriage ran parallel with the worsening situation in Europe. Gellhorn insisted on reporting the war; Hemingway insisted on staying in Cuba, sailing around the Gulf of Mexico supposedly in search of German submarines. When he realized that the action was in Europe after all, he signed on with *Collier's,* Gellhorn's employer, to cover the Normandy invasion. Gellhorn was demoted; "I have been shoved back and back," she complained to Eleanor Roosevelt. "It is quite a job being a woman isn't it; you cannot do your work and simply get on with it because that is selfish. . . . Anyhow Ernest will get there [to Normandy] and he can always tell me about it." By then, with the quarreling and drinking and competing, she knew it was over. "I want to escape from him and myself and from this personal life which feels like a strait jacket." She left him and he never forgave her. "Hell hath no fury like E.H. scorned," she wrote. But she continued to admire Hemingway; if he was an ordinary husband, he was also "a rare and wonderful type; he is a mysterious type too and a wise one and all sorts of things. He is a good man, which is vitally important. He is however bad for me."

If the breakup of her marriage was a blow to Gellhorn, Dachau in some ways was a deeper wound. "I have never been the same since," she later wrote to a friend. "It's exactly like mixing paint. Black, real true solid black, was then introduced, and I have never again come back to some state of hope or innocence or gayety which I had before." Her description in her *Collier's* article is often quoted: "We have all seen a great deal now; we have seen too many wars and too much violent dying; we have seen hospitals, bloody and messy as butcher shops; we have seen the dead like bundles lying on all the roads of half the earth. But nowhere was there anything like this. Nothing about war was ever as insanely wicked as these starved and outraged, naked, nameless dead."[2] Her account of Dachau is the opposite of her accounts of Spain and Finland: not the intrusion of horror into the ordinary world but the reverse: "Just behind the crematorium stood the fine big modern hothouses. Here the prisoners grew the flowers that the S.S. officers loved."

The shape of Gellhorn's life during the decades that followed was a double quest. She sought to experience as an eyewitness the horrors that the century of total war kept inventing. And, perhaps in reaction, she tried to find the great good place that would be her refuge from war and the boredom of St. Louis. She tried Cuernavaca, Rome, Kenya, before settling, during her final years, on a flat in London and a cottage in Wales. She never found the right man to share these places with her and the right man probably did not exist. Gellhorn's letters to her various lovers—a blur of doctors and diplomats, journalists and generals—are either manic professions of eternal love or depressive intimations of the impossibility of same. In 1954, she tried marriage again only to discover a few years later that her husband, the writer T. S. Matthews, was cheating on her. She was shocked, but Edmund Wilson, a Princeton classmate of Matthews, could have warned her: "He is always in the pants of some woman."

More fun to read about are Gellhorn's relations with men she didn't or probably didn't sleep with. She met H. G. Wells of all people in the Roosevelt White House and he took her under his wing, finding publishers and outlets for her writing, including the ill-fated lynching tale. I find myself unable to work up much curiosity about whether she slept with Wells—a point of contention among Gellhorn's biographers—though I like her riposte: "Why the hell would I sleep with a little old man when I could have any number of tall beautiful young men?" Leonard Bernstein and his piano moved into a neighboring house in Cuernavaca in 1950. "He is reported to like men (also women and goats), and is actually beautiful, which is an odd thing for a man to be, and about as natural as a 20 minute permanent wave; and full of talent and neuroses." Bernstein treasured what he called their "peculiar sexless love affair" and told Gellhorn that he had written the song "One Hundred Easy Ways to Lose a Man" in her honor.

In 1952, while living in Rome and making arrangements to adopt an Italian war orphan, Gellhorn was pursued by Bernard Berenson, then in his late eighties, eliciting this bracing tirade:

> He has a learned mind but it does not seem a mind to me; I never heard him on painting and he may be extraordinary but you know I doubt it. I doubt if one can be really profoundly extraordinary about art, unless one has a certain fire and richness inside. He hasn't; he is a little Tanagra man, spoiled all his life by smart second-rate people. He's not interesting nor inspiring; I always felt *less* of a human being after seeing him. Did I tell you that he said to me that no one had so attacked him in his life, except Gertrude Stein. I found that funny; this came after I had carefully explained to him that I didn't trust him and he wasn't my cup of tea.

She found it funny because Berenson was implying, not very subtly, that if she didn't find him attractive she must be a lesbian.

Gellhorn writes a great deal in these letters about sex and her distaste for it. Hemingway wrote to Berenson, one jilted man to another, that Gellhorn "was not built for bed."[3] Gellhorn seems to have agreed. "I didn't like the sex at all," she wrote Cary Grant's ex-wife Betsy Drake in 1972. "I daresay I was the worst bed partner in five continents. And the agile and experienced men were always shits, which didn't endear sex to me as you can imagine." She felt, she often said, like a man in a woman's body; "I think I am, very largely, a man anyhow," she wrote Rosamond Lehmann. The split in her temperament between men she liked but wasn't attracted to (Wells, Bernstein, the war photographer Robert Capa, and even Hemingway) and men she didn't much like but was (the blur of older lovers) is familiar enough in men, as Freud pointed out repeatedly. Gellhorn wondered why D. H. Lawrence wasn't satisfied with the first version of *Lady Chatterley's Lover,* "a study in boredom and marital distaste," and "went on writing it until he got that highflown pornography at the end version." Her own best fiction, such as the poignant novella based on Capa's life, *Till Death Do Us Part,* skates over the territory of sexuality.

"In a war you must hate somebody or love somebody," Gellhorn's Capa character remarks. "You must have a position or you cannot stand what goes on." Gellhorn's tendency to see the world in absolutes, which can't have helped in her relations with men, also bedeviled her later writing. Understated sympathy for the victims of World War II gave her war reporting an affecting emotional resonance. But she refused, then or after, to recognize the humanity of the perpetrators. Germans, against whom she maintained a lifetime vendetta, were simply beyond the pale. "All God's chillun hid Jews" was how she summed up German denial of war guilt.[4] The French and Italians, however, were mysteriously absolved, as though they had recovered, with the Allied victory, from some alien virus. The Israelis were always Davids, the Arabs—for whom she reserved a special venom—always Goliaths. "My belief in Israel is unwavering and I do not expect it to be faultless, unlike any other state," she wrote while covering the Six Day War. "I have never forgotten Dachau."[5]

The Russians, with their "peculiar historical genius for oppressing and being oppressed," confounded Gellhorn's stereotypes.[6] She traveled to Moscow in the summer of 1972 to meet Nadezhda Mandelstam, whose *Hope against Hope* she had greatly admired. Gellhorn described their seriocomic encounters in *Travels with Myself and Another*. Before the trip she described Mandelstam as "one human pretty damn near reaching perfection, under conditions of hell." After a few weeks of "heat, awful food, exhaustion, and deep deep boredom" in Mandelstam's company, she concluded: "She is not a bit noble and I have a failing for nobility." It was Hong Kong with Hemingway all over again, as Gellhorn's sentimental idealism clashed with what she calls Mandelstam's stoic "cunning and camouflage." What really riled her, though, was Mandelstam's support for the American military incursion in Vietnam. Mandelstam: "If North Vietnam wins, they will shoot three million people." Gellhorn: "*Why?* On what grounds do you say that?" Mandelstam: "Here they shot three million people."[7]

"I don't think I like her," Gellhorn wrote of Nadezhda Mandelstam. Reading through these five hundred pages of Gellhorn's letters, the reader may come to have mixed feelings about Gellhorn as well. Despite her virtuosity in expressing her love for the little guy, she seems never to have written to him. She preferred the gossipy round of the powerful, the beautiful, and the rich. She hated gaining weight and she hated getting old. "There are no real rewards for time passing," she wrote. She staved off the inevitable by swimming every day in her private pool with Chopin and Brahms on her record player. She kept up to date with younger writers, admiring Naipaul and Ondaatje, and made friends with a "gaggle of chaps in London all half my age." "The two suicides I know" (she was writing of Hemingway and a painter friend) "were not murdering themselves with hate, but simply leaving while there was time, from the empty ruins of life, because they knew—and I think rightly—that they had finished, and that what remained was going to be bleak and belittling." She made a final journey as a reporter—"Brazil cured me of wanderlust for some time"—and then, on February 16, 1998, at the age of eighty-nine, almost blind and suffering from cancer of the ovary and liver, she took a pill she had acquired for a quick exit, and left.

NOTES

1. Martha Gellhorn, *The Face of War* (New York: Atlantic Monthly Press, 1988), 19.
2. Gellhorn, *Face of War,* 184.
3. Carl E. Rollyson, *Beautiful Exile: The Life of Martha Gellhorn* (London: Aurum, 2002), 190.
4. Rollyson, *Beautiful Exile,* 166.
5. Gellhorn, *Face of War,* 288.
6. Gellhorn, *Travels with Myself and Another* (New York: Dodd, Mead, 1978), 264.
7. Gellhorn, *Travels with Myself,* 263.

VOLUME REVIEWED

*The Collected Letters of Martha Gellhorn*
Edited by Caroline Moorehead
Henry Holt, 2006

# The Critter Poet

GARY SNYDER WAS A CHARACTER IN A NOVEL before he published his own first book. In Jack Kerouac's *The Dharma Bums,* that vivid account of the birth of the San Francisco Poetry Renaissance and the Beat movement, there is a biographical sketch of Japhy Ryder, "the number one Dharma Bum of them all":

> Japhy Ryder was a kid from eastern Oregon brought up in a log cabin deep in the woods with his father and mother and sister, from the beginning a woods boy, an axman, farmer, interested in animals and Indian lore so that when he finally got to college by hook or crook he was already well equipped for his early studies in anthropology and later in Indian myth and in the actual texts of Indian mythology. Finally he learned Chinese and Japanese and became an Oriental scholar and discovered the greatest Dharma Bums of them all, the Zen Lunatics of China and Japan. At the same time, being a Northwest boy with idealistic tendencies, he got interested in oldfashioned I.W.W. anarchism and learned to play the guitar and sing old worker songs to go with his Indian songs and general folksong interests.

This is the beginning of the Snyder myth. For all I know, and for all that I can glean from Snyder's autobiographical writings, it is entirely true.

What makes *The Dharma Bums* a pleasure to read, forty years after its publication, is the way Kerouac, in the guise of his ordinary-Joe narrator, undercuts Japhy Ryder's humorless, self-satisfied ethos. Ray, the writer's stand-in, walks into Japhy's shack, and there is Japhy "sitting cross-legged on a Paisley pillow on a straw mat, with his spectacles on, making him look old and scholarly and wise, with book on lap and the little tin teapot and porcelain cup steaming at his side. He looked up very peacefully, saw who it was, said, 'Ray come in,' and bent his eyes again to the script." "What you doing?" "Translating Han Shan's great poem called 'Cold Mountain' written a thousand years ago some of it scribbled on the sides of cliffs hundreds of miles away from any other living beings." "Wow." Japhy proceeds to teach Ray all about Asian poetry and culture, including the proper way to have sex. When Ray walks in on Japhy, in the lotus position, making meditative love ("yabyum") to a woman called Princess, Japhy explains that "this is what they do in the temples of Tibet. It's a holy ceremony, it's done just like this in front of chanting priests. People pray and recite Om Mani Pahdme Hum, which means Amen the Thunderbolt in the Dark Void. I'm the thunderbolt and Princess is the dark void, you see."

A part of Gary Snyder's considerable prestige in the small world of American poetry is owed to the impression that he has put in the time and done the work: graduate study in anthropology at Berkeley; summers on lookout duty in national forests and parks ("The prolonged stay in mountain huts . . . gave me my first opportunity to seriously sit cross-legged"); ten years in Japan, mainly in the 1960s, doing Zen and studying Japanese aesthetics; his current rough-hewn life with his family on a hundred acres in the Sierra foothills, with a teaching appointment in English and ecology at the University of California at Davis. All this experience has gone into Snyder's poetry, the best of which manages to suppress his didactic side.

Snyder at his most moving is an elegiac poet, mourning the loss of forests, "critters" (as he calls animals), lovers, places. Snyder at his most annoying is the pedantic guy on the Paisley pillow who says, "I'm the thunderbolt and Princess is the dark void, you see." To those of us in whose early intellectual lives Snyder was a significant chapter, a return to his work after long absence can have its own embarrassments. When I was seventeen, spending a year in Japan, Snyder's *The Back Country* (1968) was one of the books that I carried everywhere with me. My favorite poem in it, which I still know by heart, was "December at Yase," the last of the "Four Poems for Robin." It begins:

> You said, that October,
> In the tall dry grass by the orchard
> When you chose to be free,
> "Again someday, maybe ten years."
>
> After college I saw you
> One time. You were strange.
> And I was obsessed with a plan.

Ten years and more go by, in which the poet considers trying to win the woman's love back. "I didn't. / I thought I must make it alone. I / Have done that." The poem concludes:

> Only in dream, like this dawn,
> Does the grave, awed intensity
> Of our young love
> Return to my mind, to my flesh.
>
> We had what the others
> All crave and seek for;
> We left it behind at nineteen.
>
> I feel ancient, as though I had
> Lived many lives.
>
> And may never now know
> If I am a fool
> Or have done what my
> karma demands.

I can't say whether this poem is any good. It's too close to me, and it too perfectly captures some of my own feelings from those days. I can see now how the poem uses little clumps of imagist detail, drawn from Pound's translations from the Chinese: "in the tall dry grass by the orchard," and how the enjambment is rather arch: "After college I saw you / One time." But, even when I was young, I knew that those last two lines about karma were a disaster. (They're crossed out in my battered copy of the book.) What they show is that Snyder, as he looks back on his early obsession "with a plan," still subscribes to one, a higher one, which he now calls "karma." All the uncertainty and the wistfulness and the delicacy of the rest of the poem is caught in the harsh headlights of "what my karma demands."

Something similar happens toward the end of what may be Snyder's best and most enduring poem, "I Went into the Maverick Bar" (from *Turtle Island,* 1974):

> I went into the Maverick Bar
> In Farmington, New Mexico.
> And drank double shots of bourbon
> backed with beer.
> My long hair was tucked up under a cap
> I'd left the earring in the car.
>
> Two cowboys did horseplay
> by the pool tables,
> A waitress asked us
> where are you from?
> a country-and-western band began to play
> "We don't smoke Marijuana in Muskokie"
> And with the next song,
> a couple began to dance.
>
> They held each other like in High School dances
> in the fifties;
> I recalled when I worked in the woods
> and the bars of Madras, Oregon.
> That short-haired joy and roughness—
> America—your stupidity.
> I could almost love you again.
>
> We left—onto the freeway shoulders—
> under the tough old stars—
> In the shadow of bluffs
> I came back to myself,
> To the real work, to
> "What is to be done."

Snyder's pleasure in being able to "pass" for a macho man is nicely rendered here, and the temptations of that life are palpable in the poem. But the rejection of "that short-haired joy and roughness" is too pat in those final two lines. One wishes this guy weren't quite so certain about the nature of the "real work," a favorite phrase of Snyder's. The revolutionary readiness of Lenin's old phrase, "what is to be done," sends a chainsaw through all that romance in the bar. Snyder knows that the dancing couples are part of the problem, and that he has the solutions. He's like the wistful revolutionary who muses, "What a beautiful church. I was baptized here. Too bad I have to blow it up."

Prescriptions for "the real work" and lists of "what is to be done" dominate Snyder's prose, much of which is collected in *A Place in Space.* On reducing world population, for example:

> Try to correct traditional cultural attitudes that tend to force women into childbearing; remove income-tax deductions for more than two children above a specified income level, and scale it so that lower income families are forced to be careful, too . . . Explore other social structures and marriage forms, such as group marriage and polyandrous marriage, which provide family life but many less children.

The decisive verbs here are *correct* and *force.* Correct those wrongheaded cultural attitudes and force those poor families to be careful.

In recent years, Snyder has become a popular speaker on the Green circuit. He is the unofficial poet laureate of the environmentalist movement. A few years ago, he exhorted the graduating class of Reed College, his alma mater: "Let's go on into the twenty-first century lean, mean, and green." (No quibble with lean and green, but why mean?) In his recent prose, Snyder is particularly attentive to the link between "endangered cultures and species." He insists that "the destruction of cultural diversity goes hand in hand with ecological destruction." So he's a strong proponent of ethnopoetics, "the study of the poetries and poetics of nonliterary peoples," which he compares to "some field of zoology that is studying disappearing species."

But, while Snyder loves nonliterary poetry, he seems to have little fondness for the literary kind, especially if it comes from the West. As he sees it, Western poetry is dominated by "the Judeo-

Christian-Cartesian view of nature (by which complex views all developed nations excuse themselves for their drastically destructive treatment of the landscape).” That’s quite a three-headed monster, the Cerberus of Western culture, but I don’t see what critters have to fear from it. Why should Jews or Christians or Descartes be held as prime suspects in crimes of ecological disaster? I’m sure Snyder has in mind some vague notion of a sinister “dualism,” as against the “holistic” conceptions of nature and humanity presumably found everywhere else on the globe. He evidently assumes that such arguments and objections no longer need to be spelled out.

Snyder’s prose is laced with American Indian sayings and Zen proverbs and Chinese epigrams, but he almost never quotes a “Western” poet. In a talk on “Unnatural Writing,” he does pause to take a swipe at two lines by Howard Nemerov: “Civilization, mirrored in language, is the garden where relations grow,” wrote Nemerov, “outside the garden is the wild abyss.” While Nemerov may be, as Snyder patronizingly calls him, “a good poet and a decent man,” he is, judging from these lines, an enemy of nature, and in need of correction:

> The unexamined assumptions here are fascinating. They are, at worst, crystallizations of the erroneous views that enable the developed world to displace Third and Fourth World peoples and overexploit nature globally. Nemerov here proposes that language is somehow implicitly civilized or civilizing, that civilization is orderly, that intrahuman relations are the pinnacle of experience (as though all of us, and all life on the planet, were not interrelated), and that “wild” means “abyssal,” disorderly, and chaotic.

Poor Nemerov, displacer of Third and Fourth World peoples, all because he suggested that language is better equipped for gardens than for wilderness. But even Whitman, whom one might have expected to garner some praise from Snyder, is chastised for his errors of thought, in a talk that Snyder delivered in Spain on the hundredth anniversary of Whitman’s death:

> Whitman is unexcelled in his attribution of a kind of divinity to ordinary (white) men and women. However, the respect and authenticity he gives to human beings is not extended to non-human creatures.

But is this true? Here's the fourteenth section of "Song of Myself" (1891–92):

> The wild gander leads his flock through the cool night,
> Ya-honk he says, and sounds it down to me like an invitation,
> The pert may suppose it meaningless, but I listening close,
> Find its purpose and place up there toward the wintry sky.

This is the Whitman who said, "I think I could turn and live with animals. . . . They do not sweat and whine about their condition, They do not lie awake in the dark and weep for their sins"; the Whitman who said, when his tread scared the wood-drake and the wood-duck, "I believe in those wing'd purposes"; who said, "And the look of the bay mare shames silliness out of me."

But Snyder has not been reading *Leaves of Grass.* His dismissal of Whitman, it turns out, is based on a cursory reading of *Democratic Vistas,* in which, according to Snyder, "we miss the presence of people of color, of Native Americans, of wilderness, or even the plain landscape." Well, then, one feels like shouting at Snyder, why don't you read Whitman's damn poetry, in which you will find all these things, and in richer and more convincing profusion than in any other American poet of his time or after?

Snyder's prose is too often chastising, moralizing, didactic. His best essay by far is called "Crawling," a three-page description of what it feels like to navigate on one's stomach through the Sierra underbrush:

> No way to travel off the trail but to dive in: down on your hands and knees on the crunchy manzanita leaf cover and crawl around between the trunks. Leather work gloves, a tight-fitting hat, long-sleeved denim work jacket, and old Filson tin pants make a proper crawler's outfit. Along the ridge a ways, and then down a steep slope through the brush, belly-sliding on snow and leaves like an otter—you get limber at it. . . . To

> go where bears, deer, raccoons, foxes—all our other neighbors—go, you have to be willing to crawl.

This is fresh and exhilarating. It reads like a poet's prose. "You can smell the fall mushrooms when crawling." There are perhaps a dozen pages like this in *A Place in Space.*

Already in that Berkeley shack, on April 8, 1956, Snyder had begun *Mountains and Rivers Without End,* a title that—as sections were published across forty years—came to seem predictive. Now Snyder has declared the poem finished, and published it in a handsome volume, with the twelfth-century Chinese scroll painting that inspired it reproduced on the endpapers. He has appended a helpful essay on the making of the poem, as well as explanatory notes and a publication record of where the many parts of the long poem first appeared.

Do the many sections of *Mountains and Rivers* comprise a single long poem? If so, it's a pretty loose and baggy one. The guiding metaphor of the structure of the poem is the gradual unfolding of the painted scroll, with the reading and viewing eye following the progress of a journey through a landscape of mountains and rivers. The book opens with a masterly description—in the tradition of ekphrasis, or writing inspired by a painting—of the scroll in the Cleveland Museum of Art that serves as Snyder's muse.

> Rider and walker cross a bridge
> above a frothy braided torrent
> that descends from a flurry of roofs like flowers
> temples tucked between cliffs,
> a side trail goes there.

Snyder doesn't ignore the seals and the writings at the end of the scroll, added by owners and connoisseurs. One of these jottings says: "Most people can get along with the noise of dogs and chickens; / Everybody cheerful in these peaceful times. / But I—why are my tastes so odd? I love the company of streams and boulders." It's clear that Snyder conceives of his poem as another such tribute, added to the scroll by a poet-connoisseur many centuries later.

*Mountains and Rivers* is best read as a sort of autobiographical journey in verse and verbal collage. Some of the earliest written sections have a distinctly period feel, with Bob Dylan rhymes—"Fat man in a Chevrolet / wants to go back to L.A."—and hitch-hiking lyricism—"Caught a ride the only car come by / at seven in the morning / chewing froze salami / riding with a passed-out L.A. whore / glove compartment full of booze, / the driver a rider, / nobody cowboy, / sometime hood, / like me picked up to drive / & drive the blues away. /We drank to Portland / and we treated that girl good." The more recently written sections arise from Snyder's current preoccupations with species loss and "cultural genocide." To my ear, the most rewarding passages are those in which Snyder imagines a world of wild nature beneath the structures of civilization, as in "Walking the New York Bedrock / Alive in the Sea of Information":

> Squalls
> From the steps leading down to the subway.
> Blue-chested runner, a female, on car streets,
> Red lights block traffic but she like the
> Beam of a streetlight in the whine of the Skilsaw,
> She runs right through.
> A cross street leads toward a river
> North goes to the woods
> South takes you fishing
> Peregrines nest at the thirty-fifth floor.

Snyder's populist take on the "cliffdwellers" in their high-rises reads like something out of an updated Dreiser: "Towers, up there the / Clean crisp white dress white skin / women and men / Who occupy sunnier niches, / Higher up on the layered stratigraphy cliffs, get / More photosynthesis, flow by more ostracods, / get more sushi, / Gather more flesh, have delightful / Cascading laughs." But when Snyder attempts to merge entirely with the world of "nature," his poetry can descend into bathos, as in his sub-Whitmanian love song to a river, "The Flowing" (1974): "The root of me / hardens and lifts to you, /thick flowing river, / my skin shivers. I quit / making this poem." Better the pithy, no-ideas-but-in-things observations of "Old Woodrat's Stinky

House" : "A venerable desert woodrat nest of twigs and shreds / plastered down with ambered urine / a family house in use eight thousand years."

Snyder discerns a tension between the mountains and rivers of his title, between "the tough spirit of willed self-discipline and the generous and loving spirit of concern for all beings." There is a similar split in Snyder as well.

His less savory side is the disciplined commissar of "what is to be done," with his endless lists of "corrections," and his self-satisfied certainty that he is living the good life while most of us are going to the dogs. But the Snyder I treasure is the wry and grizzled wilderness dweller, generously at ease in both the garden and the wild, who can cheerfully admit: "My wife Carole and I are now using computers, the writer's equivalent of a nice little chainsaw," and then add, "Chainsaws and computers increase both macho productivity and nerdy stress."

That sounds to me like the Snyder who goes into the Maverick Bar and feels at home there, and can almost love America's stupidity.

VOLUMES REVIEWED

*Mountains and Rivers Without End*
By Gary Snyder
Counterpoint, 1996

*A Place in Space: Ethics, Aesthetics, and Watersheds: New and Selected Prose*
By Gary Snyder
Counterpoint, 1995

# Lowell's Curse

ON JUNE 11, 2005, *The New York Times* ran a correction: "A picture in Weekend yesterday with the Books of The Times review, about 'The Letters of Robert Lowell,' was published in error. It showed the columnist Murray Kempton, who died in 1997, not the poet." Accidents happen, or mistakes: it wasn't made clear how the face of the acerbic columnist was substituted for the face of the famous poet. As errors go, this one could hardly approach the *Times* obituary for Herman Melville, in 1891, which identified the forgotten author as "Henry Melville." Nonetheless, it seemed starkly to register a slippage in Lowell's reputation since his death, a change of status remarked by many reviewers, including loyal friends and defenders such as Helen Vendler and Jonathan Raban. In *The New York Review of Books* for June 23, 2005, Raban wrote: "Robert Lowell's star has waned very considerably since his death in 1977, when his obituarists treated him, along with Yeats, Eliot, Auden, and Wallace Stevens, as one of the handful of unquestionably great twentieth-century poets. The publication two years ago of Frank Bidart and David Gewanter's massive edition of the *Collected Poems* did much to restore his work to public and critical view, but even now Lowell's poems are, I would guess, less widely read, taught, and anthologized than those of his two friends and contemporaries Elizabeth Bishop and John Berryman—a judgment, if that is what it is, that would have astonished serious readers of poetry between the 1950s and the 1970s."

Count me among the astonished. Except for one or two attempts to stem the tide (I remember in particular Michael Hofmann's impassioned defense of Lowell's late poetry in *The London Review of Books*), expressions of dismay have mainly been aired—at least in my reading—in the samizdat of email. Since I can't separate my own passion for poetry from my early reading of the red-covered, revised and expanded *Notebook*, in the fall of 1970 when I turned sixteen—a book that meant more to me than a thousand *Howls* or *Coney Islands of the Mind*—I can't read Lowell's letters with the distanced and rueful weighing of reputation that seems in vogue. I still remember my own shocked sense of injustice when, in September 1977, I arrived at Harvard to begin graduate school in comparative literature and learned, almost immediately, almost to the day, that the major reason I'd chosen Harvard, Lowell's presence on the teaching faculty, had come to an abrupt end, in a cab in Manhattan.

Elizabeth Bishop gave a reading at Harvard, the following spring I think, dedicated to Lowell; she read a couple of his earlier poems along with her own new elegy for Lowell, "North Haven" A year went by and Bishop was dead. A few months later, James Wright gave a reading at Harvard, dedicated to the memory of Bishop. He recited "Adam's Curse" from memory in her honor. He also read a curse on the city of Marseilles with the refrain "You wouldn't want to see it in the rain." The model for the poem, Wright explained, was Coleridge's curse on the city of Cologne, which Wright also recited from memory. And then, in March 1980, Wright was dead as well. In those days, these successive deaths of the three contemporary poets who meant most to me seemed the playing out of some curse, as though every poet I cared about was somehow *maudit*. Lowell's letters, imbued with the conviction about poetry's ultimate importance, have brought back to me that parade of readings and deaths, as elegy turned ineluctably into elegized.

Lowell never won the Nobel Prize, but his three younger friends who did—Joseph Brodsky, Derek Walcott, and Seamus Heaney—wrote elegies after Lowell's death. Each poet inventoried different things from Lowell's legacy. Brodsky and Walcott noted the propinquity of the memorial service and Boston Common; both invoked the ending of "For the Union Dead," with Brodsky, writing in English, risking overt pastiche:

Huge autoherds graze
on gray, convoluted, flat
stripes shining with grease
like an updated flag.

Walcott's elegy, published in *The Star-Apple Kingdom,* likewise registers "churches, cars, sunlight, / and the Boston Common," while asserting the traditional survival of a poet's work ("something that once had a fearful name / walks from the thing that used to wear its name").

Heaney's intimate and intuitive "Elegy" goes deeper, with Lowell serving both as a father figure granting authority on a younger practitioner ("you found the child in me / when you took farewells / under the full bay tree / by the gate in Glanmore, // opulent and restorative / as that lingering summertime") and as an example—inspiring and cautionary—of the poet's life:

The way we are living,
timorous or bold,
will have been our life.

What comes across most fully in Lowell's letters to poets is his generosity, his eagerness to seize on what is solid in new work and his honesty concerning what is not. Even to such intimidating correspondents as Ezra Pound, recipient of the first letter in this selection, Lowell doesn't flinch. Reading drafts of *Cantos* in 1956, Lowell wrote, "You beat anyone at opening windows and letting air into your poem," but then: "I wish sometimes you had a beginning, middle and end." Something else comes across in Lowell's response, in September 1975, to Heaney's "Glanmore Sonnets," the ten-poem sequence that immediately follows "Elegy" in *Field Work:*

> I've read the sonnets a good many times. Two that I like best are "The Train" and "A Drink of Water." In general, I like all your description. Your Nature pours out images with a full hand; the cup (to work this figure to death) is so often dry for me, a town man in the end. Sonnets seem in two ways perhaps the wrong form for your sequence. First the somewhat too full-dress, particularly the final couplet; then the whole sequence

> makes me think of Wordsworth, and that something that goes so well should have gone even farther. At worst, you should [be] able to mine many poems out of your many strong lines—perhaps in quatrains, or more drastic changes. I've been so long netted in my own unrhymed sonnets that I'm no judge.

*Sonnets seem in two ways perhaps the wrong form for your sequence.* Imagine getting that response from an admired elder. But Heaney must have realized that the key line in the letter was the last one quoted, about being "so long netted in my own unrhymed sonnets." Lowell was being territorial, warning a younger poet to back off from his own crisscrossed terrain. To Lowell's credit, the poems he liked best—sonnet IV ("I used to lie with an ear to the line") and "A Drink of Water," published as a stand-alone sonnet outside the Glanmore fold—were the least Lowellian. To Heaney's credit, bold rather than timorous, he followed Lowell's example rather than his advice, and published the sonnets despite Lowell's grudging praise.

Some day we will be able to read Lowell's poetry and his prose—as we read Coleridge's—apart from his breakdowns, his medications, and his marriages. His letters, as every reviewer noted, are full of such matters, "smash and vehemence" followed by rueful acceptance. "What queer lives we've had even for poets!" he wrote Berryman in 1962. "There seems something generic about it, and determined beyond anything we could do. You and I have had so many of the same tumbles and leaps. We must have a green old age. We both have drunk the downward drag as deeply as is perhaps bearable." A couple of years later, to Adrienne Rich: "As we grow older, moments of pause come, and we say, 'This too is part of it, life is inescapably this too'; and then somehow we feel it's all rich and merciful."

But I think these letters will come to matter more for other reasons. Lowell, poet of nets and whalers—who once wrote of how Wordsworth's "great clumsy structures . . . somehow lift the great sail and catch the wind"—was an inspired networker, weaving constellations of correspondents among his contemporaries. He was "hungry for company, hungry for fathers," as Saskia Hamilton writes in her smart introduction. The letters to the fathers—Pound and Williams, Santayana and Eliot—are ingratiating and bracing by turns. We can follow Lowell as he tries to shore up the foundations of his own literary ancestry, shedding Amy and James Russell and Percival Lowell—a Japan hand whom Lowell, mistakenly, places in China—for Jonathan Edwards and Melville. All this is familiar enough.

Less expected, though, is Lowell's serious engagement with American poets generally thought to be in a different tradition, especially the second strand that emerged—first at Black Mountain and then among the West Coast Beats—after Charles Olson's "Progressive Verse" manifesto of 1950. These writers claimed some of the same ancestors—Williams and Pound, especially—though one could argue that it was a different Williams (compare Randall Jarrell's selection for New Directions to Charles Tomlinson's counterselection) and a different, earlier Pound. One of the most interesting things in *The Letters of Robert Lowell* is Lowell's exchange with Allen Ginsberg during the spring of 1959. We know from Lowell's *Paris Review* interview how much his experience doing poetry readings in San Francisco alongside Ginsberg and Gregory Corso meant to his own new and looser style in *Life Studies.* This was when he was trying, as he wrote Elizabeth Bishop on March 30, "to bring together in me the Puritanical iron hand of constraint and the gushes of pure wildness."

"Dear Allen," he wrote on April 10, 1959, "I think letters ought to be written the way you think poetry ought to be. So let this be breezy, brief, incomplete, but spontaneous and not dishonestly holding back." Ginsberg had been campaigning for Dahlberg, Corso, Kerouac, Burroughs, Creeley, and Levertov. Lowell—representing the Eastern Establishment in Ginsberg's view—was surprisingly eager to read and to learn. Finding Kerouac "uninspired Joyce" and Burroughs "very real, but partially of psycho-pathic interest," Lowell was enchanted with Dahlberg's prose, "really original, almost Plutarchan and Montaignelike. He's a tremendous and good writer." Lowell added that he'd gone through Barrett's Zen Buddhist book, "fascinating, but monkish. What wonderful quotes!"

Lowell was less impressed with Creeley and Levertov, "careful, disciplined poets," though even here he seems to be looking for strengths rather than reasons for dismissal:

> If I were writing [to] them, I could truthfully say a good deal for their sensitive care. But in the rough and tumble of what is alive today? Creeley is [the] tamest imitation of Williams' tricks, tone, mannerisms, rhythms. I guess poetry as a technique means much less to me than to you. I can hear Creeley's polite, dim halting voice behind the barrage of Williams—I can just hear it, and not to much purpose, while Williams' manner drones at me in Creeley. Levertov with more observation and less skill also seems to come from Williams. Also I find everywhere a bit intangibly the humor and quirks of Pound—the hardest of masters, if you yourself are a quiet little person and so unlike him.

Then Lowell, perhaps fearing that he has gone too far, praises *Kaddish:* "It's really melodious, nostalgic, moving, liturgical. Maybe it ought to be shorter."

These judgments, generous and harsh by turns, don't seem to me territorial at all. They seem more in line with Pound's conviction that the important thing was that great poetry got written and not who wrote it. Lowell is perfectly willing to admit Dahlberg and Ginsberg to the "rough and tumble of what is alive today." Was he deaf to aspects of Creeley and Levertov? Probably. But he also rightly recognized a certain timidity and dependence in their temperaments. As he said of many of the writers championed by Ginsberg: "There's so much that is timid, conservative, intolerant of other kinds of writing." Timidity was the thing he himself had tried to banish from his life and work, as he left the comforts and confines of Harvard after a year, later left Boston ("all dandification and jelly") for New York, all the while looking to Ginsberg and Elizabeth Bishop and anyone else to break away from old styles and old modes. The way we are living, timorous or bold, will have been our lives.

VOLUME REVIEWED

*The Letters of Robert Lowell*
Edited by Saskia Hamilton
Farrar, Straus and Giroux, 2005

# Part II

# Southerners

# The Ding-Dong of Doom

POSTAGE STAMPS, THOSE QUAINT AND COLORFUL VESTIGES of a vanishing twentieth-century mode of communication, figure conspicuously in the strange career of William Faulkner. If a whaling ship, as Herman Melville famously claimed, was Melville's Yale College and his Harvard, Faulkner's Ivy League was the tiny post office at the University of Mississippi, in his hometown of Oxford, population 2,250 in 1921, the year Faulkner was named university postmaster. There, in a job he cynically treated as a sinecure for a man of leisure, Faulkner sat for days at a time reading issues, borrowed from faculty mailboxes and haphazardly returned, of the *Atlantic Monthly*, the *Dial*, and the *New Republic*—"a vast hoard of material," as Jay Parini remarks in his sturdy and well-researched new biography of Faulkner, "where he would have found much of the best in contemporary writing and thinking." Faulkner, a high school dropout whose foppish and idle ways about town earned him the nickname "Count No 'Count," held the post office job for nearly three years—steeping himself in Swinburne, Mencken, and the French symbolist poets—before being fired, in the fall of 1924, when he was nearly twenty-six. The letter of dismissal—perhaps a forgery, as Parini notes, perpetrated by Faulkner—was curt and to the point: "Neglects official duties; indifferent to interests of patrons; mistreatment of mail." Faulkner made it sound as though the decision was his own: "I reckon I'll be at the beck and call of folks with money all my life, but thank God I won't ever again have to be at the beck and call of every son-of-a-bitch who's got two cents to buy a stamp."

Faulkner later tried to minimize his reliance on all he had

learned during those years at the post office at Ole Miss, insisting instead that his truly formative education was intensely local, a matter of conversations overheard rather than magazines read. According to his own myth of himself as backwoods Balzac—a myth aided and abetted by a generation of southern critics and northern biographers—Faulkner had summoned his vision from his "little postage stamp of native soil" in Mississippi. This claim too was a forgery, of course, though Parini—a novelist and poet as well as a biographer—firmly subscribes to it. "A sense of place was everything to William Faulkner," he writes, "and more than any other American novelist in the twentieth century, he understood how to mine the details of place, including its human history, for literary effects. His novels, from the outset, are obsessed with what T. S. Eliot once referred to as 'significant soil.'" Parini compares Faulkner to the Greek mythological hero Antaeus, who needed to touch the ground to regain his powers: "Like Antaeus, Faulkner derived his strength through contact with the soil, a particular and 'significant soil,' evoked in his fiction with a fierce particularity."

This man-of-the-soil fantasy had enormous appeal for William Faulkner since—as Parini's opening chapters make clear—he was something of a deracinated drifter himself. He was born William Cuthbert Falkner, on September 25, 1897—he later added the *u* to make the name seem more aristocratic. A steady declension in fortune and status from generation to generation had left him with little "soil" to call his own. His great-grandfather William Clark Falkner, a legendary figure known as the "Old Colonel," had fought bravely but recklessly at the first Battle of Bull Run; he returned to Mississippi to oversee a plantation worked by slaves, eventually becoming, as Parini puts it, a "writer–railroad entrepreneur–lawyer–Civil War hero." His son, J. W. T. Falkner, the "Young Colonel," was an attorney and small-time politician, a University of Mississippi trustee, and a drunk—"the loneliest man I've ever known," according to one of his grandsons. The Young Colonel's son, Murry, William Faulkner's father, was a feckless depressive—"a dull man," according to Faulkner—who was happiest when drunk or on a hunting party or both. Faulkner was much closer to his mother, Maud, who had artistic tastes, liked books, and encouraged her son's slowly evolving literary aspirations.

As Murry downshifted from one absurd job to another—running a livery stable as automobiles were supplanting horses, then a gaslight business as electric lighting was coming into vogue—the family's fortunes declined and their lodgings shrank. William Faulkner's ambition—to write books that would earn enough money for him to restore the Faulkner fortunes and reclaim the Faulkner land—seems less rooted in "significant soil" than in a fantasy of recovered status. Parini is surely right that a crucial scene in Faulkner's novel *Absalom, Absalom!,* when the young and shoeless Thomas Sutpen is scornfully redirected by a black servant to the back door of a Tidewater plantation big house, "had some primal meaning for Faulkner." Sutpen's first instinct, to shoot the plantation owner and his kin, is supplanted by an epiphany of acquisition:

> It was like that, he said, like an explosion—a bright glare that vanished and left nothing, no ashes nor refuse: just a limitless flat plain with the severe shape of his intact innocence rising from it like a monument; that innocence instructing him as calm as the others had ever spoken. . . . So to combat them you have got to have what they have that made them do what he [the servant] did. You got to have land and niggers and a fine house to combat them with. You see?

Faulkner's miserable marriage to his high school sweetheart, Estelle Oldham—"pretty as a little partridge," according to his younger brother Jack—was a restoration as well; she had first turned him down to marry a successful lawyer, and Faulkner was more than willing to await his turn. She celebrated her marriage to Faulkner, in 1929, by trying to drown herself on their honeymoon. Nonetheless, the Faulkners eventually lived in a fine house in Oxford on a large tract of land with black (unpaid) servants. You see?

The view of William Faulkner as authentic voice of the southern soil has, for a long time, been the "orthodox" version of Faulkner's life and literary career. It has its origins in the southern intellectual movement of the 1920s and 1930s known as the

Agrarians or, for the journal they founded, the Fugitives—a movement, it should be said, from which Faulkner kept his distance. Poet-intellectuals such as John Crowe Ransom and Allen Tate argued that the Agrarian South should resist the deracinating effects of northern industrialism, supposedly perpetrated on an unwilling South by the victorious Yankees during Reconstruction. In arguing for their own intimacy with "the land," theirs by right of inheritance and care, they implied, and sometimes stated explicitly, that their connection to landed property ran deeper than could be claimed by late arrivals such as carpetbaggers, blacks, and Jews. Ransom, in his contribution to the Agrarian manifesto *I'll Take My Stand* (1930), invoked "the love of the tiller for the soil." The white southern farmer, he maintained, "identifies himself with a spot of ground, and this ground carries a good deal of meaning."

Parini is drawing water from the same befouled well when he refers to Oxford, Mississippi—home to a university that refused to admit black students until it was forced to in 1962—as an "organic community" and identifies Faulkner's "great subject" as "the loss of fidelity to the land and the subsequent decline of coherence in society." Parini seems aware of the reactionary impulse in these intellectual currents, and he tries to give an environmental spin to Faulkner's relations to the sacred land. "The threat of modernity, as represented by the automobile, loomed eerily," Parini remarks, "but Faulkner's attachment to horses—he rode with the hounds into the last year of his life—speaks to his innate conservatism, his wish to cling to a fading vision and way of life that could not withstand the onslaught of highways and suburbs, gas stations, and everything brought into being by the invention of the internal combustion engine."

The conviction that Faulkner is a sort of unofficial mouthpiece of the New South has led critics to persist in asking questions about his work peripheral to his major achievements. During the racial unrest of the 1950s and 1960s, Edmund Wilson and Irving Howe understandably looked to Faulkner, a liberal and a humanist, for insight into race relations in the South. Faulkner's contradictory public statements about race—he fancied himself a sort of Robert E. Lee, firmly opposed to the mistreatment of blacks but loyal nonetheless to the state of Mississippi—have made him an easy target for later critics who imagine they are making a trenchant intervention by "interrogating" Faulkner for the thousandth time on the matter of race. But surely James Baldwin had the final word in this matter, in his searing 1956 diatribe "Faulkner and Desegregation." Ridiculing Faulkner's plea for moderation, Baldwin wrote: "Why—and how—does one move from the middle of the road where one was aiding Negroes into the streets—to shoot them?" Parini makes much of the discovery, by the Faulkner scholar Joel Williamson, that the Old Colonel may have fathered a mulatto child, as though this factoid might be the source of Faulkner's recurring fascination, on display in two of his greatest novels, *Absalom, Absalom!* and *Light in August,* with miscegenation. Perhaps so, but Faulkner's main concern in those novels is with human alienation; his racially divided characters, the exotic New Orleanian Charles Bon and the Christ figure Joe Christmas, are stand-ins for his own identification with the uprooted of society.

An irony of literary biography is that the documented facts of a great writer's life too often seem pale and two-dimensional, while the author's writings by contrast seem fully realized. "A book is a writer's secret life, the dark twin of a man," Faulkner observed, "you can't reconcile them." Faulkner's life, a poor shadow compared to his novels, was not entirely without incident, in the South and elsewhere. He hung around college campuses—first Mississippi and then, tagging along with a literary friend, Yale—picking up fashionable ideas and a smattering of foreign languages. (Faulkner's first real publication was an adaptation of Mallarmé's "L'Après-Midi d'un Faune," in the *New Republic* of August 6, 1919.) During World War I, after being turned down as too short by the U. S. Army, he enlisted in the Royal Canadian Air Force instead, hoping to learn to fly planes, an abiding fascination. He returned to Mississippi pumped up with an English accent, some invented war stories (he had neither seen military action nor had he boarded a plane), and an affected limp. His first novel, *Soldier's Pay* (1926), is a rickety fantasy of a wounded soldier coming home to romantic betrayal and death. After graduating, so to speak, from the Ole Miss post office,

Faulkner spent some lively months in New Orleans amid a clutch of aspiring artists and writers, including his mentor, Sherwood Anderson, who generously believed Faulkner's story about a plane crash during the war. ("Both legs were broken, one of them in three places," Anderson reported in his charming and gullible narrative "A Meeting South," "the scalp was badly torn and some of the bones of the face had been splintered.") Faulkner wrote another—better—novel, *Mosquitoes* (1927), about bohemian life in and around New Orleans.

And then, like some act of God along the Mississippi, the floodgates of genius burst. Between 1928 and 1942—the period Faulkner called "one matchless time"—he wrote a stunning succession of masterpieces, almost one a year: *The Sound and the Fury* (published 1929), *As I Lay Dying* (1930), *Sanctuary* (1931), *Light in August* (1932). Then came a fallow interlude of a couple of years, during which he bought an airplane and finally learned to fly, wasted some time working for good pay in Hollywood on mediocre film scripts, and wasted more time on an affair with his sometime boss Howard Hawks's secretary. (Parini pardons the affair, the first of several, on the grounds that Estelle, who had lost one daughter in infancy and gave birth to another, Jill, in 1933, refused to have sex with her husband thereafter.) Faulkner then resumed the scarcely credible run of invention with *Pylon* (1935), his underrated novel about barnstorming pilots aloft and in love, *Absalom, Absalom!* (1936), *The Wild Palms* (1939), *The Hamlet* (1940), and *Go Down, Moses* (1942), in addition to assorted short stories, essays, and oddities in between.

What most needs explaining is neither the quality (extraordinary) nor the quantity (miraculous) of Faulkner's novels. The larger mystery is the sheer audacity of his imagination. And here, the South, with its supposed "tradition"—as Robert Penn Warren told Parini—of "men gathering around a campfire, drinking and smoking, remembering old times"—can't help us much. What the South gave Faulkner was, above all else, distance—an empowering and encouraging distance from publishers, critics, and especially other writers. He knew from his years of reading in the post office what the competition was. He knew what James Joyce had done and what Mallarmé had done, and what Anderson and Hemingway were doing. He knew that literary rules of decorum were made to be broken. He knew the risks (incomprehension and ridicule) and he knew the rewards (greatness). He had witnessed and sometimes experienced, in New Orleans and Hollywood, the sheer degradation and momentary exaltation that people could reach together and alone. He knew the extremities of human and literary behavior. He knew what he needed to know. Oxford, Mississippi, was quiet at night. When his courage waned, he drank. Sometimes, with the drinking, he recovered his courage and sometimes, with the drinking, he passed out or had himself checked into an even quieter hospital to dry out. And then he returned to his desk and resumed writing.

Consider *The Sound and the Fury,* his first and perhaps most lasting masterpiece. There is nothing like it in American or any other literature. Faulkner wrote it at a low point in his fortunes. He had made no money from his first two books and had received a scathing response from his editor, Horace Liveright, concerning a third—a manuscript of a historical novel that Faulkner called "Flags in the Dust" (eventually published, in truncated form, as *Sartoris*). Liveright told Faulkner he was "frankly very much disappointed by it." He specified the disappointments, rubbing it in:

> It is diffuse and non-integral with neither very much plot development nor character development. We think it lacks plot, dimension and projection. The story really doesn't get anywhere and has a thousand loose ends. If the book had plot and structure, we might suggest shortening and revisions but it is so diffuse that I don't think this would be any use. My chief objection is that you don't seem to have any story to tell and I contend that a novel should tell a story and tell it well.

"It says a great deal about William Faulkner's character," Parini remarks, "that he continued to write, and with renewed intensity, in the face of this criticism." That is putting it mildly. Faulkner didn't just continue to write; he wrote a book with even less of a "story to tell," with even less "character development," and where it can truly be said—in praise of the novel—that "the story really doesn't get anywhere and has a thousand loose ends." As

Jean-Paul Sartre wrote in his classic analysis, published during the summer of 1939: "In *The Sound and the Fury* everything has already happened."

Like Sartre and many other critics, Parini prefers the second of the four sections of *The Sound and the Fury,* the one devoted to Quentin Compson on the day he wanders around Cambridge, Massachusetts, skipping his Harvard classes, plucking the hands from his pocket watch, and preparing to commit suicide. The section has undeniable appeal. Quentin is an intellectual narrator like Stephen Daedalus, or Binx Bolling in Walker Percy's *The Moviegoer;* Percy, another Quentin enthusiast, once said that all his own novels were devoted to the task of "keeping Quentin Compson alive." All the stuff in the Quentin section about the nature of time is so beguiling that you might think (as Sartre did) that the whole novel was some rougher American version of Proust's *In Search of Lost Time.*

> When the shadow of the sash appeared on the curtains it was between seven and eight oclock and then I was in time again, hearing the watch. It was Grandfather's and when Father gave it to me he said I give you the mausoleum of all hope and desire; it's rather excruciatingly apt that you will use it to gain the reducto absurdum of all human experience which can fit your individual needs no better than it fitted his or his father's. I give it to you not that you may remember time, but that you might forget it now and then for a moment and not spend all your breath trying to conquer it. Because no battle is ever won he said. They are not even fought. The field only reveals to man his own folly and despair, and victory is an illusion of philosophers and fools.

This is grandly orchestrated and full of "big themes"; but it can hardly compare with the heartbreaking opening section, spoken or thought by Quentin's retarded brother, Benjy, or the "Once a bitch always a bitch" screed of the sadistic and bigoted third brother, Jason, later in the book. The whole Benjy chapter has an aching sense of loss, conveyed at the outset in the internal counterpoint of fence and flower. Benjy, attended by a black servant, Luster, is watching men playing golf on the pasture that used to be his but was sold to send Quentin to Harvard; he confuses the word "caddie" with his beloved sister Caddy, now lost to him:

> Through the fence, between the curling flower spaces, I could see them hitting. They were coming toward where the flag was and I went along the fence. Luster was hunting in the grass by the flower tree. They took the flag out, and they were hitting. Then they put the flag back and they went to the table, and he hit and the other hit. Then they went on, and I went along the fence. Luster came away from the flower tree and we went along the fence and they stopped and we stopped and I looked through the fence while Luster was hunting in the grass.
>
> "Here, caddie." He hit. They went away across the pasture. I held to the fence and watched them going away.
>
> "Listen to you, now." Luster said. "Aint you something, thirty three years old, going on that way."

Fence and flower are symbolic, of course, but not in any mechanical way. The fence is Benjy's boundary, prefiguring his later confinement in an institution for the insane, but it also provides comfort—"I held to the fence and watched them going away." The fence is perhaps the traditionally masculine principle, clarifying and unyielding, and linked to Jason, who will have Benjy castrated and put away. The flowers are Caddy and life itself, the ache of the lost sister and the lost pasture; Benjy later keeps a couple of flowers as a symbolic "graveyard" for his dead mother and Caddy. Faulkner's boldness lies in his decision to put the Benjy section, his tale told by an idiot, first, as though Joyce had opened *Ulysses* with Molly Bloom's monolog.

Faulkner's later novels exhibited a similar—though never repetitive—willingness to take risks. There are the fragmentary monologues of *As I Lay Dying,* belonging to the fragmented family that has banded together, as though in fulfillment of some impossible biblical prophecy, to get their coffined dead mother carried across rough country and properly buried. Again there is an inadvertently articulate retarded child: "My mother is a fish." Another child, Cash, hides his pain by methodically carpentering the coffin:

I made it on the bevel.

1. There is more surface for the nails to grip.
2. There is twice the gripping-surface to each seam.
3. The water will have to seep into it on a slant. Water moves easiest up and down or straight across.
4. In a house people are upright two thirds of the time. So the seams and joints are made up-and-down. Because the stress is up-and-down.
5. In a bed where people lie down all the time, the joints and seams are made sideways, because the stress is sideways.
6. Except.
7. A body is not square like a crosstie.

And so on, up to number 13: "It makes a neater job." I once heard Seamus Heaney interrupt a poetry-writing workshop to draw attention to this extraordinary piece of writing, a poem in itself.

Faulkner was an innovative builder of literary structures—on the bevel, so to speak—and these he bequeathed to later writers. There is the double helix of intertwined narratives of flight—an adulterous couple looking for a new life and two convicts escaping from the penitentiary—in *The Wild Palms.* (This concoction proved too audacious for Malcolm Cowley, who extracted one of the strands for *The Portable Faulkner.*) There are the brilliantly linked stories, including the most famous one, "The Bear," in *Go Down, Moses,* a form reprised in Eudora Welty's best and most bewitching book, *The Golden Apples.* And there is the sheer baroque intensity of *Absalom, Absalom!,* a great river of churning verbiage, homoerotic yearning, and miscegenation, tracing the rise and fall of the Sutpen family in the heat of a "long still hot weary dead September afternoon."

Parini lingers on some of Faulkner's most horrific scenes—the notorious corncob rape of the socialite Temple Drake in *Sanctuary* and the ghastly castration of Joe Christmas in *Light in August*—as though these are somehow the heart of Faulkner's art, grim reminders of a violent and unregenerate South. Actually, they are reminders of something else: that literary naturalism is the successor not of realism but of aestheticism. Such fantasy-laden scenes smack more of Swinburne and Rosetti than of

Dreiser. As Jorge Luis Borges wisely said of Faulkner, "His brutality is of the hallucinatory sort—the infernal, not the terrestrial sort of brutality."

The audacity and the brutality decreased during the long second half of Faulkner's career, the decades that succeeded the "matchless time." The book that inaugurated this autumnal phase of his writing was his most traditional, *The Hamlet,* which he belatedly graced with two inferior sequels, *The Town* (1957) and *The Mansion* (1959), to make up the Snopes trilogy. Balzac was his model now, as he traced the picaresque fortunes of a poor-white family on the rise, by hook and by crook, in the Mississippi hamlet of Frenchman's Bend. A meeting in the summer of 1937 with his French translator, a Princeton professor named Maurice Coindreau, seems to have confirmed the Balzac parallel. According to Parini, Faulkner told Coindreau that "the Vendée peasants of France, so movingly evoked by Balzac, had much in common with the poor white farmers of the South and that their attitudes toward life were similar, grounded in agricultural rhythms." The best defense of these uneven novels I know is by the Japanese Nobel laureate Kenzaburo Oe, who found in them a characteristic pattern, on display in *The Sound and the Fury* and *The Wild Palms* as well, of female passion paired with male innocence. "Faulkner and Dostoevsky," Oe concluded, "have created in most of their works the female archetype who is capable of sustaining a writer's maximum imagination and the 'innocent' male character who works as a medium through which his passions are realized on the page."

Coindreau's place in Faulkner's career proved far more important than providing a sounding board for half-baked notions of southern peasantry and their deep ties to the land. Coindreau's translations of *As I Lay Dying* and *The Sound and the Fury* introduced Faulkner to his most important international readers: Sartre, Camus, de Beauvoir, and Malraux. "It was the prominence of Faulkner's reputation in Europe that would finally make his Nobel Prize possible," Parini notes, "and this can be traced back directly to Coindreau's translations." Faulkner's acceptance speech for the Nobel Prize for Literature in 1949 is often quoted for its magnificent existentialist rhetoric about mankind resisting nuclear catastrophe, his rejection of the view that "when the last ding-dong of doom has clanged and faded from the last worthless rock hanging tideless in the last red and dying evening, that even then there will be one more sound: that of his puny inexhaustible voice, still talking. I refuse to accept this," wrote Faulkner. "I believe that man will not merely endure. He will prevail." But it was a quieter claim in the same speech that more securely gives voice to the sustained labor of this writer at his desk in Oxford, tirelessly inventing imaginative structures of human pain and defeat and momentary triumph. "I feel that this award was not made to me as a man," Faulkner wrote, "but to my work, a life's work in the agony and sweat of the human spirit, not for glory and least of all for profit, but to create out of the materials of the human spirit something which did not exist before."

VOLUME REVIEWED

*One Matchless Time: A Life of William Faulkner*
By Jay Parini
HarperCollins, 2004

# The War between the Tates

IN 1949, WHEN HE TURNED FIFTY, Allen Tate published an essay called "Our Cousin, Mr. Poe." In that essay, Tate confessed that as a boy of fourteen he had stared for hours at "the well-known, desperate, and asymmetrical photograph" of Edgar Allan Poe, which he hoped that he "should some day resemble." This wish, as portraits of Tate attest, was granted. But Tate's main point in the essay was not to claim some literal kinship lost in the sands of genealogical time somewhere between the vowel shift from "Allan" to "Allen." He argued, instead, that Poe, perennial butt of jests and put-downs (like T. S. Eliot's suggestion that Poe might read better in French translation), deserved a place at the table. "For Americans, perhaps for most modern men, he is with us like a dejected cousin: we may 'place' him but we may not exclude him from our board."

This seems to me roughly our present relationship to Allen Tate. Tate is always and everywhere "placed" as a reactionary southern critic and minor poet who played first fiddle (Tate actually played the fiddle) in a band of poet-critics called the Fugitives during the twenties, the Agrarians during the thirties, and, augmented with fellow travelers from England and California, the "New Critics" thereafter. These are the straw men of current academic literary criticism, the dejected cousins drinking bourbon in the corner, placed but no longer read. While there is some truth to the jibes directed their way (just as the strictures against Poe are obvious to bright fourth-graders), the Fugitive-Agrarian–New Critic contingent was far more complex and interesting than it is now given credit for. Allen Tate's achievement is both representative of their work at its best and ripe, like a distant cousin, for rediscovery. His distinctive poems, five or six of which seem permanent achievements; his impressive historical novel, *The Fathers;* his remarkable literary criticism, including some of the best essays ever written on Emily Dickinson and Edgar Poe—these won't go away.

Lately, there has been a steady trickle of publications related to Tate and his associates in what is sometimes called the Southern Literary Renaissance. (Tate, who admired only Poe and the poet Henry Timrod among earlier southern writers, suggested *Naissance* was more appropriate.) Tate's *Essays of Four Decades* are back in print. Selected letters of his poet-critic friends Robert Penn Warren and Yvor Winters, in which Tate looms large as both correspondent and subject, are appearing in stages. And Thomas A. Underwood has published volume 1 of a projected two-volume biography of Tate. The first volume brings Tate to 1938, by which time, according to Underwood's therapeutic perspective, Tate had published *The Fathers* and "had resolved many of his feelings of regional and personal orphanhood." Though Underwood doesn't say so, Tate, who died in 1979, had also published by 1938 most of the poetry and many of the strongest essays on which his reputation now rests. In volume 2, we can expect detailed accounts of Tate's notorious womanizing—"most of Tate's philandering occurred after 1938," says Underwood. Tate's conversion to Catholicism will, presumably, occupy a lot of space, along with the unfortunate injection of Jacques Maritain's neo-Thomism into his criticism. Otherwise, apart from Tate's many academic positions and honors, and his retreat from some of his most reactionary positions, it's not clear what one might look forward to in Underwood's second volume.

Based on the first volume, however, Tate is lucky in his biographer. Underwood's book is rigorously researched and sturdily written. While sympathetic to Tate and admiring of his achievements, Underwood has appropriate qualms about Tate's devotion to so-called southern ideals. He explores in detail and unflinchingly Tate's commitment until the 1950s to white supremacy ("the negro race is an inferior race," Tate wrote in a notorious letter to Lincoln Kirstein in 1933); his distaste for socializing with black writers; his opposition to the "Liberal attack" on Christian values in the Scopes trial; his flirtation with fascism as a viable blueprint for the South ("we could side with a Fascist party"). The book *is* a defense of Tate's fundamental seriousness, and of the historical importance of his stances and stands. A Freudian leitmotif is in place throughout, first sounded in the subtitle, "Orphan of the South." Tate was not an orphan—his father lived past the age of seventy—but his own imagination was so openly patriarchal that Underwood's Oedipal scheme seems for the most part internal rather than imposed. A writer who calls his only novel *The Fathers* can be expected to have some "issues" around fatherhood.

Only one thing is missing from this biography, but it is a big thing. Allen Tate was a poet, and Underwood has not written the life of a poet. There are hundreds of sentences like the following: "Before long he was not only on top of his chemistry assignments but had made the best mark in the class on a mathematics examination." But almost never do we learn anything about the circumstances in which Tate wrote a particular poem—presumably a more important event for Tate than getting a good grade in math. Tate's political and religious and psychological convictions are interesting to the degree that they served his poetry. But Underwood uses the poetry, to the extent that he mentions it at all, only to illustrate those convictions. In this regard, he has things backwards. He risks encouraging readers to dismiss the poems on the basis of politics.

Allen Tate was born in the nineteenth century, but barely, in a small town in Kentucky. Tate's father, Orley, failed in running a lumber firm, the first of many failures as he drifted around the Midwest in search of work, his growing family in tow. Orley Tate was "brutal and unpredictable," according to Underwood, a "powerfully fisted man" prone to "violence, philandering, and drinking." Allen Tate believed his father once killed a black waiter with a chair for spilling soup on him. Tate's mother, by contrast, was petite, prim, "tiny-footed." Nellie's fastidious self-image, according to Underwood, was as "a heroine of parthenogenesis in Virginia"; her father had owned eighty-one slaves and two hundred thousand acres of timber. Tate's mother and father seemed to their bemused son to embody respectively an idealized Old South and the grim realities of the New South.

Born with an enormous, Poe-like head, Tate was a sickly child, which suited his smothering mother just fine. But Orley was wary of any artsy tendencies. Young Allen took violin lessons in Cincinnati, receiving enough encouragement to consider a professional career, but Orley "didn't think it went with Kentucky." At Vanderbilt, with Nellie living nearby like Ruskin's hovering mother, Allen took up the equally sissy practice of writing verse, but balanced it with the manly habits of hard drinking and sex. When Tate ostentatiously slept with one of his girlfriends, a classmate commented: "Nobody had ever heard of anybody doing such a thing at Vanderbilt."

It was at Vanderbilt, where he enrolled in 1918, that Tate made the friendships of a lifetime, with his mentor John Crowe Ransom, recently returned from service in World War I, and with fellow students Robert Penn Warren and Donald Davidson. Ransom gave Tate a D for his first term and his "slightly bewildering" essays. Tate's poems won a better reception; while still an undergraduate he became a regular contributor and editor for *The Fugitive,* the literary magazine that he and his friends founded at Vanderbilt. What these men shared was a fierce sense of region and an equally strong conviction that the sentimental and obscurantist ways in which that region had been evoked—the "moon and magnolia" mode—were bankrupt and self-defeating. And "feminine," one might add. Against *Gone with the Wind* they advanced a hard-edged but gentlemanly modernism.

T. S. Eliot was their hero among the moderns; they were particularly drawn to Eliot's satiric quatrains in such poems as "Sweeney among the Nightingales" and "Whispers of Immortality": "Webster was much possessed by death / And saw the skull beneath the skin; / And breastless creatures under ground / Leaned backward with a lipless grin." Ransom wrote marvelous poems in this vein, and by 1925, Tate was capable of a sophisticated pastiche like "Mr. Pope," one of his finest early poems:

> When Alexander Pope strolled in the city
> Strict was the glint of pearl and gold sedans.
> Ladies leaned out more out of fear than pity
> For Pope's tight back was rather a goat's than man's.

Here was an eighteenth-century urbanity, built around wit and opposition (pearl vs. gold, fear vs. pity, goat vs. man), made available to a gentlemanly South. The rest of the poem, a tangled evocation of Pope's burial urn, isn't up to this sprightly beginning. Underwood's only comment on this key poem is to see it as a veiled self-portrait (hunchback instead of big head) in which "Allen attempted to explain how Pope became both a hater of women and a talented satirist." The poem "explains" nothing of the kind.

Tate's early poems attracted more attention in the hated North than in the South. In 1924 he went to New York for the first time and was, he told Davidson, "greatly thrilled at the mere *physique* of the city," so unlike the rural South that he loved. He was particularly impressed by the subway: "the sheer wonder of it is almost atonement for its significance as a phase of the Triumph of the Machine." Tate's host in New York was Hart Crane, with whom he had been corresponding for a couple of years. Crane's attempts to find poetic phrasing adequate to describe the modern city clearly influenced Tate's early sonnet "The Subway": "Dark accurate plunger down the successive knell / Of arch on arch, where ogives burst a red / Reverberance of hail upon the dead / Thunder . . ."

Back in the quieter South, Tate moved in with "Red" Warren in Guthrie, Kentucky, where he met Carolyn Gordon, a Chattanooga journalist and aspiring novelist. "I pissed in my pants," Tate said. "She was the most beautiful girl I had ever seen." They had sex for the first time in a local cemetery. That fall Tate returned to New York and wrote soft-core pornography for the Climax Publishing Company. He and Carolyn had stopped seeing each other in late 1924, but she announced a few months later that she was pregnant with his child. Carolyn joined him in New York, where the novelist Ford Madox Ford hired her as his typist. Tate, meanwhile, cut short his affair with the poet Laura Riding, whom he allegedly described as "all right from the neck down."

Crane, Ford, Gordon, and Riding—these were all significant writers, and suggest the charged atmosphere in which Tate was writing his own early poems. "I think we were drawn together by three things," Tate observed. "We were young, we were poor, and we were ambitious. That is, we thought that the older generation was pretty bad, and we were later going to replace them." In chronicling this crucial moment in Tate's life, Underwood makes much of a supposed "division" in Tate:

> As a Southerner in New York he tried to embrace Modernist artistic values without renouncing his affiliation with the Fugitives. . . . As a result, his career began to turn in on him; he had become a Modernist poet repressing his Southern identity. With two sets of friends, Modernist aesthetes and group-minded Southerners, he was . . . "divided against himself."

This sounds good and makes for the kind of clarity that biographers need, but it grossly oversimplifies Tate's literary situation and his actual friendships. Among the major influences on Tate's work, neither Hart Crane nor Eliot was a "Modernist aesthete," and Ransom and Warren weren't particularly "group-minded." All four poets shared a moral and aesthetic seriousness about finding a usable tradition in English poetry, and all four refused to settle for nineteenth-century verse forms or poetic diction.

It is true that Tate and Ransom disagreed about the merits of *The Waste Land.* For Ransom it was an example of precisely the sort of deracinated "cosmopolitan" mishmash that the Fugitives were out to demolish. For Tate, Eliot's poem showed how symbols might be used to express a certain attitude toward modern rootlessness. Tate's well-known "Ode to the Confederate Dead," published first in 1927, then with revisions ten years later, is, according to Tate's partly tongue-in-cheek essay on the poem, "Narcissus as Narcissus," about the chasm between modern solipsism (a contemporary visitor to a Confederate graveyard) and past heroism (the dead Confederate soldiers). Here is its solemn opening:

> Row after row with strict impunity
> The headstones yield their names to the element,
> The wind whirrs without recollection;
> In the riven troughs the splayed leaves
> Pile up, of nature the casual sacrament
> To the seasonal eternity of death.

The poem includes lines that are almost comically indebted to Eliot: "Ambitious November with the humors of the year . . . Night is the beginning and the end / And in between the ends of distraction . . . The gray lean spiders come, they come and go." (Talking, presumably, of Michelangelo.) Edmund Wilson, an editor at the time at *Vanity Fair,* returned a batch of Tate's early poems with a brief note: "I look forward to something extraordinary from you. But do try to get out of the artistic clutches of T. S. Eliot."

Wilson was wrong about these poems, however. They *were* extraordinary, taking the language of Eliot and directing it toward southern landscapes and dilemmas. Just what those dilemmas were became clearer to Tate during the decade after the Crash of 1929. The Agrarians—as they now called themselves—were not alone in believing that the United States during the twenties had bet too much on industrialization and neglected farm policy. What Tate, Warren, and others in the Agrarian group wanted to offer was something more than an enlightened economic model tied to agriculture. It was a whole vision of the good life, based on family farms and manual labor and small towns. Ritual, too, was on their agenda, and many of the most beautiful poems that arose from this Agrarian moment, like Ransom's "Janet Waking" and "Dead Boy" and Tate's "Death of Little Boys," have to do with such community-binding and kinship-revealing rituals as funerals and weddings.

The South was the region the Agrarians cared for, and in their 1930 manifesto *I'll Take My Stand,* by "Twelve Southerners," they had an unfortunate tendency to trace the ruinous industrialization of the South to the victory of the Northern invaders in the Civil War. In their view, slavery was no worse than Northern factory conditions, and in certain respects was more protective of human interests. Tate wrote admiring biographies of Stonewall Jackson and Jefferson Davis, and began another on Robert E. Lee. In more lucid moments, the Agrarians recognized that other sections of the country, such as New England, had experienced similar wrenching adjustments to industrialization and the depopulating of the countryside. An interesting revelation in Jay Parini's recent biography of Robert Frost was how close Frost felt to the

Agrarian movement, calling himself, according to Robert Penn Warren, a "Yankee Agrarian." Frost's own poems about blighted farms and the virtues of "putting in the seed" arise from some of the same anxieties and attachments as the best work of Tate and Ransom. They might have taken as their motto Yeats's lines of 1937 from "The Municipal Gallery Revisited": "All that we did, all that we said or sang / Must come from contact with the soil."

The Agrarians' hostility to those who, in their view, had no such contact with the soil—capitalists, Marxists, liberals, urban blacks, Jews—led to alliances that they had trouble explaining away. Always eager for national venues in which to air their regional passions, they welcomed a partnership with the reactionary *American Review* and its owner-editor, Seward Collins. After a hard-drinking powwow in Alabama in the spring of 1933, Tate reported that he was "astonished" to find "that Collins has the same idea we have on the Jewish nature of liberalism and on the Old Testament character of *Das Kapital.*" Collins "has worked himself into a great froth over the Jews," Tate added. "Let us not discourage him."

When Collins made it clear in an interview in early 1936 that he was a fascist pure and simple, an admirer of Hitler and Mussolini who wished to "have a king and nobles, counts, dukes, etc. in America," Tate and his colleagues backpedaled vigorously. "I am so deeply opposed to fascism," Tate wrote to the *New Republic* in May 1936, "that I should choose communism if it were the alternative to it. Both are slave-states, but the aim of fascism must be realized by force, while the aim of communism, ideally at least, looks toward order and consent."

The terms of this tepid distinction are revealing (there was no retreat on anti-Semitism), and in any case Tate continued to write for *The American Review,* having persuaded himself that the Agrarians might lead Collins away from "his fascism." Yet the steam was running out of the Agrarian movement. By the spring of 1937, aware that he was out of his depth in political matters and that his poems were being scoured for fascist tendencies, Tate wrote to Edmund Wilson that he had "resigned from agrarianism" and its "pseudo-system of practical politics." He concluded that "Ransom, Warren, and myself come a little nearer being artists than the others," and turned his attention to the safer precincts of art.

Underwood's account of Tate's political shifts and shiftiness during the 1930s is particularly welcome given the thematic arrangement of Tate's *Essays of Four Decades,* and the exclusion from the collection of Tate's most polemical political essays. The consequent scrambling of chronology makes it difficult to trace Tate's progress as a literary essayist. Still, three rough phases seem apparent. Mencken was Tate's model early on, and the brash Philistine-bashing of Tate's early essays marks his first phase, of which a good example is the strange concoction of "Remarks on the Southern Religion" (retitled "Religion and the Old South" in *Essays of Four Decades*) that Tate contributed to *I'll Take My Stand.* Adopting a baroque, abstract, smart-ass mode, Tate showed off his reading: "It is not that the scientific historian refuses to see that Pericles dressed, ate, and loved differently from Cincinnatus; it is rather that the particular instance fades away into a realm of phenomena related as cause and effect." (Tate was saying that the Old South drew from both Greek and Roman traditions.)

Eliot's criticism was an overwhelming influence on Tate's second and most fertile period as an essayist, beginning around 1932. While firming up some of Tate's less attractive prejudices against "free-thinking Jews," Eliot also inspired a more straightforward interpretive model for literary analysis. Not too long ago, Tate's essay "Tension in Poetry" (1938) was fed to graduate students as a central text of the New Criticism, which concentrated attention on "the poem itself," with minimal attention to social context or biographical detail. The essay is not much fun to read now. Tate kicks around some bad poems for a few pages, noting what he calls "failures in denotation" and "connotation." But the poems are not as bad as he claims. (Edna St. Vincent Millay's "Justice Denied in Massachusetts" clearly offends him more for its political slant on Sacco and Vanzetti than for any crimes against connotation.) A much livelier essay in a formalist mode is "Technique of Fiction," which appeared in 1944, and belongs to a third phase in Tate's criticism—looser, more personal, more confident in stating the simple pleasures of reading. In an admiring discussion of how Henry James sets his scenes in *The Wings of the Dove* and elsewhere, Tate pauses to remark: "What could be better than Milly Theale's last soiree before she becomes too ill to appear again?"

As an essayist, early and late, Tate is strongest when his self-identification with his subject is most complete, as in the fine essay on Emily Dickinson that he published in 1932. Tate steered clear of both biographical speculation and the kind of formalist ingenuity often ascribed to the New Criticism. Instead, he adopted what we would now call a cultural approach, arguing that Dickinson was born into a world of small New England towns, grounded in agriculture and religion, and found herself in the Gilded Age. "Born into the equilibrium of an old and a new order," hers was, according to Tate, "the perfect literary situation." She had the advantage of an orthodox and highly structured set of theological beliefs and intellectual traditions, namely those of Puritan New England, but since this world was on the wane, she could dwell in it without being imprisoned within it. Arguing that Dickinson was a heroic voice raised against industrialism, Tate managed to turn Dickinson into a sort of honorary southerner, "a deep mind writing from a deep culture," untouched by "the rising plutocracy of the East." In Tate's hands, Dickinson's famous poem "Because I could not stop for Death" takes on a southern coloring: a spectral cavalier taking a lady out for a spin by the Big House.

Tate wrote about Poe in similar terms, interpreting Poe's necrophilia not as a creepy psychological trait but as Poe's protest against a culture devoid of spiritual and aesthetic vitality. For Tate as critic, Dickinson and Poe were poets of "transition," caught in the moment between a world going under—the old agricultural and religious order—and another world, godless, industrial, and money-grubbing, coming into existence. As a poet himself, Tate thought of his own historical moment the same way. The Southern Literary Renaissance, he decided, had arisen at a "crossing of the ways, not unlike, on an infinitesimal scale, the outburst of poetic genius at the end of the sixteenth century when commercial England had already begun to crush feudal England."

Some such crossing of the ways is audible in Tate's own poetry, for Tate as poet has two poetic voices. One is wry and tender, in umbilical touch with childhood—and by extension the "feudal" South. The other is orotund and sublime, a key held up to the sky in hopes of thunder and lightning. The opening of "Mr. Pope" is in the former mode; the "Ode" is in the latter. In Tate's best poems, the two voices are in playful equilibrium, nowhere more poignantly than in "The Swimmers."

> Kentucky water, clear springs: a boy fleeing
> To water under the dry Kentucky sun,
> His four little friends in tandem with him, seeing
>
> Long shadows of grapevine wriggle and run
> Over the green swirl; mullein under the ear
> Soft as Nausicaä's palm; sullen fun
>
> Savage as childhood's thin harmonious tear:
> O fountain, bosom source undying-dead
> Replenish me the spring of love and fear
>
> And give me back the eye that looked and fled
> When a thrush idling in the tulip tree
> Unwound the cold dream of the copperhead.

Successful poems in terza rima, the braided rhyme scheme of Dante and of Shelley's "Triumph of Life," are rare in English. Tate's dream vision follows many of the conventions of the genre: the apostrophe to the muse; the sonorous, conjuring language, richest in the sequence of "mullein . . . palm . . . sullen"; the surveying of border regions of dream and waking, of life and death in the source "undying-dead."

Into this sublime landscape Tate introduces "The shrill companions of that odyssey":

> Bill Eaton, Charlie Watson, "Nigger" Layne
> The doctor's son, Harry Duesler who played
> The flute; and Tate, with water on the brain.

Seemingly random matter-of-fact details—the flute player and the hydrocephalic head—undergo a mythical change in this dreamscape of water music:

Dog-days: the dusty leaves where rain delayed
Hung low on poison-oak and scuppernong,
And we were following the active shade

Of water, that bells and bickers all night long.
"No more'n a mile," Layne said. All five stood still.
Listening, I heard what seemed at first a song.

The song turns out to be the hoofbeats of a posse coming down the hill. After a beautifully modulated Homeric simile—"Then, as sleepwalkers shift from a hard place / In bed, and rising to keep a formal pledge / Descend a ladder into empty space, // We scuttled down the bank below the ledge"—the boys awake to the stark geometry of a lynching. A stranger on horseback and the sheriff drag the body back to town.

My breath crackled the dead air like a shotgun
As, sheriff and the stranger disappearing,
The faceless head lay still. I could not run

Or walk, but stood. Alone in the public clearing
This private thing was owned by all the town,
Though never claimed by us within my hearing.

Though "The Swimmers," first published in 1953, rightfully belongs in the sequel, Underwood gives some attention to the "race theme" in the poem, and adduces it toward the end of the book as evidence for Tate's adoption during the 1950s of more progressive views on race. "I wasn't born with virtue in these matters," Tate wrote; "I have had to acquire it."

"The Swimmers" isn't a good poem simply because of its progressive views on race, however. And anything obvious that it has to say about southern guilt is less interesting than what it has to say about shame and childhood secrets, and how a sense of community is sometimes built, like an oyster with a painful grain of sand, around such secrets. Its power derives from the life of its language, from Tate's sure grip on oneiric evocation, narrative drive, and telling detail. It was Tate's unerring skill in knowing that "scuppernong" and "Harry Duesler who played the flute" belonged there that makes this poem a key portent of what came to be known, a decade later, as "confessional poetry." Robert Lowell as a teenager pitched his tent on Tate's Tennessee lawn in 1937, and his poetry, with its trust in the public resonance of autobiographical detail, remained tethered to Tate's. What finer tribute to Tate's "Ode" could there be than Lowell's Yankee counterpoint, "For the Union Dead"?

Underwood wants us to believe that Tate was a better novelist than poet. He claims that *The Fathers* is "the most important work of [Tate's] life" and "the crowning achievement of his career," but such judgments are more indicative of Underwood's distaste for poetry than of the peculiar virtues of Tate's novel. Tate wrote the book during the 1930s, in several fits and starts. When he finally finished it, he had to splice its sometimes disparate writing together. It is a Civil War novel, more centrally concerned with divisions among a couple of Southern families—loosely based on Tate's ancestors, in and around Washington, D.C.—than with Yankees and Rebels. The Buchans are an old Virginia family rooted in the soil. The Poseys of Georgetown are urban, Catholic, mercantile. Tate doesn't settle for a simple opposition, though, of a noble Old South of the soil versus a crass New South of money. The patriarch of the Buchans wants to preserve the Union, and a Posey is the hero of the novel. The novel is told from the perspective of Lacy Buchan, looking back at events that occurred many decades earlier, and there is no one that Lacy admires more than the wheeler-dealer George Posey. Among the vivid scenes, or tableaux, that make up the book, the opening, when Lacy is a youngster of fifteen at his mother's funeral, is particularly poignant. Here is the old Agrarian subject of the kith and kin gathered around a community-binding ritual:

> It was only today as I was walking down Fayette Street towards the river that I got a whiff of salt fish, and I remembered the day I stood at Pleasant Hill, under the dogwood tree. It was late April and the blossoms shot into the air like spray. My mother was dead. Crowds of the connection had arrived the night before; and I had come, a boy of fifteen, after breakfast, out into the yard. Under the tree I could still taste the salt of the roe

herring that Aunt Myra Parrish had kept serving to the kin and friends from Washington and Alexandria.

It is bracing to find, in the latest volume of Robert Penn Warren's letters, that Warren thought this "a fairly stereotyped way of opening: the business of the smell of herring seems to be a kind of dodge for getting into the story." He urged Tate to cut the passage.

*The Fathers* is the story of a man who sells his own mulatto half-brother to buy a prize mare, then kills his own brother-in-law to avenge the death of that same half-brother. Miscegenation and rape suggest Faulkner's influence, but it's Fitzgerald and Gatsby who surprisingly preside here. George Posey is guilty of greater transgressions than Gatsby, but he, too, is a "stranger" adrift who shows in the end more dignity and honor than the rooted Buchan family he marries into. The Buchans could be the Buchanans, blue blood and attitude, but it's Posey/Gatsby who carries the day. (Tate sets a scene in Gadsby's Tavern—a broad hint of what he's up to.) *The Fathers* is consistently interesting and entertaining to read—there's a sustained evocation of Poe and a cameo by Henry Adams, "a great snob even then"—and it's certainly as good a plantation novel as Willa Cather's contemporaneous *Sapphira and the Slave Girl.* But if *The Fathers* is Tate's "crowning achievement," Tate's reputation is in trouble.

Underwood's book ends on a bathetic note. He tells how happy Tate was when he had finished *The Fathers,* and how it suddenly seemed to dawn on him that he had a daughter of his own. He quotes a letter of Tate's: "I finished the novel the night of the 21st: the last incident was on July 21st 1861. Nancy became a woman on the 21st. The book will appear on Sept. 23rd, her birthday. The moon seems to favor it." "Looking forward rather than backward," Underwood concludes, "Allen Tate was no longer an orphan but a father." In other words, the completion of *The Fathers* "brought a symbolic end" to his own childhood, allowing him to acknowledge his daughter. It seems more likely that, like other busy fathers, Tate simply didn't make time for his daughter—until, that is, he finished the time-consuming novel and Nancy was old enough to be amusing.

I would rather leave Tate during the 1930s on another, less triumphal note, struck in a short poem to Robert Penn Warren called "Brief Message":

> This, Warren, is our trouble now:
> Not even fools could disavow
> Three centuries of piety
> Grown bare as a cottonwood tree
> (A timber seldom drawn and sawn
> And chiefly used to hang men on),
> So face with calm that heritage
> And earn contempt before the age.

There is more than a hint, in that hammering plain style, of Raleigh and Yeats, but the cottonwood tree—the wayward rhythm in the line in which it is mentioned, and the specialized parenthetical knowledge about its uses—is all Tate's. A young man looks lucidly at the South during the depression: no religion, no money, a burden of guilt, a bareness of culture, and hostility all around. Under the circumstances, Tate and his friends, those dejected cousins, did pretty well.

VOLUMES REVIEWED

*Allen Tate: Orphan of the South*
By Thomas A. Underwood
Princeton University Press, 2000

*Essays of Four Decades*
By Allen Tate
ISI Books, 1999

# The Family Man

DURING THE HALF CENTURY SINCE HIS DEATH in 1955, James Agee has maintained a saintly aura, though it remains unclear just what sort of martyrdom he suffered. He had in excess what used to be called "advantages." Born into comfortable circumstances in Tennessee in 1909, he was educated at Exeter and Harvard and employed by the Luce empire at *Fortune* and *Time.* Among his closest and most loyal friends were influential editors and publishers, many of whom he had known at school. Tall and rangy, Agee was as photographs attest spectacularly good-looking, attractive to both women and to men. As a writer, he was a quick study and a dazzling stylist, adept at many forms and many voices. His vices were those of his generation: alcohol, womanizing, a marauding egotism. Not quite a *poète maudit*—for where is the curse in a Harvard education or a Luce paycheck?—Agee settled for the lesser role of the bad boy in powerful organizations; he had a temper tantrum when the *Fortune* editors tampered with his piece on the cultivation of orchids. And yet, the sense of martyrdom persists. His friend and *Time* colleague Robert Fitzgerald called the callous on Agee's right middle finger "one of his stigmata as a writer."

Agee was a talented poet, a more than talented writer of fiction, a journalist of extraordinary range and ambition, and a film critic of genius. Like many writers, he probably wished those gifts had been distributed differently; a year before his death he told the photographer Helen Levitt that poetry had been his true vocation.[1] The curve of Agee's career from early promise—his book of poems, *Permit Me Voyage,* won the Yale Younger Poets award for 1934, when Agee was twenty-five—to midlife collapse now seems, in Robert Lowell's phrase, the "generic life" of the World War II generation of writers: Delmore Schwartz, John Berryman, and Randall Jarrell. The evidence that Agee accomplished a remarkable body of work before his death at age forty-five—he died as Lowell did of a heart attack in a New York taxi—fills two packed volumes from the Library of America. I miss the best poems (none, good or bad, are included here), and I would have been happy to have more *Fortune* features—the one on Saratoga, for example, or "The Great American Roadside"—instead of a clutch of perfunctory book reviews from *Time*. Still, these volumes properly showcase Agee's wondrous film criticism and his sometimes baffling magnum opus (with the photographer Walker Evans), *Let Us Now Praise Famous Men,* and so they do justice to a significant if still puzzling literary career.

Early and late, Agee's great theme was the family, perhaps because he had such a precarious sense of his own. His father died in a car accident when Agee was five, a loss immortalized in his excruciatingly poignant posthumous novel, *A Death in the Family*. Agee's parents were mismatched in a way familiar from D. H. Lawrence—the laborer husband and the cultivated wife from town. The one-car accident occurred as Agee's father was returning from the mountains above Knoxville, where he had grown up and still felt most at home. Early on in *A Death in the Family,* father and son have lingered in a movie theater watching a Chaplin film—"That horrid little man!" according to the mother. Afterward, they sit down in silence on an outcropping of limestone "like a great bundle of dirty laundry," in an empty lot overlooking the lights of Knoxville. "He felt that although his father loved their home and loved all of them, he was more lonely than the contentment of this family love could help; that it even increased his loneliness, or made it hard for him not to be lonely." Agee's widowed and pious mother took up residence on the grounds of the St. Andrew's School, run by Episcopal monks near Sewanee, Tennessee. A married priest there, James Flye, became Agee's mentor and surrogate father; another monk became his stepfather. The hothouse mood of the school, with its Holy Week rituals and anxious boys ("I thank Thee that I did not wet the bed this night—enough to get caught"), is vividly captured in Agee's novella *The Morning Watch.*

At Exeter and then at Harvard, Agee seemed to be in a hurry, as though all prizes would vanish at midnight. Precocious in all things sexual and literary, he progressed from infatuation with a male classmate at Exeter to an affair with a female librarian several years his senior. The pattern held with a more serious relationship at Harvard, with a chemistry professor's daughter six years older—this was Agee's first wife, Via. Meanwhile, he was elected president of the Exeter *Monthly* and the *Harvard Advocate,* wrote the class ode for his Harvard graduation in 1932, and made friendships with Exeter alumni Lincoln Kirstein and Dwight Macdonald and, at Harvard, with the poet-translator Robert Fitzgerald. He was lucky to take two courses with the great I. A. Richards, circling from residence in China back to Cambridge, whose brilliance in reading poetry and fiction was not lost on Agee. As Fitzgerald wrote: "When [Richards] spoke of the splendors of Henry James's style or of Conrad facing the storm of the universe, we felt that he was their companion and ours in the enterprise of art."

In that enterprise Agee was already well embarked by graduation. A summer spent as a migrant worker in Nebraska and Kansas—the first of Agee's "experiments in misery," as Stephen Crane had called them—gave Agee material for two expertly deployed short stories published in the *Advocate.* In the first of these, "Death in the Desert," the narrator bums a ride in a crowded car, and a quarrel erupts between the driver, Joe, and his wife over Joe's refusal to pick up a black man half-crazed and desperately entreating help on the desert road. The power in the story lies in how the narrator shifts the guilt back onto himself:

> The fact that, according to Joe, the car was crowded already became, for a time, very important to me. I was the extra man in the car. I was the reason why an exhausted Negro remained in the desert near death. I could offer my place; I could refuse to ride any farther, unless something were done to help him. I realized, all the while, that my presence here had nothing to do

> with Joe's refusal to take him in, and at length this truth reduced that sport of conscience to its logical absurdity. I knew, quite soon, that there was nothing for me to do; yet I felt compulsion to say what his wife had tried to say, and a great deal more. In purely abstract argument I had talked myself red-eyed and ready for murder, on this matter of the Negro and his place; and now, when I was involved in actuality, I could say nothing and do nothing; and my silence made me confederate in a monstrous wrong.

Like much of Agee's early work the scene has Christian resonances—no room at the inn and the Good Samaritan. As so often in his writing, he has placed himself as the odd man out in a family setting. In its compassion and effort to get the narrator's feelings fully told, "Death in the Desert" seems to me to owe less to the minimalism of Hemingway (the "godfather" of Agee's stories, according to Fitzgerald) than to Sherwood Anderson's stories of adolescence such as "I Want to Know Why."

If Agee's poems are less assured than his prose, it may be in part because American poetry between the wars was less assured than American prose. Agee wanted to fit American idiom to inherited verse forms. His natural mentors, by region and dialect, should have been the southern formalists John Crowe Ransom and Allen Tate. Instead, Agee chose as his model Hart Crane, who committed suicide during the spring of Agee's Harvard graduation; he also admired such I. A. Richards touchstones as Marvell and Hopkins. The title of Agee's *Permit Me Voyage* is drawn from the third section of Crane's beautiful sequence "Voyages." Agee's title poem begins:

> Take these who will as may be: I
> Am careless now of what they fail:
> My heart and mind discharted lie
> And surely as the nervèd nail
>
> Appoints all quarters on the north
> So now it designates him forth
> My sovereign God my princely soul
> Whereon my flesh is priestly stole.

Robert Fitzgerald thought the neglect of Agee's poems was due to their explicit Christian themes, but kindred material did not prevent Eliot's "Ash Wednesday" or Tate's Christmas sonnets from getting a hearing. A bigger hurdle is that Agee's poems fail to cohere around a single sensibility; they read like an anthology by different hands. The best by far are lullabies, such as the poem that begins "Sleep, child, lie quiet, let be" and the lovely "Theme with Variations," which begins with the quatrain "Night stands up the east: / Day glides down the west: / Lax in his fur the beast / The bird with brow in breast." The fourth variation draws its erotic charge from the Tennessee woods:

> Where now the lizard and the rinded snake
> That skipped and slurred their lengths and lusted in the heat?
> Where the lean bugs that on the water break
> Their rapid dances and each other eat?
>
> The lithe-tongued butterfly where now is he
> That chanced his bright wings on the unequal air?
> Where the mean hornet and the sweet-groined bee:
> Now they are under night how may these bloodless fare?

It was Agee's good luck that Archibald MacLeish—a poet, a Yale man, and one of the founding editors of *Fortune*—encouraged Agee to gather his early poems together and submit them to the Yale Younger Poets series, for which MacLeish himself conveniently served as judge. The bounties of *Fortune,* where Agee worked from 1932 until 1939, were a mixed blessing, but mainly one feels a blessing. The smart and efficient editors allowed Agee to show off his orchestral prose when appropriate, as in the gorgeous opening blasts of his magisterial piece on the Tennessee Valley Authority:

> The Tennessee River system begins on the worn magnificent crests of the southern Appalachians, among the earth's oldest mountains, and the Tennessee River shapes its valley into the form of a boomerang, bowing it to its sweep through seven states. Near Knoxville the streams still fresh from the mountains are linked and thence the master stream spreads the valley

> most richly southward, swims past Chattanooga and bends down into Alabama to roar like blown smoke through the floodgates of Wilson Dam, to slide becalmed along the crop-cleansed fields of Shiloh, to march due north across the high diminished plains of Tennessee and through Kentucky spreading marshes toward the valley's end where finally, at the toes of Paducah, in one wide glass golden swarm the water stoops forward and continuously dies into the Ohio.

When they tried to curb his excesses, as in the flat, overlong, and leering piece on the orchid business, they were probably right to do so. Agee's 1934 piece on cockfighting, with a footnote on how boxing gloves derived from the protective muffs fitted over the roosters' spurs, is much more interesting; both articles, with their probing of the mysteries of tight communities, seem in retrospect preparation for Agee's *Fortune* assignment of 1936 to cover the struggle of southern sharecroppers during the depression.

Agee's writing always had most authority when he was drawing on his native landscape, finding the "master stream" pulsing near Knoxville. Earlier in 1936, before taking on the sharecropper assignment, Agee had written one of his best things, a lyrical evocation of his childhood called "Knoxville: Summer 1915," published in *Partisan Review* in 1938 and later appended to *A Death in the Family*. "We are talking now of summer evenings in Knoxville, Tennessee," it begins, "in the time that I lived there so successfully disguised to myself as a child." Agee's evocation of men in the evening watering their lawns is lyrically beautiful and mysterious beyond any obvious symbolism: "the fathers of families, each in his space of lawn, his shirt fishlike pale in the unnatural light and his face nearly anonymous, hosing their lawns." As so often in Agee's work, one detects the ache attached to families, and the longing for something transcending paternal loneliness, achieved for a moment then lost in a vision of the family gathered on the lawn:

> On the rough wet grass of the back yard my father and mother have spread quilts. We all lie there, my mother, my father, my uncle, my aunt, and I too am lying there. . . . By some chance,

> here they are, all on this earth; and who shall ever tell the sorrow of being on this earth, lying, on quilts, on the grass, in a summer evening, among the sounds of the night.

One can see why Samuel Barber was moved to do a setting of "Knoxville: Summer 1915" for soprano and orchestra in 1947, though the music was already there for all to hear.

In July, 1936, Agee and the photographer Walker Evans spent three weeks with three tenant families in Hale County, Alabama. *Let Us Now Praise Famous Men* was the four-hundred-page fulfillment of Agee's *Fortune* assignment on sharecroppers, and it hardly needs saying that the results did not meet the expectations of the editors, who were happy to cede Agee the rights to try to turn his mushrooming article into a book. The book was eventually published in 1941 and sold only six hundred copies, despite Lionel Trilling's judgment that it was a "great book" and "the most realistic and important moral effort of our generation." Reissued by Houghton Mifflin in 1960, with a foreword and additional photographs by Walker Evans, *Let Us Now Praise Famous Men* finally found its audience. "Agee worked in what looked like a rush and a rage," Evans wrote. "In Alabama he was possessed with the business, jamming it all into the days and the nights. He must not have slept." The contrast between Agee's feverish prose and the dignified, daguerreotype-like quiet of Evans's frontal portraits of family members, cabins, and shoes is one of the great strengths of the book.

Agee actually developed two kinds of prose for the occasion. One closely resembles the lyricism of "Knoxville: Summer 1915," as in the aria fifty pages in: "All over Alabama, the lamps are out. Every leaf drenches the touch; the spider's net is heavy. The roads lie there, with nothing to use them. The fields lie there, with nothing at work in them, neither man nor beast." Agee's dreamlike meander through New Orleans, "stirring, rattling, and sliding faintly in its fragrance," almost sounds like Kerouac: "taxis are still parked along Dauphine Street and the breastlike, floral air is itchy with the stilettos and embroiderings above black blood drumthroes of an eloquent cracked indiscoverable cornet, which exists only in the imagination and somewhere in the past, in the broken heart of Louis Armstrong."

Agee's other voice, inspired by a careful and envious study of Evans's astringent photographs, is patient, understated, dedicated to the task of exhaustively describing all that is there to see:

> On the floor at center, two by two, toes to the wall, a pair of woman's black slippers, run-over at the low heels. A pair of workshoes, very old, molded to the shape of the feet. A pair of girl's slippers, whited over scrubbed clay and streaked again with clay. A pair of little-boy's high black shoes, broken at the toes and worn through the soles, the toes curled up sharply; looped straps at the heels: thick clay scrubbed off . . . These shoes, particularly those of the children, are somewhat gnawn, and there are rat turds on the floor.

Beneath the description, however, were indignation and sorrow, the groundswell of Agee's populism. That sympathy never veered into Communism—"The Party fished in vain for Agee," as Fitzgerald dryly remarked. And while Agee was firmly on the side of the tenant farmers against the predations of Capitalism, his deeper theme was not the struggle of the working man but the persistence and survival of families.

In his portrait of shoes—the woman's, the man's, the girl's, and little boy's—and in many other passages, Agee's pent-up longing for family happiness found its way into *Let Us Now Praise Famous Men,* the original title of which was "Three Tenant Families." The image of a family assembled on a quilt from "Knoxville: Summer 1915" became an obsession for Agee. He convinced himself that one of the young sharecroppers, whom he called Annie Mae, shared his fantasy of spending "her last few days alive having a gigantic good time in bed . . . with Walker and with me, whom she is curious about and attracted to, and who are at the same moment tangible and friendly and not at all to be feared, and on the other hand have for her the mystery of glamour almost of mythological creatures." One of the most depressing passages in Laurence Bergreen's 1984 biography of Agee records the all too literal working out of this fantasy, when Agee persuaded Evans to make love to Agee's second wife, Alma, while Agee sat at the foot of the bed sobbing. Of the intricacies of Agee's love life perhaps the less said the better, except to remark that his relatively successful third marriage, to the Austrian émigrée and *Fortune* staffer Mia Fritsch, coincided with his most equable and fruitful period, when he reviewed films at *Time* and then, from 1942 to 1948, served as regular film critic for the *Nation.*

James Agee on film is one of the glories of American or any other criticism. In his reviews he managed to steer clear of both intellectual puffery (film as high art) and slumming in pop culture. He recognized from the start that there were films of consuming quality and interest and that the steady and intelligent gaze he had directed at Walker Evans's photographs and at tenant farmers' shoes could yield passages of writing more assured than anything in *Let Us Now Praise Famous Men.* When reviewing a film allowed him to sneak up on some gigantic reputation like Shakespeare's (Laurence Olivier's *Henry V*) or Hemingway's (*The Killers*), Agee found fresh things to say about both the film and the source. Hemingway's talk, so magical on the page, "sounds, on the screen, as cooked-up and formal as an eclogue." Olivier's Crispin's Day oration before battle "is not just a brilliant bugle-blat: it is the calculated yet self-exceeding improvisation, at once self-enjoying and selfless of a young and sleepless leader, rising to a situation wholly dangerous and glamorous, and wholly new to him."

Agee's film criticism sounds like that too, a calculated yet self-exceeding improvisation. Its culmination is the twenty-five-page essay he wrote for *Life* in September of 1949 entitled "Comedy's Greatest Era." Agee's premise was simple: "As soon as the screen began to talk, silent comedy was pretty well finished." In a Bob Hope film, "the fun slackens between laughs like a weak clothesline." What Agee loved in silent movies was the same thing he loved in nineteenth-century daguerreotypes and New Orleans jazz, an unself-conscious authenticity of the kind Friedrich Schiller called "naive" rather than sentimental. Agee began his essay in a mock-analytic mode: "In the language of screen comedians four of the main grades of laugh are the titter, the yowl, the bellylaugh and the boffo. The titter is just a titter. The yowl is a runaway titter. Anyone who has ever had the pleasure knows all about a bellylaugh. The boffo is the laugh that kills." Agee examined the smiles of the great comedians: Harold Lloyd's "thesaurus of smiles" which "could at a moment's notice blend prissiness, breeziness and asininity" or Buster Keaton—the "most deeply 'silent' of the silent comedians"—whose smile "was as deafeningly out of key as a yell." The twitchings of Harry Langdon's clueless face "were signals of tiny discomforts too slowly registered by a tinier brain; quick, squirty little smiles showed his almost prehuman pleasures, his incurably premature trustfulness." And then there was Chaplin, some kind of ultimate for Agee: "Of all comedians he worked most deeply and most shrewdly within a realization of what a human being is, and is up against."

From writing about films Agee yielded to the temptation to help make them. He collaborated with John Huston on *The African Queen* and worked on the screenplay (rewritten by the director, Charles Laughton) of *The Night of the Hunter,* a gothic fairy tale about a brother and sister in flight from a nightmare stepfather. Still photogenic, Agee played some bit parts, too, typecast as a drunk in his own adaptation of Stephen Crane's "The Bride Comes to Yellow Sky" in 1951 and, the following year, as a poet in a TV dramatization of Lincoln.

By the early 1950s, Agee was famous and in demand but he was also dying. He suffered his first heart attack in 1951 and had serious heart trouble thereafter. The sense of urgency so evident in his youth returned in spades. He turned down Huston's offer to write an adaptation of *Moby-Dick,* working instead on an original screenplay about Gauguin. He worked relentlessly on his novel, *A Death in the Family,* aware, surely, of the title's potentially double meaning: "I add Agee's death to his hero's and can't forget the epitaph," Robert Lowell wrote in 1958. One of the last things Agee wrote was a final, ironic lullaby—to be sung by the crowd "like middle-aged Sunday School children"—solicited but turned down by Lillian Hellman for the musical *Candide:*

> Purest child, our hearts we leave thee,
> All we hope and hold most dear;
> Shining one, we must believe thee,
> Fair one, fare where we would fear.

Agee had his demons; but if you consider what he accomplished in a scant quarter century, it's hard to think of him as a martyr to anything beyond, in his own words, what a human being is, and is up against.

NOTE

1. Robert Fitzgerald, editor, *The Collected Short Prose of James Agee* (Boston: Houghton Mifflin, 1968), 91.

VOLUMES REVIEWED

*Let Us Now Praise Famous Men, A Death in the Family, Shorter Fiction*
By James Agee
Library of America, 2005

*Film Writing and Selected Journalism*
By James Agee
Library of America, 2005

# Love in the Ruins

"NO WARMER AND MORE SECRET BOOKS THAN THESE TWO," the Austrian novelist Peter Handke wrote of Walker Percy's first novels, *The Moviegoer* and *The Last Gentleman,* both of which he translated into German. "And the secret is not made, cooked—it is not cheap mystery, it is felt and developed with writing, work." Handke and Percy shared a couple of "secrets," including the deaths of their mothers by suicide. They also had in common a certain obliqueness in their literary situations, writing out of tradition-steeped Catholic regions (Austria and Louisiana) on the periphery of larger (German and American) national literatures. But more important—it's what makes Handke's remark so refreshing—there is an awareness in both writers of the sheer hard work of writing, if anything like true warmth and true secrecy are to be won. "One waits," as Percy once wrote, "not for the Muse, fuck her, but until one finds a new language, because that's about what it takes, the language is about dead."

By birth and upbringing, Walker Percy (1916–1990) seemed destined to mourn the vanished glories of the Old South. The Percys of Alabama and Mississippi were aristocrats, if anyone was. Among the congressmen and the war heroes whom the family produced in successive generations, however, there lurked a pervasive melancholy. Percy's father and grandfather died of self-inflicted shotgun blasts. His mother drove her car off a country bridge and into a bayou—a mysterious performance that Percy, thirteen at the time, came to consider a suicide. The orphaned boys—Walker, Phin, and Roy—were adopted by their much older bachelor cousin, William Alexander Percy, and came of age in his imposing house, full of books and paintings and a well-used piano, on Percy Street in Greenville, Mississippi.

Will Percy—"the most extraordinary man I have ever known," in Walker's estimation—was a poet in the yearning Romantic vein. To keep a poem free from "irrelevant photographic details," he once advised, "you set it in some long-ago time." He is best known for his wonderful memoir, *Lanterns on the Levee,* which appeared in 1941, as good a guide to the mind of the South, the white South, as you are likely to find. Though he was in touch with such "Agrarian" poets as Allen Tate and John Crowe Ransom, and he shared their resentment of the encroaching industrial godless North, Will Percy found the modernist technique of their verse unattractive. Asked for his opinion of Ransom's famous "Bells for John Whiteside's Daughter," the third stanza of which runs, "The lazy geese, like a snow cloud / Dripping their snow on the green grass, / Tricking and stopping, sleepy and proud, / Who cried in goose, Alas," Uncle Will drily responded: "That's not the way geese act."

It was rumored that Walker's mother had killed herself when Will Percy rebuffed her advances. She may have misconstrued the sexual preferences of this infinitely charming man who refused to have Faulkner visit again after he showed up drunk for a tennis match. Uncle Will determined that the Percy brothers must have playmates, and invited a local boy of Walker's age called Shelby Foote, whose dark good looks reminded Will of the young Proust, to come by. It was the beginning of a lifelong friendship between Percy and Foote, the literary record of which can be found in Jay Tolson's fine edition of the Foote-Percy correspondence. (Percy was particularly lucky in this friendship. Foote was a talented and precocious novelist who had much to teach Percy later on. His three-volume history of the Civil War remains an underrated masterpiece, even as Foote himself has become a celebrity for his starring role in Ken Burns's *The Civil War.*)

Percy went off to Chapel Hill in 1933 with his head filled with the saintliness of Robert E. Lee and the sensibleness of segregation. When Foote, who also attended UNC, pushed the virtues of integration, Percy exploded: "Shelby, you call yourself a Southerner!" Percy flunked his placement exam in English composition when he imitated the Benjy section of Faulkner's *The Sound and the Fury*. He was a comfortable frat boy who was noticed, when he was noticed at all, for his passion for General Lee. Foote, by contrast, was rejected by the same fraternity when it became known that he had a Jewish grandparent. On graduation, Walker decided to become a doctor; his grades, never outstanding, were adequate for enrollment at Columbia's medical school.

Then came the great divide in Walker Percy's life. While his brothers and Shelby Foote went to war, he came down with tuberculosis, a few months into his Bellevue internship, in the spring of 1942. As he lounged about the famous cabins of the Trudeau Sanitorium on Saranac Lake in the Adirondacks, he found (as he recounted many times to many interviewers) that science could not answer the questions about life and death that suddenly tormented him. So out went the science books and in came Sartre and Heidegger and Kierkegaard. "After twelve years of scientific education," he later wrote, "I felt somewhat like the Danish philosopher Soren Kierkegaard when he finished reading Hegel. Hegel, said Kierkegaard, explained everything under the sun, except one small detail: what it means to be a man living in the world who must die."

Percy maintained in retrospect that tuberculosis was "the best thing that ever happened to me." In the space of four or five years, he returned to the South, gave up his medical career, and, supported by a generous trust fund, began writing in the two genres that would occupy him for the rest of his life: novels, of which he eventually published six, and philosophical essays, often dealing with the gap between scientific and existentialist models of brain function, and occasionally with less technical subjects, such as the aesthetics of drinking bourbon. ("Bourbon does for me," he wrote, "what the piece of cake did for Proust.") In 1946, Percy married Mary Bernice Townsend ("Bunt" to her husband and friends), a medical technician; both of them converted to Catholicism a couple of years later. They lived briefly in New Orleans, the setting of several of Percy's novels, then moved to a small Louisiana town above Lake Pontchartrain, where Percy lived for the rest of his life.

Much of the criticism and biography of Percy have centered

on his explanations of that small detail overlooked by Hegel: what it means to be human and mortal. His books, so redolent of the South and southern mores, have often been reduced to American versions of ideas already developed in Camus or Sartre—"alienation," "the absurd"—or in Catholic theology. Such intellectual debts are obvious, and Percy made no attempt to conceal them, but they distract attention from Percy as a writer, as a creator of what he called "new language." Scholars have plumbed his philosophical essays for more big ideas, again at the expense of a careful sounding of the novels. Many of Percy's most ardent admirers have wanted to see in him a saint or a spiritual guide. Percy was grateful for Robert Coles's early study of his work, but he confided to Foote that he didn't recognize himself in the book: "I think it is because Coles is projecting a good deal of himself, a kind of good-hearted Colesian decency which may apply to him but not exactly to me." Later books have continued this tendency. The portentous title of Jay Tolson's excellent and very readable biography, *Pilgrim in the Ruins,* which appeared in 1992, is symptomatic.

Patrick Samway's new biography continues the trend, paying minute attention to every documentable moment—the annual retreats, the visits from priests, the donations to religious orders—of Percy's spiritual life. With its five-hundred-page bulk, Samway's biography is of the every-fact-that-fits variety. If you want to know where and from whom Percy bought his cars, or who his Finnish publisher was, or who starred in *The Unsinkable Molly Brown* when Walker saw the show in New York, this is the book for you.

In fairness, it is no small thing to gather all the facts and all the documents about a famous person and assemble them in a reliable order. More log than life, Samway's book will be of great value to anyone seriously interested in Percy. Still, it is shapeless except in its chronological structure, graceless and sometimes bizarre in its phrasing, and full of non sequiturs. The reader is rewarded from time to time with a sentence such as this one: "Walker once made a bittersweet discovery after having problems with his large bowel, that too much drinking at the Boston Club had been the cause." What exactly was "bittersweet," the bourbon or the discovery? Sometimes Samway's file cards seem unedited, just folded any old way into the narrative. A paragraph describes the letter of recommendation that Percy wrote for Jason Berry, who worked in Mississippi on the gubernatorial campaign of Charles Evers. "Berry visited Walker and they talked for several hours, especially about the dynamics of a young white man working among blacks. Later Berry's and Percy's concerns seemed to merge as each, in his own way, wrote about pedophilia." Huh?

Samway studied with Joseph Blotner, the long-winded biographer of Faulkner and Robert Penn Warren. "Reading Blotner's Faulkner with interest," Percy writes Foote in the spring of 1974. "Don't mind details the reviewers deplored. Pity is, he has to leave out the most interesting stuff: F's relation to Estelle, how come Jill hated life at home, sexual relations with Joan and Jean, etc. Neccesary [sic] reticence of course but pity anyhow." How, then, does Samway treat "the most interesting stuff" in Percy's life? With indirection and innuendo. There are peculiar pockets of reticence amid all his data. He mentions unspecified "marital troubles" during Percy's late fifties and sixties, and dutifully documents—with little interpretation—his friendships with attractive and intelligent young women. Samway quotes a rueful letter to Foote, in the key of Philip Larkin's "Annus Mirabilis" ("Sexual intercourse began / In nineteen sixty-three / Which was rather late for me"), about how the "new Bohemia" is too late for "literary seniors" like them:

> Explain why it is that the girls did not exactly knock each other down to get at me when I needed them most but that in this my sixty-eighth year to the Lord, I am propositioned regularly by handsome thirtyish lady-girls, three in recent months, an editor, a photographer, a P-R lady—who have in common only that they don't fool around at all. Their seductions have been almost totally unsuccessful . . . Explain women. Have women gone crazy? What does a handsome, fine-assed, thirtyish lady-girl want with a skinny, bald-headed, sixty-seven-year-old writer?

Samway's gloss is typically flat-footed: "Walker's question was not rhetorical: he knew literary success or celebrity attracted too many women." Concerning that tantalizing bit about the seductions being "almost totally unsuccessful," Samway has nothing to say. He discounts the rumors about Percy's relations with one young woman, but he starts his own rumors about another. "If his friendship with Lyn Hill was raising eyebrows, his friendship with thirty-one-year-old Jo Marie Gulledge was hardly noticed." Hardly noticed, that is, except by the sharp-eyed Samway.

More surprisingly, Samway has little to say about Percy's novels, offering neither plot summaries nor his own judgments. He quotes instead, in great thickets of one-liners, from contemporary reviews. His account of *The Moviegoer* moves from what is known about the writing of it—here the Foote-Percy correspondence is particularly revealing—through the editorial handling of it (including the championing of the novel by Stanley Kauffmann, then an editor at Knopf), to its publication, its reception, and the National Book Award in 1962. As to the meaning of the book, its achievement or shortcomings, Samway is silent. Perhaps this is the kind of self-effacement one should be grateful for in a biographer. But books are big events in the life of a writer, and you can't make sense of the life—the real life—without making sense of the books.

Of Percy's six novels, at least three still reward attention. *The Moviegoer* has preserved all its charm. Even in its approach to "big ideas," it is whimsical rather than pompous. The philandering moviegoing Binx Bolling's concepts of "certification" (experiences and places rendered real by being represented in movies), "repetition," and even the much commented-upon "search" are the half-baked and humorous musings of a man with a meditative tilt of mind.

> What is the nature of the search? you ask . . . The search is what anyone would undertake if he were not sunk in the everydayness of his own life. . . . The movies are onto the search, but they screw it up. The search always ends in despair. They like to show a fellow coming to himself in a strange place—but what

> does he do? He takes up with the local librarian, sets about proving to the local children what a nice fellow he is, and settles down with a vengeance. In two weeks' time he is so sunk in everydayness that he might just as well be dead.

Time has been less kind to *The Last Gentleman.* Maybe its clunky evocations of Gide and Mann seemed vital in 1966, when Joyce Carol Oates, reviewing it for *The Nation,* found its "highly whimsical kind of picaresque . . . altogether richer and more intriguing than . . . *The Moviegoer.*" The novel is almost unreadable now, cloying in its account of its young hero's sexual longings for a two-dimensional deb called Kitty, unfocused in its social satire of New York City. It has patches of vitality, and almost all of these have to do with the South and southernness—as when the alienated hero from Alabama becomes an honorary member of a clique of Ohioans. When Percy tries to generalize, and takes on The Human Condition, the characters flatten into symbols for this or that aspect of fallen, post-Christian man. The settings—north and south—are mostly abstract; they're theater sets, and nothing like the richly rendered detail of New Orleans in *The Moviegoer,* or the later *Love in the Ruins.*

Shelby Foote hinted at the problem when he objected to the long epigraph from the Catholic existentialist thinker Romano Guardini concerning the end of the modern world. ("The world to come," Guardini concludes, "will be filled with animosity and danger, but it will be a world open and clean.") "I don't know that I'd use the quotes at the outset," Foote wrote. "The one from Kierkegaard (sp) is o.k. because of brevity, but the second is all too explicit in a work so utterly implicit. I don't much like epigraph quotes anyhow; they remind me of crutches—or, worse, those Algebra books with the answers printed in. It doesn't need propping up at all, which this long quote seems to me to do."

The fact is, the props are already there in *The Last Gentleman.* It's a wonder that Percy thought it needed a sequel, which turned into *The Second Coming* (1980). *Love in the Ruins* (1971) is a skillful rehash of *The Moviegoer,* with the premonitions of the end of modern life made explicit. For a vision of the apocalypse, set in bombed-out New Orleans, the narrative is surprisingly down-to-earth and racy. The first-person narration, Percy's natural voice, serves him well again. This novel also spawned a sequel—as though the end of the world just kept on going—in *The Thanatos Syndrome* (1987).

It's a minority opinion, but I believe that the most enjoyable of Percy's novels is *Lancelot* (1977). Percy's rantings at the modern world are given wonderful voice in the murderer Lancelot Lamar, who has deliberately burned his meticulously restored plantation house to the ground, with his adulterous wife and a movie crew inside. Looking back on his married life from his cell, Lamar recalls: "Later we lived by sexual delights and the triumphs of architectural restoration. Truthfully, at that time I don't know which she enjoyed more, a good piece in Henry Clay's bed or Henry Clay's bed."

Late in life, Percy realized that he was now "the oldest male Percy in history; 57, so what lies ahead is virgin territory; imagine a Percy with arthritis! senility! Parkinsonism, shuffling along, fingers rolling pills, head agoing! I don't know whether I'm looking forward to doing a great thing like Kant and Spinoza and Verdi in the 1980s or whether I'll jump in the Bogue Falaya next week with a sugar kettle on my head." But Percy did great things. He once suggested that his books started "where Faulkner left off . . . with a Quentin Compson who didn't commit suicide. Suicide is easy. Keeping Quentin Compson alive is something else."

VOLUMES REVIEWED

*Walker Percy: A Life*
By Patrick Samway, S.J.
Farrar, Straus and Giroux, 1997

*The Correspondence of Shelby Foote & Walker Percy*
Edited by Jay Tolson
Doubletake/Norton, 1997

# A Sense of Place

Eudora Welty has chronicled the legends and landscape of her native state of Mississippi with such tireless brilliance that she herself has become a legendary fixture of that landscape. As a young and unknown writer, she was an enthusiastic cicerone to the likes of Henry Miller (exploring the South for his "Air-Conditioned Nightmare" of depression America) and the Anglo-Irish novelist Elizabeth Bowen. Who wouldn't want to be shown around the ghost towns of the old Natchez Trace—the buffalo track turned Indian trail turned pioneer road—by Eudora Welty? In the following passage, from a vivid travel essay of 1944 called "Some Notes on River Country," she summons up a vanished world from the landscape of the Trace:

> Winding through this land unwarned, rounding to a valley, you will come on a startling thing. Set back in an old gray field, with horses grazing like small fairy animals beside it, is a vast ruin—twenty-two Corinthian columns in an empty oblong and an L. Almost seeming to float like lace, bits of wrought-iron balcony connect them here and there. Live cedar trees are growing from the iron black acanthus leaves, high in the empty air. This is the ruin of Windsor, long since burned. It used to have five stories and an observation tower—Mark Twain used the tower as a sight when he was pilot on the river.

We see in the mind's eye both the ruin and the empty air, but also a second layer of fantasy: the floating lace, the fairy animals, the five stories, and Mark Twain in the tower. In such passages, Welty gives us what Wallace Stevens called "Nothing that is not there and the nothing that is."

Like Goethe in Weimar or Emerson in Concord, Eudora Welty, who died in 2001, became one of the obligatory sights of a tour of Mississippi. So V. S. Naipaul, making his "Turn in the South" in 1988, paid a formal call on her in Jackson. They talked about the presence of the frontier in her stories, and the temperament of the southern frontiersman. "Scare everybody, outwit everybody, beat everybody, kill everybody—that's the frontiersman's mentality," Welty explained. Then she quickly added that the violence in Mississippi was "not nearly as frightening as the Northern—urban—brand." (Her much celebrated story of the murder of Medgar Evers, "Where Is the Voice Coming From?" is to some degree an attempt to blame southern racism on the rednecks, descendants of those "kill everybody" frontiersmen.) Naipaul, so conscious of the cultural privations of his own Caribbean homeland, wondered if living in "a frontier state" had been a limitation for Welty "as a writer, and as a woman writer." Characteristically she dodged the second part of the question—she always refused the designation of "woman writer"—and reassured Naipaul that the "great variety of people" in Mississippi had given her plenty to write about. "In a place that hasn't changed much you get to know the generations. You can see the whole narrative of a town's history or a family's history."

Her own family history is woven into two late works, a tightly plotted novella of 1972 called *The Optimist's Daughter* and her relaxed autobiographical memoir, first delivered as a set of lectures at Harvard, called *One Writer's Beginnings* (1984). Both these performances are thoroughly literary, crafted, and cagey about intimate details. Welty will write till the cows come home about the commanding presence of her father, a native Ohioan (and thus something of a latter-day carpetbagger) who made good as an insurance executive in Jackson. Her mother's Yankee upbringing on a mountaintop in West Virginia, with a slew of left-handed, banjo-picking brothers, is another scenario Welty never tires of. She ends her memoir with an often quoted summation: "As you have seen, I am a writer who came of a sheltered life. A sheltered life can be a daring life as well. For all serious daring starts from within." There's a quiet allusion here to a once famous novel of the South by Ellen Glasgow called *A Sheltered Life,* a novel in which the title is ironic. (The South must overcome its "sheltered" past and enter the modern, merciless world of technology and commerce.) There's also a fierce protection of privacy in Welty's phrasing: don't look for the daring because you'll never find it. As Welty proclaimed in 1972, the same year she published *The Optimist's Daughter:* "Your private life should be kept private. My own I don't think would particularly interest anybody, for that matter. But I'd guard it; I feel strongly about that. They'd have a hard time trying to find something about me."

Welty's defiance hasn't deterred Ann Waldron, the author of an unauthorized but perfectly friendly and respectful new biography of Welty. Waldron notes that all was not sweetness and light in Welty's upbringing; the shelter didn't cover strains in the senior Weltys' marriage and serious psychological problems for Welty's two brothers. Waldron tactfully dances around the issue of Welty's "sexuality," a term Welty would probably find unbearable. She notes Welty's close relationships with gay men and lesbian women, especially such haughtily aristocratic writers as Katherine Anne Porter and Elizabeth Bowen, and quotes some lush passages from Welty's correspondence with Bowen. ("I miss and will miss and have missed you . . . it's so strange, isn't it, the crisscross where and when we are with all we love and must love.") Then Waldron concludes, correctly, that "no one knows the truth about Eudora's sexuality"—a sentence that sounds faintly parodic, as though invented by "Eudora" herself for the opening line of a story. The overarching theme of Waldron's biography is that of the ugly duckling: the tall and gawky and odd-looking girl with a gift for comedy who makes her way through high school and college and a stint doing PR for the WPA before settling on writing stories that didn't sell and then eventually did. (As Welty traveled around Mississippi for the WPA she also took a lot of photographs, though she was never, as is often said, a "WPA photographer.")

The kind of writer Eudora Welty had turned herself into by the 1930s was fairly familiar during the previous generation, sometimes called the golden age of the American short story.

Such fin de siècle short story writers as Stephen Crane or Kate Chopin or Jack London could whip up a story in nothing flat, designed for a certain magazine and often for a particular time of year. That was the age of the Christmas story, of which O. Henry's "The Gift of the Magi" is merely the most enduring. Stories that heralded the coming of spring, often with an Easter theme (Welty's "Livvie," a romance ending with "the bursting light of spring," is a perfect example), or the fall colors, or the trials of winter are ubiquitous in these writers' work. They were genre writers, as comfortable in the conventions of the Civil War story or the "Negro story" or the tale of Old New England (or Old New Orleans or Old California) as their editors were in asking for more just like the last one. This was also the age of the "surprise ending," that durable invention of Poe by way of Maupassant that could suggest either the accidents of the universe or God's sure plan. At a certain point you could feel the surprise coming on, like a storm. Once in a while, though, a story would go on longer than usual, the storm would blow over, and something like a novel would emerge: *The Red Badge of Courage; The Awakening; The Call of the Wild.* But really these were long stories, "novellas," lacking the complex architecture of plot and interlocking characters of the European novel as practiced by Henry James or Edith Wharton. And sometimes, as in Chopin's *The Awakening,* the surprise ending was delayed but still there, snapping the story shut like a box.

You can see the surprise-ending machinery skillfully put to use in Welty's first published story, "Death of a Traveling Salesman." Disoriented by illness, a shoe salesman runs his car into a ditch and dazedly seeks refuge in a broken-down farmhouse inhabited by an old half-wit woman and her menacing son. He suspects a conspiracy to rob or kill. But no, he suddenly realizes, in a searing moment of clarity. The woman is young, and pregnant to boot. The salesman, Bowman, has stumbled into a greater mystery than the conspiracy he feared. "There was nothing remote or mysterious here—only something private. The only secret was the ancient communication between two people." The surprise ending, turning a thriller plot into a sentimental evocation of love in the hard-bitten thirties farm-country, allows Welty to reaffirm her belief in the sacredness of privacy.

Welty's familiar and much anthologized "A Worn Path" combines the primitivizing conventions of the Negro story, as practiced by Crane and Chopin, with the Christmas story, the traditional message of which is that even the lowest—the poor, the outcast, the overlooked—will find a way to celebrate. (This is the perennial Christmas surprise, from Dickens to O. Henry and on to the Grinch.) An old black woman from the rural outback walks all the way to the town of Natchez.

> It was December—a bright frozen day in the early morning. Far out in the country there was an old Negro woman with her head tied in a red rag, coming along a path through the pinewoods. Her name was Phoenix Jackson. She was very old and small and she walked slowly in the dark pine shadows, moving a little from side to side in her steps, with the balanced heaviness and lightness of a pendulum in a grandfather clock.

She walks through the countryside through most of the day, having strange encounters with man and beast along the way. By the time she walks into town—"There ahead was Natchez shining"—she has forgotten why she came. She wanders mechanically into a doctor's office, and one attendant explains her history to another. "She doesn't come for herself—she has a little grandson. She makes these trips just as regular as clockwork. She lives away back off the Old Natchez Trace." Her grandson, it turns out, swallowed lye many years ago. There's some doubt as to whether he's even still alive. Phoenix takes the bottle of medicine, accepts a nickel of extra charity—"It's Christmas time, Grandma," says the attendant—and informs the doctor's office staff that she's "going to the store and buy my child a little windmill they sells, made out of paper . . . I'll march myself back where he is waiting, holding it straight up in this hand." She walks out of the doctor's office and, regular as the clock that is the story's reigning metaphor, starts the long way home.

Almost nothing in "A Worn Path" marks it as of our century. It has an 1890s feel, with its "indomitable" and allegorically named mother figure, its Christmas theme (including allusions to the journey of the magi), its sad little sappy brave ending. It could have been published in *A Youth's Companion* or *St. Nicholas,* those staples of youthful uplift. "A Worn Path" is nonetheless an important story in Welty's early work. In it she has already discovered the archetypal Welty plot. A person goes down a well-traveled road and strange things start to happen. It is important that the road be well traveled, "worn." The deeply cut Natchez Trace becomes Welty's favorite setting. Welty likes well-traveled roads for two reasons. First, they are haunted.

> I have never seen, in this small section of old Mississippi River country and its little chain of lost towns between Vicksburg and Natchez, anything so mundane as ghosts, but I have felt many times there a sense of place as powerful as if it were visible and walking and could touch me.

Second, they are a suggestive analog of the storyteller's procedures, which are always twice told, to go where everyone has gone before.

But Welty had reservations about "A Worn Path." When it was chosen for the 1941 O. Henry Prize anthology (the first of countless reprintings of this beloved story), she remarked that she thought another of her stories of that year, "Powerhouse," was much better. She paired the stories at the end of her first collection, *A Curtain of Green* (1941), as though inviting the reader to compare them. "A Worn Path" wins over readers because of its very worn-ness. We know where that old woman is going with her pinwheel held high. "Powerhouse," by contrast, is an early example of one of the stubbornly distinctive and harder-to-sell stories that Welty has written throughout her career. Her identification with the main character in Powerhouse, a jazz pianist modeled on Fats Waller, is far more intense than her endearing and distancing account of Phoenix. Following Phoenix along the path, Welty takes few risks of tone or topic. In "Powerhouse," though, she dares herself to match the improvisatory genius of her protagonist. This entails mucking around in black speech and white, profanity and innuendo, and what we now call ethnic stereotyping. Welty adopts an arresting point of view—a sort of sympathetic, over-the-shoulder narration fully responsive to the force that is Fats:

> Powerhouse is playing!
>
> He's here on tour from the city—"Powerhouse and His Keyboard"—"Powerhouse and His Tasmanians"—think of the things he calls himself! There's no one in the world like him. You can't tell what he is. "Nigger man"?—he looks more Asiatic, monkey, Jewish, Babylonian, Peruvian, fanatic, devil. He has pale gray eyes, heavy lids, maybe horny like a lizard's, but big glowing eyes when they're open. He has African feet of the greatest size, stomping, both together, on each side of the pedals. . . . Improvising, coming on a light and childish melody—*smooch*—he loves it with his mouth.

The story is more portrait than plot. Powerhouse plays a set at a white dance, takes his entourage down the street to a black dive, where he receives a telegram that his wife has jumped from her apartment window—"Brains and insides everywhere, Lord, Lord." Powerhouse blames the death on his old nemesis, the wonderfully named and surely imaginary Uranus Knockwood ("Ain't ever seen it wrote out in any print, even for horse racing"), then returns to play another set.

In "Powerhouse," Welty's fun is our fun. Her admiration for Powerhouse is so evident in every line that you feel, well, she just wants to *be* Powerhouse. Welty and Waller are one. It's easy to see how William Faulkner, eager to encourage a promising young writer, could get confused about just who this Eudora was. During the wartime spring of 1943, Welty received a mash note from Faulkner, perhaps the writer she most admired. "Dear Welty," he wrote. "You are doing fine. You are doing all right. I read THE GILDED SIX BITS, a friend loaned me THE ROBBER BRIDEGROOM. I have just bought the collection named GREEN something, haven't read it yet . . . You are doing very fine. Is there any way I can help you? How old are you? Do you mind telling me about your background. My address is below."

Living in the same state as Faulkner, Welty once said, was

"like living near a great mountain, something majestic." Her excitement over the letter was only slightly dampened by the fact that the one work of hers that Faulkner specifically claimed to have read, "The Gilded Six Bits," was in fact written by Zora Neale Hurston. Actually, the bourbon-abetted confusion with Hurston—the African-American virtuoso of the thirties, trained in anthropology at Columbia, who collected folklore in Florida and Haiti and practiced voodoo in New Orleans—goes beyond the similarly exotic names, Zora and Eudora. For really Welty and Hurston were thirties writers with similar ambitions. Each had a WPA-era thirst to find some authentic rooted realm of cultural vitality outside the collapsing cities. Each found in the voices of black women and men, and black music, an echo of this authenticity. Each was deeply enmeshed in folklore, building stories and novels around tales twice told. *The Robber Bridegroom,* lent to Faulkner by a friend, is just this kind of story, an eighty-page fairy tale of loud talkers, tricksters, and rakish lovers.

A tour de force like "Why I Live at the P.O." taps a similar, improvisatory source as "Powerhouse," but it's a narrower achievement. Perhaps Welty's most popular story (it gave the name "Eudora" to a widely used email program), it employs a similarly explosive central character, this time rendered in a cascading first-person rant:

> I was getting along fine with Mama, Papa-Daddy and Uncle Rondo until my sister Stella-Rondo just separated from her husband and came back home again. Mr Whitaker! Of course I went with Mr Whitaker first, when he first appeared here in China Grove, taking "Pose Yourself" photos, and Stella-Rondo broke us up. Told him I was one sided. Bigger on one side than the other, which is a deliberate, calculated falsehood: I'm the same.

That delicious riff on one-sidedness is as good as any of Powerhouse's inventions. But this poor-white comedy is safer ground for Welty, and she allows herself to condescend to these awful people in ways that she resolutely avoids in her zestful evocation of Powerhouse.

In these early stories, Welty takes us all around her native state, using material gathered during her WPA itinerancy. She is drawn to wandering musicians and photographers, freak-show performers and con men. They are at once stand-ins for her, the roving storyteller, and enactors of the "worn path" and freak-show performance of the short story itself. Stories like "Petrified Man" and "Keela, the Outcast Indian Maiden" don't take a Diane Arbus line on freaks as marginalized victims, alienated and alone. Welty's grotesques tend to be figures of energy and survival, in charge of their fate. Ugly ducklings, they have found ways to trade on their oddity, turning hard luck into hard cash.

Welty's wanderers regularly come upon haunted places—ruined houses and ghost towns and worn paths—but she doesn't derive from them the usual narratives of southern Gothic fiction. The geography of Mississippi ultimately interests Welty more than its history, and she has no time at all for the great Gothic and tragic mother-vein of the Civil War. "I hate the Civil War," she once told an interviewer. "I hate it. I have never read *Gone with the Wind.* I'm totally ignorant about the Civil War. . . . But I just hate it, all those hideous battles and the terrible loss." The reference to *Gone with the Wind* is the giveaway clue here, as though the Civil War and Margaret Mitchell's novel were somehow the same thing. It's not so much the battles and losses that Welty hates—she called one of her novels *Losing Battles,* but it's not about the war—as the literary treatment of it in nostalgic historical novels, of which there were many during the thirties besides *Gone with the Wind.* As a displaced Yankee of sorts, Welty may also have found the Civil War an awkward subject while growing up. She tends to portray herself in her stories as a midwesterner, like the Chicagoan in *The Optimist's Daughter,* or the young woman in "No Place for You, My Love" who assumes "a serious, now-watch-out-everybody face, which orphaned her entirely in the company of these Southerners."

Welty will use the Civil War at times as a marker of great age, as when she describes the young husband's clothes in "The Death of a Traveling Salesman: "He wore muddy blue pants and an old military coat stained and patched. World War? Bowman wondered. Great God, it was a Confederate coat." Likewise, in "A

Worn Path," when Phoenix can't remember why she walked all the way to town, she explains that she never went to school: "I was too old at the Surrender." Such Civil War references, rare in Welty's later writing, are themselves a convention of 1890s tales, but in Welty's stories they have the effect of distancing the Civil War, placing it in a remote and irrecoverable realm, rather than invoking its continuing effect on the South. Welty only risked one Civil War story, "The Burning" (1950), and it's not a very good one. It probably started as a sort of correction of Margaret Mitchell's account of Sherman's raid. Jackson was the first Southern town that Sherman burned, and Welty's portrait of helpless white ladies from a "big house" and their more resourceful black slaves is a far cry from plucky Scarlett O'Hara. "The Burning" won an O. Henry award, and the Civil War historian Shelby Foote asked to include it in a collection of Civil War stories. Welty told him it was the worst story she'd ever written.

Welty's objections to historical fiction went beyond nostalgia, however. She had, you might say, an epistemological objection to it. She simply didn't believe that the historical past was available to fiction, and she said so on several occasions and in different ways. "I never could understand how people could write historical novels with real people speaking," she once said. At other times, as in her essay "Place in Fiction," she called the historical novel a contemporary version of the fairy tale: "Of course we shall have some sort of fairy tale with us always—just now it is the historical novel." Welty's practice implied that the storywriter had only two genuine options in representing historic events. One was frankly to acknowledge the fairy-tale status of such re-creations. *The Robber Bridegroom* (1942), Welty's lively and sweet-spirited novella of Natchez Trace lowlife and romance, is a fairy tale from start to finish. In a pan in the *Times,* Lionel Trilling scowled about how Welty had tried to "translate the elements of European fairy tales into the lore of the American frontier,"comparing it to the "coy mystifications" of Virginia Woolf. (Welty, who admired Woolf, didn't mind the comparison.)

The other option was to acknowledge the unavailability of history, and to weave this tension into the very fabric of the story. Welty's "First Love" is her supreme example of this strategy. In it she adopts the perspective of a deaf-mute twelve-year-old boy who witnesses Aaron Burr's preparations for and subsequent escape from his trial for treason in Washington, Mississippi. We cannot hear Burr's words in the intense nocturnal conversations witnessed by the boy, nor can we hear the boy's actual account of them. The past is as sealed and silent as Aaron Burr.

> There was a kind of dominion promised in his gentlest glance. When he first would come and throw himself down to talk and the fire would flame up and the reflections of the snowy world grew bright, even the clumsy table seemed to change its substance and to become a part of a ceremony. He might have talked in another language, in which there was nothing but evocation. . . . Lights shone in his eyes like travelers' fires seen far out on the river.

Welty invents a charged language of homoerotic longing, centered on gesture and glance: "One of the two men lifted his right arm—a tense, yet gentle and easy motion—and made the dark wet cloak fall back. To Joel it was like the first movement he had ever seen, as if the world had been up to that night inanimate."

A related story, also collected in *The Wide Net and Other Stories* (1943), is "A Still Moment." Three real-life wanderers—the painter Audubon, the itinerant preacher Lorenzo Dow, and the bandit and murderer James Murrell—encounter one another by chance in a clearing along the Natchez Trace. Murrell is about to murder Dow when Audubon appears. Suddenly, a white heron swoops down, and all three men are transfixed by the aura of the bird. This is the still moment of the title.

> What each of them had wanted was simply *all.* To save all souls, to destroy all men, to see and to record all life that filled this world—all, all—but now a single frail yearning seemed to go out of the three of them for a moment and to stretch toward this one snowy, shy bird in the marshes. It was as if three whirlwinds had drawn together at some center, to find there feeding in peace a snowy heron. Its own slow spiral of flight could take it away in its own time, but for a little it held them still, it laid quiet over them, and they stood for a moment unburdened.

The heron is like Wallace Stevens's jar in Tennessee: "The wilderness rose up to it, / And sprawled around, no longer wild." Again, history at its truest doesn't talk; it is a series of epiphanal "still moments." "A Still Moment" was, as Welty noted and Waldron reports, "the only time her writing was based on facts she had read instead of living people she had observed." "A Still Moment" was Welty's favorite among her stories and it's easy to see why. It has lost none of its freshness and strangeness. Indeed, the Natchez Trace stories from Welty's second collection, *The Wide Net and Other Stories,* remain a neglected treasure in her collected works.

Reading through *The Wide Net* collection in 1944 with an eye to reviewing it, Robert Penn Warren wrote to his close friend the critic Cleanth Brooks.

> Welty is an extremely interesting gal. I'm not inclined to think that she has gained ground in her last book, but she has plowed the same ground a little more deeply. I've been trying to define her basic theme. Fumbling in results as yet. Alienation, perhaps. All main characters are "cut-off" characters. Deaf boy. Women sex-starved, to use the tabloid word. Artists afraid of world. Little girl looking across the street at big girl. Or perhaps, not merely alienation, but vicariousness. Well, this is certainly fumbling.

Despite his discomfort with Welty's lesbian-inflected story of little girl and big girl, "The Winds," Warren does a nice job here of identifying some of Welty's dominant themes, themes that would become even clearer in her next collection, the seven linked stories of *The Golden Apples* (1949). This echo chamber of a book, following the blighted but comical lives in a derelict town, is built around allusions to poems of W. B. Yeats. It is like a loose-limbed novel, though Welty refused (against her publisher's request) to call it one. One of the stories, "June Recital," is among her best; it is a sort of pendant to "Powerhouse," with an old-maid itinerant piano teacher, a Yankee of German origin, going slowly mad with longing for art and love. *The Golden Apples* displays the "gained ground" Warren was looking for, but it's finally a bit too acquiescent to the strictures of New Critics like Warren and Brooks. Its elaborate echoes of Yeats and careful piling up of imagery show the good student of New Critical "texture," the lessons carefully learned.

It is more difficult to make a strong case for Welty's full-length novels. Sentence by sentence, they have the same improvisatory brilliance as her short stories, but they tend to lack a compelling structure. Two short novellas, *The Robber Bridegroom* and *The Optimist's Daughter,* are perfectly satisfying, and have the onward propulsion of her stories. But the longer performances, *Delta Wedding* and *Losing Battles,* go on and on, with short-story characters who try and fail to take on the depth and complexity of novel characters. Welty likes to build her novels around family gatherings—weddings, funerals, reunions—where characters are introduced as they arrive. In *Losing Battles,* her novel about up-country Mississippi rural white folk, the characters just keep arriving. There are so many—thirty or so in all—that she provides a list of them at the start of the novel, along with such extras as "various descendants and cousins and married kin of the Beechams." They tell each other stories, catching up (and catching the reader up) on one another's past lives. The main narrative, which we have to put together from the piecemeal revelations of a circle of gossips, concerns Jack Renfro, who may or may not be about to be released from the state penitentiary for a comical crime involving his attempts to retrieve his mother's wedding ring.

The first hundred pages of *Losing Battles* are lively and fun to read, with Jack's picaresque escapades taking up most of the narrative. We assume that the tale—which might be called "Waiting for Jack"—will end when Jack finally comes home. Welty (as Waldron informs us) thought so too, till she opened a folder in which she had stashed some post-arrival ideas and decided to go with it, creating a short story of five hundred pages. The title comes to seem like an admission of narrative exhaustion. Welty allows herself no internal description of her characters; we learn about them from what they say and do, and from what others say about them. But she indulges in the most baroque efflorescence of metaphor in describing settings and props, and these, finally, are the true pleasures of the novel. Here, for example, is the opening, which is typical of the novel as a whole:

> When the rooster crowed, the moon had still not left the world but was going down on flushed cheek, one day short of full. A long thin cloud crossed it slowly, drawing itself out like a name being called. The air changed, as if a mile or so away a wooden door had swung open, and a smell, more of warmth than wet, from a river at low stage, moved upward into the clay hills that stood in darkness.
>
> Then a house appeared on its ridge, like an old man's silver watch pulled once more out of its pocket.

There's a figure of speech in every line, and each of those metaphors and similes—the flushed cheek, the called name, the open door, the silver watch—suggest aspects of the human drama about to be played on this animated stage. The pleasures of *Losing Battles* are of this local, almost miniature, variety, as when a farm road—another well-worn path—at the beginning of the novel lies in the morning light "the color of a human palm and still more groined and horny and bare."

Richard Ford and Michael Kreyling, the editors of the handsome and expertly annotated Library of America volumes, have wisely limited themselves to the stories Welty herself collected. They have just as wisely ignored her tinkerings and revisions, sometimes forty years after the fact, for her *Collected Stories of Eudora Welty* (1980). The nine essays selected here include such delights as "A Pageant of Birds," an account of a costume celebration of birds in a black church in Jackson. I would have welcomed some of Welty's photographs, such as the ones she took of the bird pageant, but that seems outside the scope of the Library of America. (The family photographs in *One Writer's Beginnings* are retained.) It's hard to imagine a better or more respectful way to publish Welty more or less entire.

Welty's extraordinary popularity at the moment is intriguing. Once formidable southern competitors like Carson McCullers (whom Welty despised) and Welty's mentor Katherine Anne Porter seem to have lapsed into partial eclipse. The Christian armature of Flannery O'Connor's stories has not worn well. Other short story masters who cover some of the same territory as Welty, such as Peter Taylor, are hardly read at all today. But every new anthology of American short stories includes something of Welty's, and every aspiring short story writer knows a few of her stories almost by heart. I suspect some of this adulation is for the wrong reasons. Welty allowed a sentimental, dear-old-endearing-Eudora aura to surround her, an impression confirmed by the ingratiating *One Writer's Beginnings.* She's known as the author of such affection-inspiring crowd-pleasers as "Why I Live at the P.O." and "A Worn Path," while tougher, better pieces of writing get little attention. I think some readers who love Welty will be surprised at the sheer volume of her almost complete works—imagine, two tomes of almost a thousand pages each! And if they were to read through them, there will be more surprises still.

VOLUMES REVIEWED

*Stories, Essays, & Memoir*
By Eudora Welty
Selected and annotated by Richard Ford and Michael Kreyling
Library of America, 1998

*Complete Novels*
By Eudora Welty
Selected and annotated by Richard Ford and Michael Kreyling
Library of America, 1998

*Eudora: A Writer's Life*
By Ann Waldron
Doubleday, 1998

# Poet in the Sun Belt

RANDALL JARRELL THOUGHT OF THE POET AS "a sort of accident-prone worker to whom poems happen." Jarrell wrote reviews, children's books, translations, and a comic novel; but his letters make clear that he lived for the accidents. In times of safety, when no poems came, he was despondent. When he was young the poems happened in abundance. He published four books of poems in nine years, from 1942 (when he was twenty-eight) to 1951, but he had to wait nine more years before he had enough poems for his next book, *The Woman at the Washington Zoo,* of which more than a third consists of translations of German poems. His last collection, *The Lost World,* was published a few months before his death in 1965. Jarrell's life and death are still shrouded in mystery, while his reputation as a poet is uncertain.

It is part of the mythology of his generation of poets—which included John Berryman, Delmore Schwartz, and Robert Lowell—that Jarrell's death was a suicide. A sentence from A. Alvarez's *The Savage God* places Jarrell in august company: "Cesare Pavese and Paul Celan, Randall Jarrell and Sylvia Plath, Mayakovsky, Esenin and Tsvetayeva killed themselves"; and Robert Hass, in a moving elegy to Jarrell, vows "to somehow do honor to Randall Jarrell, / never to kill myself." A selection of letters probably should not have an argument but this one does: Mary Jarrell, the poet's second wife, is convinced that her husband's death was an accident. She calls her selection "autobiographical," but this is not altogether so, in view of the lengthy attention she gives to Jarrell's death, where her commentary supplants his text. She tells the story again. It was night; he was wearing a dark coat and dark gloves as he walked by the side of a North Carolina highway; the driver testified that Jarrell "lunged in the path of the car" (though the coroner's report casts doubt on this). Still, no new recital of the circumstances is likely to persuade the reader that it was an accident, since the real difficulty is to understand Jarrell's mood at the time.

During the month before his death Jarrell wrote to Robert Penn Warren about the hellish spring and summer he had just lived through. "I've always wanted to change, but not change into what you become when you're mentally ill. I was badly depressed last summer and, in getting out of that, got elated and unreasonable, and stayed in the hospital, recovering, from about March 1 to July 1." For this period, letters are scant, and Mrs. Jarrell's commentary can hardly be considered impartial. But two events stand out. In March Jarrell wrote to Michael di Capua, his editor: "I don't know whether Mary has told you; but she and I are separated and will be divorced after a while." In April, when he was, according to Mrs. Jarrell, "in such unrelieved depression that shock treatments were being considered, Jarrell cut his left wrist in a suicide attempt." A reconciliation followed. Jarrell told Warren, "It feels awfully good to be home with Mary again." But his wrist didn't heal properly, and Jarrell returned to Chapel Hill for treatment. It was then that the accident or suicide occurred. The letter to Warren, which precedes this second treatment, concludes:

> I haven't written any poems, but I've been thinking so much about the passage of time, and what it's like to live a certain number of years in the world, that I think it's sure to turn into some poems in the long run.

The reader will have to judge whether passages like this sound desperate or hopeful. But if death came as an accident to Jarrell, it seems to have come the way he thought poems did. As he wrote in "90 North," "I die or live by accident alone."

Jarrell was fifty-one when he died. During his life he seemed the least likely of his contemporaries to die young. He was "almost without vices," as Lowell said. In the company of a generation of poets given to excess Jarrell neither smoked nor drank. Until his last years he showed no signs of madness; indeed, according to the reports of friends he seems to have suffered from an almost maddening sanity. Even his divorce from his first wife seemed painless. As one correspondent wrote, "Your divorce seems to be the most calmly and humanely conducted of any that I know of." Jarrell stayed in excellent physical condition by playing tennis expertly; during the war he won the doubles championship of Tucson and was runner-up in singles, and he played in tournaments all his life. He also loved his job of teaching. "I'd pay to teach," he liked to say. When he wrote Elizabeth Bishop in 1957, "Probably both of us will live to be eighty-three," this seemed a reasonable guess, at least for himself, though he added, "The world is full of bombs and airplane crashes."

Jarrell had every chance to become a "southern poet" and didn't. He was born in Nashville in 1914 and attended high school and college there. He made his first contribution to the cultural life of Nashville when he was twelve, modeling for the statue of Ganymede that adorns the full-scale replica of the Parthenon in Centennial Park. Jarrell's mentors at Vanderbilt were the Fugitive poets John Crowe Ransom, Allen Tate, and Robert Penn Warren. They encouraged him to write by exhortation and example; the first letter in the volume is to Warren, and it begins, "Here are the poems." Jarrell didn't share their politics, however: he had no interest in the restoration of an agrarian society, and their vision of a southern aristocracy, established around family tradition, held no appeal for him. His own middle-class parents (his father was "a partner in Kramer-Jarrell Portrait Pictorialists") were divorced when he was a child, and the nearest he came to being part of a family was the year he spent in Hollywood with his grandparents (whom he called Mama and Pop), after the separation. He didn't hate the South but he didn't have much to say about it either. When Tate suggested the subject to him in 1945 Jarrell wrote back: "The only Southern subjects I ever thought of writing about are you, Red, and Mr. Ransom—your poems, I mean."

If Tate, Ransom, and "Red" Warren can be considered the last southern poets, Jarrell may be the first poet of the Sun Belt.

Almost all the letters in this collection were postmarked in the cities of that loosely defined waist of the nation, where labor and fuel are cheap, and men read *Road and Track* and watch professional football on television—two of Jarrell's passions. Except for some visits to "the northeast, that wretched direction," and a few years in Washington, D.C., and Gambier, Ohio, Jarrell spent most of his life in Nashville, Austin, Tucson, Laguna Beach, and Greensboro, North Carolina. "I wish you could see the football here," Jarrell wrote to Tate from Austin, where he took one of his first teaching jobs and met his first wife, Mackie, a fellow English teacher. During the war he was stationed at various army bases in Texas and Arizona, serving mainly as an instructor in celestial navigation, and he asked Mackie to send him the newspaper accounts of the University of Texas practice games.

What Jarrell called "my army poems" are distinctive for their gentle empathy with the boys of the sunny cities who were asked to fight in a war that seemed at first like a sport—

> In our new planes, with our new crews, we bombed
> The ranges by the desert or the shore,
> Fired at towed targets, waited for our scores—

and to the end had some of the abstract, impoverished feel of a high school geography class:

> *We read our mail and counted up our missions*—
> In bombers named for girls, we burned
> The cities we had learned about in school—
> Till our lives wore out.

After the war Jarrell served for a year as literary editor of *The Nation,* on the strength of the reviews and poems he had written while in the army. He loathed New York, finding relief in the ballet and the proximity of Forest Hills ("I spent much of last week at the tennis matches, which mitigated New York, for a little, a little"). He avoided New York parties where he would be subjected to the narrow confines of New York literary gossip. Of Delmore Schwartz he wrote, "He thinks that Schiller and St. Paul were just two *Partisan Review* editors." In a letter to Lowell he reported: "I wrote a funny poem about a man who was born in New York City and died there."

The city of Greensboro, which Jarrell called "one more version of pastoral," was his refuge for almost twenty years, from 1947 to 1965. He taught at the Women's College of the University of North Carolina, an institution he viewed with the same merciless affection he directed toward the fictional college of Benton, in his novel, *Pictures from an Institution.* "The average North Carolina girl talks as if she were an imbecile with an ambition to be an idiot," he wrote to Margaret Marshall, the literary editor of *The Nation;* and when people asked him what his students were like, he referred them to his poem "A Girl in a Library":

> If someone questioned you, *What*
>         *doest thou here?*
> You'd knit your brows like an orangoutang
> (But not so sadly; not so thoughtfully)
> And answer with a pure heart, guilelessly:
> *I'm studying. . . .*
>         If only you were not!
> Assignments, recipes, the *Official Rulebook*
> *Of Basketball.*

But Jarrell felt implicated in this vision of half-educated athletic health—"One sees in your blurred eyes / The 'uneasy halfsoul' Kipling saw in dogs'. / One sees it, in the glass, in one's own eyes." He often complained of his own faulty education. "Indeed I don't read Greek," he wrote Hannah Arendt, "it's a wonder I read English."

Jarrell is often praised by critics for his understanding of women, and especially for the poems—"The Face," "Next Day," "The Woman at the Washington Zoo"—in which he adopts a female persona. He told Allen Tate he had a "semifeminine mind"; but the cost of this empathy seems to have been a curiously protective, asexual, and almost avuncular attitude toward women. He adored little girls, and didn't much like to see them grow up. When they did anyway, he addressed them as "Baby doll." Like many other men, Jarrell seemed happiest when he was telling a woman what to read. While teaching at Salzburg in the summer of 1948 (it was his first visit to Europe and he seems to have left Mackie at home to take care of the cat), he fell in love with one of his students. They refrained from sex, "out of deference to his marriage," according to the editor, but on his return Jarrell bombarded her with seventy love letters, several of which seem to be little more than long reading lists ("Isak Dinesen, *Out of Africa;* Christina Stead, *The Man Who Loved Children;* Evelyn Waugh, *Decline and Fall;* Dostoievski, *The Idiot*"). To another woman correspondent he wrote, "Telling things to read is something I can hardly make myself finish." Reading was more than a passion for Jarrell, however. It was a shrine he visited daily. He said that in libraries he felt "soothed and calm and secure," like "a baby come back to the womb." He simply wanted the women he cared for to be able to join him there.

Jarrell was such a prude and at the same time such an avid reader of Freud that one is surprised he isn't more lucid about his own repressions. "Last night Blackmur was pretty bad," he reported from Princeton. "He does so enjoy talking about awful or unseemly things." Jarrell could joke about his own squeamishness—"Me for Queen Victoria, as far as Public Life is concerned"—but his friends respected it. According to Mrs. Jarrell, Lowell "took care not to use the fashionable four-letter words with Jarrell that he used with others." Jarrell's letters abound with words like *golly* and *dovey* ("a dovey Colonial house like Cleanth's") and *crazy about;* some of Rilke's poems are "honeys." He seems particularly reluctant to talk about his body, and Mrs. Jarrell quotes, apparently in agreement, Lowell's curious remark about her husband: "His body was a little ghostly in its immunity to soil, entanglements and rebellion."

When the bodies and minds of his friends rebelled, Jarrell was distant and unhelpful. He wrote to his Salzburg student in 1949:

> The poet who was my particular friend among poets—Robert Lowell—has had a bad "nervous breakdown" and is in a mental hospital. I had a pathetically irrational letter from him last week. You have such a helpless bewildered feeling when something like this happens.

When Lowell was hospitalized again, in 1954, Jarrell, according to his wife, "found it distasteful to be even minimally involved in this crisis." Such clouds had no place in the Sun Belt. Ten years later Jarrell, to his surprise and horror, began to experience manic symptoms quite similar to Lowell's, symptoms that were at times endearing. While introducing Hannah Arendt as a guest lecturer in Greensboro, Jarrell talked for twenty minutes about meeting Johnny Unitas, the quarterback of the Baltimore Colts. When Jarrell tipped a waitress fifteen hundred dollars, arrangements were made for his admission to Memorial Hospital in Chapel Hill.

Jarrell is rarely a good letter writer and never a great one. He did not enjoy writing letters, nor did he give much care to them. His letters assume a tie made some other way; they almost never try to establish one. It is therefore unfortunate that one of Jarrell's closest friends, Peter Taylor, refused to relinquish his letters for this volume. The editor has chosen four hundred letters from twenty-five hundred, and still one finds every few pages a letter that is in Jarrell's words "a perfect banyan tree of weekday-names and dates." Many of the letters are really cover letters, wrapping paper for poems or articles or letters to the editor. Mary Jarrell and her assistant, Stuart Wright, provide helpful notes between the letters, identifying articles, poems, and people alluded to, but the principles of selection are hazy. The editor tells us that "only the most literary and autobiographical portions of Jarrell's nearly one hundred love letters to Mary von Schrader [Jarrell] have been excerpted and presented," but we never learn what exactly Mrs. Jarrell means by "literary" (well written? dealing with literary topics?) or "autobiographical" (Mrs. Jarrell sometimes provides so much commentary that the volume seems biographical); and the recipient is probably not the best editor of love letters.

Some of Jarrell's finest letters resemble (and sometimes were) early drafts of reviews. There are brilliant, often line-by-line analyses of poems in letters to Adrienne Rich and to Lowell ("In 'The Crucifix' I think 'the worldly angels strip to tease / and wring a world of bathos from their eyes' isn't good: I think its tone is a little too timely and tawdry for the tone of the rest." Lowell cut it). It is often said that Jarrell was the best poetry critic of his generation, but this isn't quite true. He was the best poetry reviewer. He didn't change the ways we read the poets of the past, as for example Northrop Frye or William Empson or R. P. Blackmur consistently did. His famous essay "Some Lines from Whitman" helped rescue its subject from the rigid formalism of the New Criticism, but it is less a work of criticism than a masterpiece of instructive quotation ("To show Whitman for what he is one does not need to praise or explain or argue, one needs simply to quote").

The two brilliant essays on Frost in *Poetry and the Age* (1953), his first and best collection of essays, are perhaps an exception, for Jarrell really discovered Frost for serious readers of poetry, and showed them how to read him. It is hard now to believe that poems like "Design" and "Home Burial" and "Acquainted with the Night" were hardly known when Jarrell wrote "The Other Frost," but it is true. In 1963 Jarrell wrote a wonderful letter about Frost to Lowell and Elizabeth Hardwick:

> He'd stay with us in Greensboro and talk all day—for one interesting, awful, and touching day about nothing but his family. . . . I existed for him just as the person who'd written those pieces about his poetry. . . . He felt I was an Indian who'd sold him, *given* him, Manhattan Island, and he was willing to keep me on a special little reservation in return. I felt that he talked more like poetry than anybody else I'd ever heard, that his voice made other voices sound a little high in comparison, so what did I care whether he was right or wrong? (He actually *said* that his writing had had all the success he wanted it to, so what did he care what happened with nuclear weapons?) The only cultural try I ever made with him was to read him four or five haiku that I thought close enough to his couplets for him to like; and he really did like them.

For ten or fifteen years Jarrell was the best reviewer of poetry in America. Not only did he protest the neglect of some of the best older poets—Frost, William Carlos Williams, and Marianne Moore—but he also had an uncanny sense of who the central poets of his own generation were. He detected Lowell's promise early, and his continuing enthusiasm helped Lowell to keep it. After the publication of Lowell's first book, in 1944, Jarrell wrote confidently (but also coaxingly), "Some of the best poems of the next years ought to be written by him." In the fifties, while others were praising Berryman and Schwartz and MacLeish, Jarrell singled out Elizabeth Bishop, telling her: "I like your poetry better than anybody's since the Frost-Stevens-Eliot-Moore generation." His letters reveal the enthusiast behind the reviewer's mask. Jarrell's dominant emotion when reading a good poem was gratitude. "Gee, your poems are wonderful," he wrote to Bishop.

Jarrell judged bad books with angelic ruthlessness; his quips are remembered like good jokes while their victims are forgotten. He called one book of poems "non-Euclidean needlepoint" and remarked that another gave "the impression of having been written on a typewriter by a typewriter." But his cruel reviews were unconsciously cruel. He seems to have felt that he was weeding the garden of poetry, and that everyone would be grateful to him for doing the dirty work. He was bewildered when poets complained. "It is always hard for poets to believe that one says their poems are bad not because one is a fiend but because their poems are bad," he wrote in a letter to the editor in 1948. Jarrell gradually tired of reviewing. He announced his change of heart to Lowell in 1949: "We live in a reviewing criticizing age that doesn't give a damn for works of art, mostly—why should I help it along? I'll write articles occasionally about what *I like* and all the rest can just die quietly without any help from me."

While working on one such piece he wrote to Mary, "It's funny that Whitman could say both the wonderful things and the goofy junk." This is roughly what critics have found funny in Jarrell's work. The wonderful things are in the reviews and articles, they have argued; the goofy junk is mainly in the poems. In Helen Vendler's laconic formula, "Jarrell . . . can be said to have put his genius into his criticism and his talent into his poetry." But this seems to me to overrate the criticism and underrate the poetry. What is lacking in Jarrell's poetry is a feel for, or a trust in, the density and texture of language. One almost never feels that a poem of his has grown around the sound of a single word or cluster of words, as one does, for example, with the poems of Frost and Hardy and Rilke (all poets that Jarrell loved, though mainly for their *dramatic* genius, their ability to find fit words for the characters in their poems). Jarrell prefers to exploit quotation, misquotation, and allusion, resources on which his criticism draws as well. "Next Day," one of his best poems, begins:

> Moving from Cheer to Joy, from Joy to All,
> I take a box
> And add it to my wild rice, my Cornish game hens.
> The slacked or shorted, basketed, identical
> Food-gathering flocks
> Are selves I overlook. Wisdom, said William James,
>
> Is learning what to overlook. And I am wise
> If that is wisdom.
> Yet somehow, as I buy All from these shelves
> And the boy takes it to my station wagon,
> What I've become
> Troubles me even if I shut my eyes.

The melancholy wit, the ambivalent pleasure in brand names and the props of suburban America, the expertly placed quotation—these are all characteristic of Jarrell's best poems.

Jarrell found in the German language the density he never found in English. "The most wonderful thing of all is the flavor of the common, ordinary words," he wrote to Mary, "and that you'd never taste if it were your native language" (unless you were Frost or Hardy, one is tempted to add). He never learned much German, however. "Alas, my German isn't a *bit* better," he complained to Hannah Arendt, "if I translate, how can I find time to learn German? if I don't translate, I forget about German." His method of translation was to rely less on the original than on previous translations. His version of Chekhov's *Three Sisters,* since he knew no Russian, was written *against* "seven already existing bad English translations." This is why his versions betray so little resistance from the original; the English language hasn't had its feathers ruffled. This is particularly (and damagingly) true of Jarrell's posthumously published *Faust,* while his most satisfying translations are from Rilke's short poems; with the help of a dictionary and a native speaker like Arendt, Jarrell could master some of the language of the original. (The narrator of *Pictures from an Institution,* who also translates Rilke, remarks: "You can always get a German to help you with the German, but who is there to help you with the English?")

For Jarrell Germany was above all the country of childhood. He felt at home among Grimm's fairy tales, furry animals, and the evanescent children in the Rilke poems he had translated: "to think about the little pale / Face that shone up from the water, sinking: / O childhood, O images gliding from us / Somewhere. But where? But where?" The surprise, and sense of breakthrough, in the poems in *The Lost World* is the retrieval of Jarrell's own childhood, and the discovery that *his* Germany, so to speak, was Hollywood, and the year he lived there with his grandparents. His madeleine turns out to be tapioca pudding:

> This spoonful of chocolate tapioca
> Tastes like—like peanut butter, like the vanilla
> Extract Mama told me not to drink.
> Swallowing the spoonful, I have already traveled
> Through time to my childhood.

The fairy-tale properties of southern Germany are translated to Southern California: "When I was twelve we'd visit my aunt's friend / Who owned a lion, the Metro-Goldwyn-Mayer / Lion. I'd play with him, and he'd pretend / To play with me." Jarrell's poems about Salzburg are less "Märchen-like," kitschy, and uncanny than his description of Hollywood:

> On my way home I pass a cameraman
> On a platform on the bumper of a car
> Inside which, rolling and plunging, a comedian
> Is working; on one white lot I see a star
> Stumble to her igloo through the howling gale
> Of the wind machines. On Melrose a dinosaur
> And pterodactyl, with their immense pale
> Papier-mâché smiles, look over the fence
> Of *The Lost World.*

Jarrell is most unguarded in the poems of *The Lost World.* One passage seems to prefigure his own death:

I believe the dinosaur
Or pterodactyl's married the pink sphinx
And lives with those Indians in the undiscovered
Country between California and Arizona
That the mad girl told me she was princess of—
Looking at me with the eyes of a lion,
Big, golden, without human understanding,
As she threw paper-wads from the back seat
Of the car in which I drove her with her mother
From the jail in Waycross to the hospital
In Daytona. If I took my eyes from the road
And looked back into her eyes, the car would—I'd be—

Nothing in the letters helps us much with passages like this; and yet, if we are to make sense of Jarrell's life, we have to make sense of the poems. A selection of his letters can hardly be autobiographical when the only autobiography he left is in his poetry. His biographers, who are certain to be at work soon, will not be able to ignore the letters; but if their narratives are to be of any value, they will have to begin and end in the poems.

VOLUME REVIEWED

*Randall Jarrell's Letters: An Autobiographical and Literary Selection*
Edited by Mary Jarrell
Houghton Mifflin, 1985

# Part III

# The Union Reconsidered

# American Jeremiad

1.

The generation of American writers that came of age around 1840—the men and women who initiated what we now think of as a national literature—aspired more to youthful vigor than to the "classic" status of ancient Greece and Rome, so dear to the generation of the Founding Fathers. A sense of expanding frontiers, buttressed by expansive ideas borrowed from European romanticism, impelled them. They wrote enthusiastically of "Young America," spelled nature with a capital *N* (and sometimes without an *e,* like some pagan divinity unleashed from the Black Forest), and refused to be, in Emerson's pejorative word, "retrospective."[1]

"The American Scholar," Emerson's Phi Beta Kappa address to Thoreau's graduating class at Harvard College during the summer of 1837, is full of appeals to youth:

> Meek young men grow up in libraries, believing it their duty to accept the views, which Cicero, which Locke, which Bacon, have given, forgetful that Cicero, Locke, and Bacon were only young men in libraries, when they wrote these books.

The classics of Greece and Rome, the great books of Great Britain, were merely "the sere remains of foreign harvests." Thoreau took the lesson to heart. "I have lived some thirty-odd years on this planet," he wrote in *Walden,* "and I have yet to hear the first syllable of valuable or even earnest advice from my seniors." The hemlocks surrounding Walden Pond better represent these writers' aspirations than the faux-Roman columns and obelisks on the Mall in Washington.

With regard to which of their own books might survive, becoming classics in their turn, nineteenth-century American critics were youthfully confident and, in our view, often wrong. Who now reads those bosky American epics "Evangeline" or "The Song of Hiawatha" except for laughs? Aside from *The Scarlet Letter,* recognized then and now as a masterpiece though for shifting reasons, it is remarkable that some of the books we treasure most survived oblivion. *Walden* and *Moby-Dick* were commercial failures, all but ending their authors' careers. Emerson backed off from his initial enthusiasm for *Leaves of Grass* ("I should have enlarged the *but,*" he remarked, when he learned that Whitman had published his private letter of congratulation in the *New York Tribune*); Emily Dickinson, with pride or prudence, said she had not read Whitman but was "told that he was disgraceful." Dickinson herself stowed her nearly two thousand poems, of which a mere ten were published in her lifetime, in a drawer and instructed her sister to burn her papers at her death. Such messages entrusted to bottles eventually floated to shore, to join our confident (and probably wrong) judgments about our own contemporaries.

It is striking that so many of the nineteenth-century American works we now consider unquestionably important—including four of the five books (*Walden, Leaves of Grass, The Scarlet Letter,* and *Moby-Dick*) identified by Denis Donoghue as "the American classics"—were published during a scant five years, from 1850 to 1855. Other remarkable books, such as *The House of the Seven Gables, Uncle Tom's Cabin,* and Emerson's *Representative Men,* appeared during the same period. Two major issues dominated American society during this transitional moment, one political and one religious. The political issue was of course slavery—and many of these works have something to say about slavery. Thoreau was an ardent abolitionist and Mark Twain's two major novels *Huckleberry Finn* and *Pudd'nhead Wilson* look back on this period from a postwar perspective.[2]

The religious crisis is more difficult to characterize but no less significant: the breakup of the old Puritan certainties, and the consequent embrace of a new revivalism on the one hand—sometimes called the Second Great Awakening—and a new religious liberalism on the other, associated with Emerson, William Ellery Channing, and Henry Ward Beecher, Harriet Beecher Stowe's brother. Much of the scorn heaped on their "seniors" by these midcentury American writers derived from their sense that the previous generation had botched the spiritual and political challenges of its time. "Each age," Emerson had warned, "must write its own books," and by the 1920s, a new group of youthful writers—Hemingway, Fitzgerald, Dos Passos, Faulkner, and Pound—found American literature from before the Civil War still not American enough. "Hawthorne, the others," Faulkner told a seminar of Japanese students, "they were Europeans, not Americans." Amid confident talk of America's "coming of age," only Mark Twain seemed part of a "usable past," while earlier writers like James Fenimore Cooper seemed impossibly remote, relics of a national childhood. "We like to think of the old-fashioned American classics as children's books," D. H. Lawrence wrote in 1923, in his *Studies in Classic American Literature.* But Lawrence, with his Old World perspective on what was distinctive in American writing, thought Americans ignored these books at their peril. Lawrence proposed to take a fresh look at *Moby-Dick* and at the "little thin volumes" of Hawthorne, Poe, and the rest, and what he discovered was a literature of extremity, beyond anything in the supposedly modern literature of the early twentieth century:

> The furthest frenzies of French modernism or futurism have not yet reached the pitch of extreme consciousness that Poe, Melville, Hawthorne, Whitman reached. The European moderns are all *trying* to be extreme. The great Americans I mention just were it. Which is why the world has funked them, and funks them to-day.

Denis Donoghue's *The American Classics* is very much in Lawrence's mode: a stranger from abroad reads the neglected American classics to tell us what they say, and in doing so he promises to tell us who we are. There are no surprises among the five books that Donoghue identifies as the American classics: the four already mentioned and *Adventures of Huckleberry Finn.* Donoghue aims neither to shore up the "canon"—that supposedly agreed-upon list, underwritten by publishers, critics, and professors of literature, of the important American books—nor to undermine it. These are the books, he believes, that have lasted and can speak for American culture; if books replaced the heads on Mount Rushmore, these would be the books. Familiarity itself is the criterion; these five books "make available to readers—or have a good chance of doing so—a shared cultural experience, something," Donoghue adds, "in which American society is otherwise impoverished."

Just as some politicians have suggested that Ronald Reagan's head should be added to Mount Rushmore, some readers may feel that Donoghue's list—"five white men," as he concedes—is unduly short. His criteria for exclusion are sometimes expressed, sometimes not. He argues that since no single work of Emerson's or poem by Dickinson has come to stand for those writers, neither writer can be considered "classic." Presumably Poe, a French classic though not securely an American one, is excluded on the same technicality. Donoghue sneers at Fenimore Cooper (a favorite of Lawrence), whose "nearly unreadable" novels have a prestige that can only be explained by "the need of American readers to feel that they have made their peace with the native Americans." He dismisses *Uncle Tom's Cabin* on the old charge that it is propaganda, though critics more formidable than Donoghue, such as Edmund Wilson and Constance Rourke, have found it to be far more complex than that—"a much more impressive work than one has ever been allowed to suspect," Wilson wrote in *Patriotic Gore.* As for American literature after Mark Twain, Donoghue—following T. S. Eliot's lead—finds twentieth-century American society too fragmented to produce anything truly classic. His students, he writes, prefer Ayn Rand's tirades or *To Kill a Mockingbird;* Donoghue himself may prefer *The Waste Land* and *Absalom, Absalom!,* but such books are not, in Donoghue's word, "privileged" as his five books are.

Donoghue characterizes *The American Classics* as "a chapter of autobiography" and gives it the subtitle "a personal essay." He invites readers to set the work slightly aside from his twenty-odd books of literary criticism, including such memorable interventions—Donoghue has always had a knack for the sharp and timely corrective—as *The Arts Without Mystery* and *Speaking of Beauty,* vigorously argued books in which he attempts to rescue the concepts of the mysterious and the beautiful from pseudoreligious Victorian rhetoric. In stressing the personal and the autobiographical in *The American Classics,* Donoghue excuses himself from systematic argument while allowing for idiosyncrasy and cantankerousness. As such, *The American Classics* can be viewed as a sequel to his affecting memoir *Warrenpoint* (1990), which described his upbringing as the son of a Catholic policeman in the Royal Ulster Constabulary in Northern Ireland and his rigorous education in Catholic schools there. Having come to America in his "middle years," and having taught for decades at New York University, Donoghue wanted to discover what it meant that these five books have been accepted by American culture as the cardinal books. What does this acceptance say of the culture? How do American readers use them; in the service of what causes?

In Donoghue's view, the question has assumed a renewed urgency in the light of recent American policies abroad: "Afghanistan, Iraq—and what next?—Israel's Sharon triumphant in Bush's Washington, the Palestinians brushed aside, the American empire enforcing itself commercially and militarily." You might think that Donoghue would want to send American readers back to the American classics in order to recover some better vision of national purpose. But he is convinced that the seeds of disaster in current American foreign and domestic policy are patent in the American classics themselves. For Donoghue, the American classics are symptoms, not touchstones.

2.

To many readers, Henry David Thoreau has seemed exemplary in his understanding of how human beings might peacefully coexist with plants and wild animals. His experiment on Emerson's woodlot at Walden Pond, beginning on July 4, 1845, has inspired many for its seemingly "green" demonstration of how lightly we might live on the land. A passage such as the following is typical of Thoreau's tact, and his nuanced concern regarding human depredation in the wilderness:

> What is a country without rabbits and partridges? They are among the most simple and indigenous animal products; ancient and venerable families known to antiquity as to modern times; of the very hue and substance of Nature, nearest allied to leaves and to the ground,—and to one another; it is either winged or it is legged. It is hardly as if you had seen a wild creature when a rabbit or a partridge bursts away, only a natural one, as much to be expected as rustling leaves. The partridge and the rabbit are still sure to thrive, like true natives of the soil, whatever revolutions occur. If the forest is cut off, the sprouts and bushes which spring up afford them concealment, and they become more numerous than ever. That must be a poor country that does not support a hare.

Thoreau adopts here a strange, almost grass-level perspective, making the kinds of distinctions—winged or legged, rustling leaves or rustling animals—with which a vulnerable creature, a mole or vole, might assess a potentially dangerous intruder. But Donoghue, who regards *Walden* as an "abrasive" book, is not seduced. He has found another passage in which Thoreau relishes the resilience of Walden Pond, despite the inroads of woodcutters, ice-men, and the nearby railroad. "Of all the characters I have known," Thoreau writes,

> perhaps Walden wears best . . . where a forest was cut down last winter another is springing up by its shore as lustily as ever.

The passage seems innocuous enough, but such sentiments, according to Donoghue, "allow Thoreau to feel that the despoiling of forests and rivers doesn't matter, he can be assured—as President Bush is—that they will grow back again, with nothing lost." If Thoreau could be summoned from the grave, Donoghue implies, he would support drilling for oil in Alaska and the laying of mining roads in our national parks. The Thoreau who was skeptical of vaunted technological progress has made little impression on him.

As for living unobtrusively on the land, Donoghue is equally indignant:

> In *Walden* Thoreau had not a word of sympathy for James Collins and his family, miserably poor Irish emigrants, to whom he paid four dollars and twenty-five cents for their shack on condition that they vacated it by five o'clock the following morning.

Far from being an experiment in ecologically sensitive living, Walden, according to Donoghue, was really a landgrab, a cynical ploy of gentrification. It is true that Thoreau seems contemptuous of the Irish workers squatting on Emerson's land; he is more sympathetic to American Indians and African-American slaves. But Donoghue neglects to say that Collins was working on the Fitchburg Railroad, whose Concord branch was apparently complete when Thoreau approached him, and that Collins seemed happy to get some cash for his shack before moving along to the next spur of the railroad for more work.

Donoghue thinks that Thoreau's highhanded treatment of James Collins is typical of classic American writers, who preach a good line about democracy and their fellow men while hypocritically sticking it to them in private. It is almost Donoghue's biggest complaint against Thoreau and Emerson that they were unsociable. Thoreau "wrote essays on friendship and love" but was "not an especially likable man" and "did not like people." Likewise, "Emerson had very little interest in people at large." The charge is certainly true of both Emerson and Thoreau. "Philanthropy is almost the only virtue which is sufficiently appreciated by mankind," Thoreau observed. But Donoghue confuses dislike of philanthropy with misanthropy. Emerson and Thoreau felt that a self-satisfied interest in "people at large" tended to blind philanthropists to people as individuals. "The philanthropist," according to Thoreau, "too often surrounds mankind with the remembrance of his own cast-off griefs as an atmosphere, and calls it sympathy."

Even Walt Whitman, who really does seem to like "people at large," doesn't do so in a way acceptable to Donoghue. Of Whitman's beautiful poem about a young woman longingly watching "twenty-eight young men bathe by the shore," Randall Jarrell once wrote that there was "such tenderness and subtlety and understanding that . . . Chekhov himself couldn't have treated it better." Not at all, Donoghue rejoins; the woman is really just a stand-in for Whitman, who is guilty in the poem of "the reduction of third person to first."

Donoghue's real concern in these passages is a wider indictment of American democracy and its callousness toward the poor and oppressed. He thinks that there is a conflict between Emersonian individualism and true democracy: "Like Thoreau, Emerson fears and therefore affects to despise society." Donoghue is hardly the first critic to suspect Emerson of being at best a reluctant democrat. But Donoghue insists that anyone who admires Emerson's call for self-reliance is guilty of complicity with American injustice. Stanley Cavell and George Kateb, a philosopher and a political scientist who have written respectfully of Emerson, are, in Donoghue's blistering words, "notably complacent about the American character of the democracy they enjoy. They have apparently forgotten that the regime of George W. Bush and John Ashcroft contrived not only to interpret the USA Patriot Act illiberally but to keep an American citizen, José Padilla, indefinitely in solitary confinement without charge. Not to speak of the use to which the Bush administration has put Guantánamo Bay."

He chides Cavell for writing (in 1990, long before it was possible to recall Ashcroft, let alone forget him) that American society is characterized by "good enough justice." Donoghue sees an opening: "To which it is necessary to reply: there is never good enough justice." Is it really necessary to reply in this way? Donoghue ignores or seems to ignore that Cavell is alluding to the psychoanalytic thinker D. W. Winnicott's notion of "good enough mothering": despite individual shortcomings, most mothering, in Winnicott's view, is "good enough," and mothers should not feel guilty of falling short of perfection. American judges and juries are certainly imperfect, and miscarriages of justice can have disastrous consequences, but what better judicial system does Donoghue have in mind?

Donoghue interprets all of the "American classics" in this post–September 11 way. "So how would I propose to read *Moby-Dick* now, now meaning since September 11, 2001, and the rise of George W. Bush as president and commander in chief?" *Moby-Dick* is useful, he persuasively argues, because it resists the kind of "simple allegory of good and evil" that the Bush administration sees as operative in the world. In a similar vein, Donoghue offers a new solution to an old conundrum: how to interpret the disturbing final chapters of *Adventures of Huckleberry Finn,* in which Huck, so sympathetic to the runaway slave Jim's suffering in the first part of the novel, is drawn into Tom Sawyer's fantasy-driven schemes to humiliate Jim. In suggesting that this section of the novel shows how the "taint" of racism in American society can reassert itself at any time, Donoghue asks us to read as tragedy chapters written as farce. Donoghue grudgingly concedes that slavery was eventually deemed "morally repellent" by "a national and international zeitgeist" and "later (however haltingly) by the Supreme Court. . . . But the racist prejudice that made the war and the legislation necessary has not ceased."

However one might agree with such assertions, they do little to illuminate *Huckleberry Finn.* Some of Donoghue's best pages are not about racism at all but instead concern Mark Twain's deification of the Mississippi River, which inspired in turn his fellow Missourian T. S. Eliot's moving evocation of the river in the opening lines of "The Dry Salvages":

> I do not know much about gods; but I think that the river
> Is a strong brown god—sullen, untamed and intractable,
> Patient to some degree, at first recognised as a frontier;
> Useful, untrustworthy, as a conveyor of commerce;
> Then only a problem confronting the builder of bridges.

"The particular merit of Eliot's reading of *Huckleberry Finn,*" Donoghue remarks, "is that it respects the work as a poem, a work of fiction, and discourages readers from thinking that it is primarily a tract or an editorial." Exactly right, but it has not discouraged Donoghue from finding a tract in the concluding chapters of the novel.

3.

Most puzzling of all is Donoghue's indictment of Hawthorne. When I recently reread *The Scarlet Letter,* I found it wasn't quite the book that I remembered—great books never are. I felt that I had the gloomy costume drama and its four main characters firmly in mind: Hester Prynne and her weak-willed lover, the Rev. Arthur Dimmesdale; Hester's cuckolded husband, the scholarly physician Roger Chillingworth; and little Pearl, the offspring of Hester's illicit love for Dimmesdale. But this time I noticed how strongly Hawthorne insisted on the English origins of his cast of immigrants, how recently they had embarked on what Perry Miller called the American "errand into the wilderness."[3] And I noticed, too, how Hawthorne asked us to acknowledge what a bad marriage Hester had made with her Casaubon-like husband, who had sent her ahead to the New World while he completed some important research of his own. "Thou knowest that I was frank with thee," she tells him of their marriage, when Chillingworth confronts her on her adultery. "I felt no love, nor feigned any." To which Chillingworth, equally forthright, replies:

> It was my folly, and thy weakness. I,—a man of thought,—the book-worm of great libraries,—a man already in decay, having given my best years to feed the hungry dream of knowledge,—what had I to do with youth and beauty like thine own!

In its account of lofty expectations spectacularly unmet, and improvised arrangements cobbled together in the breech, *The Scarlet Letter* prefigures many American immigrant narratives. Abraham Cahan set *Yekl,* his 1890s version of *The Scarlet Letter,* on Hester Street in lower Manhattan.

For Donoghue, however, *The Scarlet Letter* is a parable of the

American refusal to admit mistakes. Donoghue wants Hester Prynne punished for her sin. He wants her to take poison like Emma Bovary or jump in front of a train like Anna Karenina. He is shocked that she gets off scot-free: "There is not a hint of remorse, contrition, or confession." In the generational conflict at the heart of the novel, Donoghue sides with Chillingworth and the punitive Puritan ministers. (D. H. Lawrence, by contrast, thought the young lovers worried too much about their elders' disapproval: "If they had had the honest courage of their own passion, there would have been no sin.") Donoghue is impressed by how "strikingly impoverished in ritual and symbolism" Hawthorne's imagined Puritan community is. It seems perverse of Donoghue, however, to keep repeating that Catholicism has clear answers to the problem of sin when, as Perry Miller long ago observed, what was "persistent" in the thinking of New England "from the covenant theology . . . to [Jonathan] Edwards and to Emerson is the Puritan's effort to confront, face to face, the image of a blinding divinity in the physical universe, and to look upon that universe without the intermediacy of ritual, of ceremony, of the Mass and the confessional."

It is always rash to question Hawthorne's sense of history—one finds so often that he has been there before you. Donoghue is disappointed that in *The Scarlet Letter* Hawthorne "conceives of sin as a social transgression only." But when Donoghue wonders why Hawthorne reduces sin to its social effects, the reduction is not in Hawthorne, who read the Puritan sermons with great care, but in the Puritans themselves. Hawthorne was particularly drawn to those recurrent New England sermons on social backsliding that Perry Miller identified as "jeremiads," consisting of a doleful "public review of the shortcomings of the society." If you compare the jeremiads of the founding generation of immigrants and the later generations, "you will be struck by the fact," wrote Miller in *Errand into the Wilderness,* "that the second and third generations had become oriented toward the social, and only the social problem."

In an irony that Hawthorne might have appreciated, Denis Donoghue set out to write in *The American Classics* a blistering and up-to-date attack on the shortcomings of current American culture and society: our intolerance for the poor; our racism; our cavalier treatment of the environment; our conviction that September 11 means never having to say we're sorry. In doing so, however, he has unwittingly produced only the latest installment of the earliest distinctively American literary genre. Donoghue has endeavored, as Perry Miller said of earlier ineffectual attempts, "to fire again the once-shattering blunderbuss of the jeremiad."[4] Some readers will no doubt be grateful for Donoghue's quixotic attempt to demonstrate that "the classic books do not offer any resistance to the determination of American culture to go for power, conquest, the empire of globalization—the new version of slavery." But surely one may view with dismay the policies of the Bush administration without believing that Whitman and Hawthorne are complicit in the spread of American power abroad. What is just as troubling is that Donoghue does not seem to recognize the deep insight into conventional American hypocrisy in the works of Hawthorne and Thoreau and the feeling for democratic experience in Whitman's poems and in such a book as *Specimen Days*. It is understandable that a critic should be appalled by the brutalism of recent American policies; but it is regrettable that voices that should be heard in the works he discusses are drowned out by the passion of personal protest.

NOTES

1. For the significance of the year 1837 for Emerson, Lincoln, John Brown, and the leaders of the literary and political movement known as "Young America," see Edward L. Widmer, *Young America: The Flowering of Democracy in New York City* (New York: Oxford University Press, 1999), 3–5. For "Natur," see chapter 9 of Louisa May Alcott's *Jack and Jill*: "You, sir, are a model of a man fresh from Natur's mould. A true-born child of this free hemisphere; verdant as the mountains of our land."

2. From the first chapter of *Walden*:

> I sometimes wonder that we can be so frivolous, I may almost say, as to attend to the gross but somewhat foreign form of servitude called Negro Slavery, there are so many keen and subtle masters that enslave both north and south. It is hard to have a southern overseer; it is worse to have a northern one; but worst of all when you are the slave-driver of yourself.

3. Perry Miller, *Errand into the Wilderness* (Cambridge: Belknap Press of Harvard University Press, 1956).

4. See *Nature's Nation* (Cambridge: Harvard University Press, 1967), 115. On page 64 of *The American Classics,* Donoghue refers to this book as "Nation's Nation."

VOLUME REVIEWED

*The American Classics: A Personal Essay*
By Denis Donoghue
Yale University Press, 2005

# Patriotic Gore

I.

ULYSSES S. GRANT AND WILLIAM TECUMSEH SHERMAN, the men with the exotic names who turned the Civil War decisively in the North's favor, are sometimes credited with putting an end to the romance of war. The once popular Southern novelist John Esten Cooke lamented that in modern warfare as conducted by the Union forces, "where men are organized in masses and converted into insensate machines, there is nothing heroic or romantic or in any way calculated to appeal to the imagination." One looks in vain among the Northern victors for the flair and dash of the Confederate heroes—the wily guerrilla raider John Mosby, celebrated in a poem of Melville's, or Jeb Stuart sporting an ostrich plume in his cap.

The North, to be sure, was not without its distinguished martyrs. Colonel Robert Gould Shaw led his black troops in the doomed charge on Fort Wagner, giving Boston Brahmins a fit subject for their fantasies of leadership and martial heroism. Another Bostonian, Colonel Thomas Wentworth Higginson, led a black regiment to occupy Jacksonville, Florida, ordering that no houses be destroyed or plundered—"Sherman's 'bummers' not having yet arrived," Higginson noted proudly. When the town went up in flames anyway, Higginson insisted that it was the white reinforcements who had torched the wooden buildings and not his own well-mannered troops. Preparing for departure, he returned through the smoke-filled streets to the house where he had been billeted to pluck a tea rose for his lapel.[1]

The grim conditions of the final stages of the war put an end to such sentimental gestures, as Lincoln turned to the implacable generals who understood that victory was a matter of superior numbers and superior technology. Sherman knew well that he couldn't compete with the young hotheads of the South according to their own methods. "War suits them," he wrote, "and the rascals are brave, fine riders, bold to rashness, and dangerous subjects in every sense. . . . These men must all be killed or employed by us before we can hope for peace."

For Sherman, the romance of war lay neither in the battlefield bravura of the Confederate cavalry nor in the idealized antislavery causes espoused by Boston Brahmins, but rather in what he called "the grand and beautiful game of war." It was a game for which he was well suited. The son of a lawyer with Connecticut roots who admired Tecumseh, the great chief of the Shawnees, Sherman had grown up in the frontier state of Ohio—"an untamed animal just caught in the far West," he called himself—and attended West Point, from which he graduated in 1840. Sherman was never an abolitionist; he fervently opposed using black soldiers during the war as well as giving the vote to blacks. He felt at ease in the South, where he had taken part in mop-up operations against the Seminoles in Florida before serving in Mobile and Charleston, where he had friends among the leading families. When he taught at a military academy in Louisiana in 1860, he suggested to his wife back in Ohio that they might purchase slaves to run the household. She was appalled. Sherman's view of the rebellious South was not ideological; in his view, the South needed to be disciplined for its ill-advised decision to secede from the Union.

Like Grant's, Sherman's early service in the war was undistinguished, and he almost gave up the "beautiful game" after some setbacks along the Mississippi, when he was much maligned in the newspapers for overestimating Confederate troop strength in Kentucky, for his harsh treatment of civilian supporters of the Confederacy in Memphis, and for what Edmund Wilson called "a certain insouciance in his efforts to protect property."[2] Relieved of his command in late 1861, sullen and suicidal, Sherman developed a lifelong hatred of the press. Many, including his wife, feared that he was insane. When he returned to the battlefield, as Grant's main lieutenant, he was openly determined to pursue the game of war according to his own convictions.

What secured Sherman's fame was the great campaign beginning in the spring of 1864, when he crisscrossed the state of Georgia, first taking Atlanta, then marching to Savannah—the "March to the Sea"—then back up the coast through the Carolinas to Raleigh and final victory. Throughout this campaign, Sherman, affectionately called "Uncle Billy" by his troops, showed a zeal for technological and tactical innovation. His troops were so skilled in the demolition and rebuilding of railroads, bridges, and tunnels that one Confederate claimed that Sherman carried an extra tunnel with him. Sherman's huge army of sixty-two thousand on the march was self-sustaining, moving a dozen miles a day and cutting a swath twenty-five to sixty miles wide through the countryside, while drawing provisions from farms and plantations along the way—the work of the so-called "bummers." The regular troops were followed by a second army of freed slaves and sympathizers, a constant annoyance to Sherman who, on one occasion, removed the pontoon bridges from a river so that this band of camp followers was left behind—to face the dangers of drowning or of vindictive Confederate raiders and slaveholders.

Sherman clearly relished the imaginative ways in which he subdued and terrorized the countryside—German generals in World War II read his vivid *Memoirs* with care—but he retained a strict sense of the rules. When in his view they were broken, he was outraged and vengeful. On the road to Savannah, a young Union officer's foot was blown to pieces by a land mine planted in the road. "This was not war, but murder," Sherman wrote. In response, he ordered a group of Confederate prisoners "armed with picks and spades" to "march in close order along the road, so as to explode their own torpedoes, or to discover and dig them up." When the prisoners hesitated, Sherman was delighted: "I . . . could hardly help laughing at their stepping so gingerly along the road." The reader of Sherman's *Memoirs* finds his sympathies shifting back and forth in this horrible scene, from the young officer's suffering to the hapless prisoners. But Sherman's laughter can only appall.

E. L. Doctorow includes both of these disturbing episodes, the pontoon bridge and the land mine, in *The March,* a sprawling historical novel that takes Sherman's exploits and what Doctorow calls "the brutal romance of war" as its subject. The Civil War has been the great mother lode of historical fiction in America, from *The Red Badge of Courage* to *Gone with the Wind,* Gore Vidal's *Lincoln,* and, more recently, *Cold Mountain.* No American novelist of the twentieth century has done more than Doctorow—the author of nine novels in addition to short stories, critical essays, screenplays, and a play—to enliven the historical novel, already by the 1930s a musty sideline in American literature.

Doctorow has brought to what had been a conservative genre a conceptual vigor and a narrative excitement that have affinities with experiments of his own generation of fabulists—John Barth, Donald Barthelme, and Kurt Vonnegut. He has had a special interest (as in *Loon Lake* and *Billy Bathgate*) in the gangsters and hoboes of the depression. His best novel remains the highly entertaining *Ragtime,* with the outsized personalities Stanford White, J. P. Morgan, Emma Goldman, Houdini, and the rest inhabiting the sepia-tinged turn-of-the-century New York of the Gilded Age. The Civil War has turned up only tangentially in his books. So it is with much anticipation that one turns to Doctorow's novel about the national cataclysm that gave rise to the Gilded Age.

Like all Doctorow's work, *The March* is stylishly written—his model, here as elsewhere, is F. Scott Fitzgerald—but it seems, despite its considerable length, a smaller, less ambitious book than one might have expected in view of his subject. What seemed bracingly experimental in some of Doctorow's previous novels, the combination of historical and fictional characters and fates in surprising ways, seems merely conventional in *The March.* Doctorow recasts some of the most closely examined events in American history: the uncertain beginnings of the march in Georgia; Lincoln's reelection, based in large part on Sherman's success in taking Atlanta; the endgame of the war; the assassination of Lincoln; the controversy over the terms of surrender and reconstruction. Toward the end of the novel, Doctorow gropes for the significance of the march itself, both as a historical event and as some kind of metaphor for grand human effort. The publication of this novel in the aftermath of September 11 and while the nation is again at war raises a tantalizing question: Why Sherman, and why now?

2.

The narrative of *The March* begins in confusion, when the settled life of the fictional Jameson plantation in rural Georgia is disrupted by the impending arrival of Sherman's army:

> At five in the morning someone banging on the door and shouting, her husband, John, leaping out of bed, grabbing his rifle, and Roscoe at the same time roused from the backhouse, his bare feet pounding: Mattie hurriedly pulled on her robe, her mind prepared for the alarm of war, but the heart stricken that it would finally have come, and down the stairs she flew to see through the open door in the lamplight, at the steps of the portico, the two horses, steam rising from their flanks, their heads lifting, their eyes wild, the driver a young darkie with rounded shoulders, showing stolid patience even in this, and the woman standing in her carriage no one but her aunt Letitia Pettibone of McDonough, her elderly face drawn in anguish, her hair a straggled mess, this woman of such fine grooming, this dowager who practically ruled the season in Atlanta standing up in the equipage like some hag of doom, which indeed she would prove to be.

The headlong dash of this opening sentence, as though punctuation itself is gone with the wind, is meant to convey Sherman's merciless uprooting of a whole civilization. From now on everyone and everything will be on the move. "And I know him!" Letitia screams of General Sherman. "He has dined in my home. He has lived among us. He burns where he has ridden to lunch, he fires the city in whose clubs he once gave toasts." It will be another seventy pages, however, before we get a glimpse of Sherman himself, with his battered cap and a cigar stub in his mouth, riding nonchalantly on his small horse.

Meanwhile, Doctorow introduces a cast of invented folk to

connect, as though by contagion, the famous names and places. Some of these come from previous novels, by Doctorow and other writers; some seem lightly disguised historical characters. Doctorow has fun with their names. Two slaves are called Jake Early and Jubal Samuels, evoking the Confederate general Jubal Early. A spirited slave girl called Pearl seems to have stepped out of *The Scarlet Letter*—in her red shawl threaded with gold she even dresses like Hawthorne's illegitimate scamp. The Boston-bred Lieutenant Clarke rescues Pearl from slavery without quite acknowledging her sexual allure. At Milledgeville, capital of Georgia during the war, another group of loosely connected characters joins Doctorow's traveling show: an efficient Union army surgeon with a bloodied saw in his hand; a judge's daughter who asks the surgeon's help with her dying father; two bedraggled Confederate soldiers, incarcerated for desertion and dereliction of duty, who have escaped from the Milledgeville prison.

In these opening sections, Doctorow develops a single idea: that as a civilization is uprooted its members are given the chance to invent themselves anew. Light-skinned Pearl puts on a Union uniform and serves briefly as a drummer boy, then as Sherman's mascot, and finally, along with the judge's daughter, as a nurse assisting the army surgeon. The escaped Confederate soldiers, Arly and Will, dress up as Yankees and bring off a series of picaresque escapades, stealing cash from a church collection to pay for a visit to a brothel before going on to more serious acts of mayhem. Even Uncle Billy, the West Point professional soldier, undergoes a transformation: "Sherman affected the sloppy uniform, and shared the hardships, of the enlisted man."

Amid the steady attrition of the march, we're never quite sure who the main characters are and which ones are subsidiary—just as we are reasonably certain that Lieutenant Clarke is a durable hero, Doctorow kills him off, replacing him with another noble Northerner, Stephen Walsh, who carries Pearl to freedom. Meanwhile, Doctorow continues to introduce significant characters late in the novel: a British journalist, a Mathew Brady–like photographer and his black assistant, and, in an affecting portrait, Abraham Lincoln, "the amassed miseries of this torn-apart country made incarnate."

We are meant to feel that this ebb and flow of characters reflects the turbulence of the march, a "floating world," as Emily Thompson, the judge's daughter, puts it. At the same time, Doctorow seems to distrust the possibility that a shaped narrative can emerge from the ongoing "march of life," which has no goal or consummation. In the past he has had recourse to a closing violent cataclysm of some kind, as in the ending of *Ragtime* when the black Coalhouse Walker is shot by the police. The historical record has given him an obvious climax to the march in the assassination of Lincoln, but since Lincoln's death is expected, Doctorow has contrived a parallel plot involving a threat to Sherman's life to intensify the sense of an ending.

The sturdiest, most fully imagined characters in the book are Arly Wilcox, a half-cracked Confederate master of disguise and escape, and the Union army surgeon Wrede Sartorius. Sartorius and Wilcox are in some sense opposites—the one unchangeable and imperturbable under the most horrific conditions, the other Protean in his shifting personalities and mercurial escapes—but they both thrive in the nomadic world of the march. Arly joins a long line of illusionists and con artists in Doctorow's fiction, most memorably Houdini in *Ragtime.* The German-born Dr. Sartorius, trained in medicine at Göttingen, is a more complicated character. He introduces advances in medical treatment on the battlefield, but in his zeal for modern methods he seems a little too impervious to the sufferings around him. He doesn't get the girl, Emily, but whether this is a failing in her or in him (he wonders at one point whether he doesn't resemble, in his lack of feeling, one of his patients, who has a spike lodged in his brain) is never quite made clear.

What is most unnerving about Dr. Sartorius, however, is that we have met him before, as the sinister medical researcher in Doctorow's gothic novel *The Waterworks,* set in New York during the aftermath of the Civil War. We are meant to believe that the sympathetic army surgeon of *The March* turned into the nightmare figure, half Dr. Frankenstein and half Dr. Mengele (all mad doctors are German) of *The Waterworks.* This little in-joke does nothing to make Sartorius convincing in *The March,* however; nor do Sartorius's unlikely predictions of penicillin, blood transfusions, and X-rays. In a similar narrative sally, we meet, during the pontoon bridge incident, the parents of the ragtime pianist and sympathetic terrorist Coalhouse Walker Jr. from *Ragtime.* Doctorow may be reminding us that a major theme in *Ragtime* is a rich white family's redemption through the adoption of a black child—a theme reworked in various ways in *The March.*

But there is only one dominating character in Doctorow's novel, and that is the march itself. For the Southerners in its path, the march is like some supernatural disaster unleashed on the countryside:

> When the sound of this cloud reached them, it was like nothing they had ever heard in their lives. It was not fearsomely heavenmade, like thunder or lightning or howling wind, but something felt through their feet, a resonance, as if the earth was humming.

For Sherman and his men, by contrast, the march is a kind of visionary alternative to the settled life of city and farm. It is "the new way to live," as Arly says, and a constant injunction to live "in the present as if there were no future," as Sartorius is said to live. Doctorow adopts both these perspectives, noting the hardships imposed on the South by the "bummers" while writing sympathetically of Sherman's hatred of "city governance and dealing endlessly with whining civilians."

As Sherman argues with Secretary of State Stanton about the terms of surrender, with Stanton pushing for a more punitive treatment of the South, we are invited to share in Sherman's exultation in the meaning of the completed march:

> Though this march is done, and well accomplished, I think of it now, God help me, with longing—not for its blood and death but for the bestowal of meaning to the very ground trod upon, how it made every field and swamp and river and road into something of moral consequence, whereas now, as the march dissolves so does the meaning, the army strewing itself into the isolated intentions of diffuse private life, and the terrain thereby left blank and also diffuse, and ineffable, a thing once again, and victoriously, without reason, and, whether

> diurnally lit and darkened, or sere or fruitful, or raging or calm, completely insensible and without any purpose of its own.

This baroque elaboration of the Gettysburg Address ("we can not dedicate—we can not consecrate—we can not hallow—this ground. The brave men, living and dead, who struggled here, have consecrated it . . .") tempts us to forget the atrocities wrought by both sides along the route of the march.

In offering so many divergent views of the march, Doctorow has conveyed some of the complexity of the historical event, but what, finally, does the march signify for Doctorow himself? Perhaps the divergent views are themselves the point. In his Massey lectures at Harvard, published in 2003 as *Reporting the Universe,* Doctorow maintained that a "multiplicity of witness" was crucial to a free society: "A true democracy endows itself with a multiplicity of voices and assures the creation of a self-revising consensual reality that inches forward over the generations to a dream of truth."

But this merely postpones the question, for what "dream of truth" about our national history does *The March* move toward? Is Sherman's march to the sea meant to be a metaphor for Manifest Destiny, the American empire expanding and consuming what first Native Americans and then African-American slaves have sown? Is Sherman, with his contempt for poor blacks and his single-minded concentration on "the mission," some sort of stand-in for President Bush? Is he meant as an ironic reminder that emancipation was largely the work of men who didn't give a damn about the slaves? Is Pearl, daughter of a slaveholder and a slave, meant to be a hopeful embodiment of a better, more inclusive America? None of these possibilities seems particularly convincing, and whatever light Doctorow thought to shine on our own difficult times remains diffuse at best. Indeed, two other novels by Doctorow—the apocalyptic *City of God* (2000) and *Ragtime,* with its family fortune built on patriotic flags and fireworks—seem more incisive anticipations of September 11 and Bush's America than *The March.*

It is one of the many ironies of the Gilded Age that General Sherman, scourge of Georgia, became a popular figure in the postwar South as he urged policies of reconciliation and forgiveness. If it were not for his distaste for bureaucracy and the press, he probably could have joined, had he wished to do so, the other Union generals elected to the presidency. His popularity was still high in 1903 when Augustus Saint-Gaudens's gilded monument of Sherman was installed at the southeast entrance of Central Park. The statue—in which the mounted general is preceded by a crowned figure bearing an olive branch—lacks the simple nobility of Saint-Gaudens's monument for Colonel Shaw and his black soldiers on Boston Common. There is something conflicted in the Sherman monument, "a certain ambiguity," as Henry James (whose younger brother Wilkinson had been grievously wounded in Shaw's doomed charge) noticed when he contemplated the statue in 1904, a year after its installation:

> Its idea, to which I have alluded, strikes me as equivocal, or more exactly as double; the image being, on the one side, and splendidly rendered, that of an overwhelming military advance, an irresistible march into an enemy's country—the strain forward, the very inflation of drapery with the rush, symbolizing the very breath of the Destroyer. But the idea is at the same time—which part of it is also admirably expressed—that the Destroyer is a messenger of peace, with the olive branch too waved in the blast and with embodied grace, in the form of a beautiful American girl, attending his business. And I confess to a lapse of satisfaction in the presence of this interweaving—the result doubtless of a sharp suspicion of all attempts, however glittering and golden, to confound destroyers with benefactors. The military monument in the City Square responds evidently, wherever a pretext can be found for it, to a desire of men's hearts; but I would have it always as military as possible, and I would have the Destroyer, in intention at least, not docked of one of his bristles. I would have him deadly and terrible, and, if he be wanted beautiful, beautiful only as a war-god and crested not with peace, but with snakes.

There is a kindred ambiguity in E. L. Doctorow's novel about the irresistible march. It concludes on a sentimental note, with Pearl, now of age, and her husband-to-be, the New Yorker Stephen

Walsh, marching toward the great city with some of Sherman's glittering aplomb. He will read law, like Oliver Wendell Holmes. She will go to medical school and, at Walsh's urging, "let the world catch up to you." What seems a pathetic fallacy lifted from the closing paragraph of Stephen Crane's *Red Badge of Courage* seals the happy ending: "There was still a scent of gunfire in the trees, and they were glad to come out into the sun again." This is the reassuring image of the beautiful American girl with the olive branch rather than that of the bristling war god crowned with snakes. Doctorow may have wished to preserve the ambiguity, the mixing of destroyers and benefactors. But in the comforting resolution of *The March,* it is an ambiguity without pain or peril.

NOTES

1. On Robert Gould Shaw, see chapter 10, "The Martyr and His Friends," in George M. Fredrickson, *The Inner Civil War* (New York: Harper and Row, 1965). For Higginson's tea rose, see *The Complete Civil War Journal and Selected Letters of Thomas Wentworth Higginson,* ed. Christopher Looby (Chicago: University of Chicago Press, 2000), 120.

2. Edmund Wilson, *Patriotic Gore* (New York: Oxford University Press, 1962), 182. Wilson's chapter on Sherman is particularly revealing of the inner conflicts in the man.

VOLUME REVIEWED

*The March*
By E. L. Doctorow
Random House, 2005

# Friends by Chance

IF SNAKES, AS EMILY DICKINSON ONCE SAID, prefer a boggy acre, American literary biography must be crawling with them. Size counts in American biography; wade in for twenty pages and you sink to your knees. The English do it differently and better. English biography, like so much else in contemporary British intellectual life, is an invention of Bloomsbury. Lytton Strachey's *Eminent Victorians* (1918) swept like a dry wind through what Virginia Woolf called the "parti-colored, hybrid, monstrous" two-volume Victorian lives. The traits we associate with Bloomsbury's "new biography"—an amused curiosity about the ties between private and public behavior; an approach to individual temperament informed but not infested by Freudian ideas; a dryness of tone more given to irony than enthusiasm—remain characteristic of the best English biographies. Stylistically, Bloomsbury owed much to French writers—Flaubert, Stendhal, and Proust—though not to French biographers. The French don't really *do* biography though they do autobiography—which as a modern genre Montaigne and Rousseau pretty much invented—extraordinarily well.

Modernism never really happened to American literary biography. You would have to go back far, to Henry James's incisive *Hawthorne* (1879), for something comparable to Strachey. It is a book best known for James's claim that a biography of Hawthorne is all but impossible, not only because so little happened in Hawthorne's quiet life but because so little *could* happen in a land so sketchy, so lacking in "complex social machinery," as the United States of Hawthorne's time. Perhaps James's

*Hawthorne* came too early to be a significant influence. James's own later biography of the sculptor William Wetmore Storey is more a loose collection of documents with commentary than a book—it is precisely the kind of baggy, respectful volume Strachey set out to destroy. And James's life of his brother William, as Rachel Cohen reminds us in *A Chance Meeting,* turned into an account of his own childhood and family instead, *Notes of a Son and Brother.*

In retrospect, James's shift from biography to autobiography seems symptomatic of the best American writing. Henry Adams could have been a brilliant biographer, of his illustrious friends John Hay or Clarence King; he wrote a brilliant autobiography instead, and so did Gertrude Stein, though his of himself is in the third person while hers is a first-person autobiography of someone else—her companion, Alice B. Toklas. American literature, like French literature, can boast magnificent examples of autobiography, beginning with Benjamin Franklin and John Woolman and including such more or less real-life adventures as *Typee, Walden, The Country of the Pointed Firs,* and *Armies of the Night.* But as for literary biography, one sees the wisdom of the editors of the Library of America in excluding it altogether from our American Pléiade. English professors will continue to mention reverently Leon Edel's multivolume *Henry James* and Richard Ellmann's *James Joyce* as monuments—monuments they are, stately and a bit lifeless on the shelf.

To achieve something new in literary biography, American biographers have either had to school themselves in the methods of Bloomsbury, as Janet Malcolm has done to excellent effect, or to revisit the sources of whatever we have of a native tradition, as Jean Strouse and Louis Menand and Nicholas Delbanco, among others, have done. For all of these writers and for Bloomsbury, too, the example of Henry James looms large, as both a theorist of biography in such iconic texts as *The Aspern Papers,* and as the writer in our literature who has gone most deeply into the interconnectedness of human lives. It is not an accident that many of our most interesting biographers now eschew the single life, and insist instead on the relational aspect of lives lived—that we are who we know and love and befriend and betray. Rachel Cohen, in her cunningly crafted and meticulously written *A Chance Meeting,* has drawn on both these strands of biographical vitality, the Bloomsbury line and the Jamesian line, and has produced, in this her first book, something fresh and unexpected and promising.

What Cohen has written is not so much a group biography as a sort of evocative matrix of writers and artists over time, with exhilarating overlap and cross-reference:

> The thirty people gathered here met in ordinary ways: a careful arrangement after long admiration, a friend's casual introduction, or because they both just happened to be standing near the drinks. They saw each other first in a photography studio, or a magazine office, and they talked for a few hours or for forty years. Later it felt to them, as it often does, entirely by chance that they had met and yet impossible that they could have missed each other.

Cohen's title comes from an appealing bit of memoir by Willa Cather, in which Cather recounts her chance encounter, in 1930, in a hotel in the South of France with the eighty-four-year-old niece of Gustave Flaubert. For the deeply reactionary Cather, Madame Grout is the embodiment of everything she admires in European culture, and a reminder of all those "absent things" James, in his book on Hawthorne, lamented in crass America:

> She was not an idealist; she had lived through two wars. She was one of the least visionary and sentimental persons I have ever met. She knew that conditions and circumstances, not their own wishes, dictate the actions of men. In her mind there was a kind of large enlightenment, like that of the many-windowed workroom at Croisset [of Flaubert], with the cool, tempered northern light pouring into it.

With her thirty characters and thirty-six "chance meetings," Rachel Cohen is in search of a kindred many-windowed enlightenment.

At first glance, the reader might mistake *A Chance Meeting* for a more casual and politically correct version of Edmund Wilson's documentary literary history *The Shock of Recognition* (1955). In both books, the march of American writing is presented as a series of encounters among writers, though Cohen's writers met at parties or offices while Wilson's writers "met" by reading one another's books. (When Emerson actually met Whitman, he somewhat regretted his initial enthusiasm about *Leaves of Grass.*) Inevitably, many of the same writers figure in both books—Whitman, Mark Twain, Howells, the James brothers. Neither book tries very hard to unsettle the established canon of American literature, though Cohen's is the updated canon that now includes far more women (Wilson's book is subtitled "The Development of Literature in the United States Recorded by the Men Who Made It") and people of color (none in Wilson). Even in this regard, however, Cohen does not stray far from Wilson's narrative. She introduces both W. E. B. DuBois and Gertrude Stein (absent in *The Shock of Recognition*) as students of William James, and James Baldwin as an admirer of Henry James. Ulysses S. Grant, about whom Cohen writes compellingly, owes much of his contemporary reputation as a writer to Wilson's championing of Grant's *Memoirs* in *Patriotic Gore.*

But Cohen's *A Chance Meeting* is not really an attempt to redraw the map of American literature. Except for a few conversations with the photographer Richard Avedon, it is not based on original research; Cohen has gone where good literary biographies could take her. She is not in the business of burnishing the reputations of neglected figures. Her choices of twentieth-century American poets—Hart Crane, Marianne Moore, Langston Hughes, Elizabeth Bishop, Marianne Moore—will antagonize no one. Her slightly more idiosyncratic choice of prose writers from the same period—Willa Cather, Gertrude Stein, Zora Neale Hurston, Baldwin, and Mailer—is almost as safe. There are a couple of surprises, Carl Van Vechten and Katherine Anne Porter, but you can't write about the social landscape of the Harlem Renaissance without including Van Vechten, whose writings, in any case, interest Cohen less than his photographs. And Porter, who hosted Hart Crane during a rough patch in Mexico and came late to admire Cather, whom she never actually met, provides a useful thread for Cohen's "intertwining." Cohen's selection of "artists," mainly portrait photographers with a handful of oddball others (Duchamp, John Cage, Joseph Cornell) mixed in, is surprising in other ways—no Sargent or Saint-Gaudens, no abstract expressionists, no Fairfield Porter or Larry Rivers.

Cohen offers some beguilingly arbitrary rules for inclusion or exclusion. Her writers and artists "were born in America," they "lived in cities," they "spent quite a lot of their time visiting and talking." So, no Faulkner, or any other writers based in the South, and no Frost or Dickinson, holed up in Amherst. Henry Adams and Edith Wharton are excluded for the dubious reason that "the people in this book were interested in social reality, but by and large they did not document it." (If DuBois and Mailer did not document social reality, however, what exactly were they up to?) Cohen's true and perfectly defensible criterion is the one she offers last: "Finally, and fundamentally, I wrote about people whose company I felt I had an instinct for."

As one reads *A Chance Meeting,* one comes to trust Cohen's instincts—the book preserves a delicate balance between the apparently random (the "chance" of her title) and the obsessive. One also comes to see that her real subject is not "American literature" or "American culture," or some implied argument about the period bookended by the Civil War and the civil rights movement. It is true that she goes into the Harlem Renaissance in some depth, but here her choice of figures invites closer scrutiny. She rightly chides Carl Van Vechten, in his unfortunately named novel *Nigger Heaven* and elsewhere, for his patronizing preference for "primitive" themes in black writing and art. She might have added Sherwood Anderson's *Dark Laughter,* and the whole genre of such novels that celebrated the happy-go-lucky "Negro life." But Cohen seems to lean in the same direction when she celebrates Zora Neale Hurston's brand of zaniness (itself a pose), as dramatized in such books as Hurston's collection of African-American folklore *Mules and Men,* and scolds Jessie Fauset—an admirable novelist—for her primness and dull parties: "these were formal and less fun . . . and besides there was never much to drink." She doesn't seem to see that Fauset and DuBois embraced formality and sobriety in order to counter precisely the kinds of stereotypes of happy, hard-drinking blacks perpetuated by the likes of Van Vechten and Anderson.

Cohen's true subject, however, is a more private hoard of concerns, artfully arrayed across the whole canvas of the book. One of her concerns is the nature of collectors and collecting—the processes by which we gather the objects and people we "have an instinct for." She is, like Baudelaire and Poe and many photographers and painters, a physiognomist of sorts—a "collector of people," as she calls Richard Avedon—with an overriding interest in the variety and meaning of human faces. And finally, she is a student of the nature of friendship. A poignant admission in her introduction records the genesis of *A Chance Meeting:* "a solitary year spent driving around the United States" with a trunk full of books by Henry James, Willa Cather, and the rest. And what did she want to learn from these writers during her solitary *Wanderjahr*? "I cared most to know how they felt about friendship."

Cohen's opening "chance meeting," not really by chance and not exactly a meeting, takes place on the August day in 1854 when Henry James's father decided to have a daguerreotype taken of himself and his eleven-year-old son in the studio of the photographer Mathew Brady on lower Broadway in New York.

> They had come in from the country. It was August, the attractions of the summer house had begun to wane, and Henry James, Sr., had discovered that he had a bit of business at the New York *Tribune*—that he had, pressingly, to see a gentleman about an idea. He had kissed his wife and collected his small son, Henry, Jr., and they had taken the ferry. Once they were under way, the senior James had been seized with the happy thought of presenting Mrs. James with a surprise, a daguerreotype of the two of them. When Henry James, Jr., wrote about that day dears later, he couldn't quite remember but was affectionately certain that his father, despite his love of surprises, would have given away the secret the moment they returned: "He moved in a cloud, if not rather in a high radiance, of precipitation and divulgation."

This handsomely deployed opening paragraph starts many of the hares in Cohen's hunt. There is at the outset the idea of the attractions of the city. There is the hovering question about what really happened, and how memory has its own claims to reality: "he couldn't quite remember but was affectionately certain." There is the countervailing kind of evidence of the past provided by the photograph, a "fragile enterprise," according to Cohen, in which Brady's soft voice and gentle movements coaxed something special from his sitters—exposed them, you might say. "His presence calmed his subjects and allowed them as they waited for the exposure, to settle into themselves, so that the depth of their experience was evident on their faces." (Cohen's own prose, an unlikely hybrid of Cather's restrained clarity and Stein's slightly wayward accretions, is itself calming and patient of exposure.) And there is the theme of collecting, both in Brady's outrageously ambitious and nearly successful project of "photographing every well-known or influential American of his day," and in Cohen's own culling of scenes and quotations—that "high radiance of precipitation and divulgation"—from this calm moment when James-père "collected his small son" before the war.

When we see Brady again in *A Chance Meeting,* he is photographing General Grant in 1864. Still a "completist," according to Cohen, Brady is assembling the other great collection for which he is known: his photographs, and those by his gifted assistants, of Civil War soldiers and battlefields. "Always driven, he became a recording fury, pushing, pushing, pushing to get people into his collection before they went to the grave." It is characteristic of Cohen's eye for coincidence (another kind of "chance meeting") that Grant, as captured by Brady's camera, "wore a long coat with nine buttons running down each side" and that Henry James, Jr., sitting for the same camera ten years earlier, wore "a narrowly cut coat with a long row of nine bright buttons." The buttons were an embarrassment for James. The English novelist Thackery had scrutinized the nine buttons on a visit to the James family and remarked that were James to go to England, he would surely be addressed as "Buttons."

The impact of the Civil War on participants and noncombatants runs through the first ten or so chapters of *A Chance Meeting* and remains a leitmotif throughout. Among the best chapters is one entitled "William Dean Howells and Annie Adams Fields and Walt Whitman." The point of the chapter is that Howells, whom Cohen writes affectionately about, somehow missed the great drama of his age. (In this regard, the theme of the chapter resembles Henry James's great stories "The Beast in the Jungle" and "The Jolly Corner.") In his strenuous efforts to make his way as a literary man, Howells, a bright boy from Ohio, cultivated Boston literary insiders like the publisher James Fields and his wife, Annie. Howells got his wish, and became the consummate Boston insider himself, turning down Whitman's poetry for the *Atlantic* and reviewing *Leaves of Grass* as a nightmare; the reader "goes through his book, like one in an ill-conditioned dream, perfectly nude, with his clothes over his arm."

When Howells actually met Whitman, by chance, at Pfaff's saloon on lower Broadway in August 1860, he didn't know what to say—and Cohen finds in this missed opportunity both a key to Howells's career and a turning point in American literary history. As Cohen sums it up:

> It was the moment before the cataclysm that was to divide the age of Lowell and Holmes from that of Whitman. But for William Dean Howells, his encounter with Whitman was somewhat less thrilling than it had been to stand in the Fieldses' library and talk of writers "whose names were dear to me from my love of their work." And to Whitman it was likely another night at Pfaff's.

Howells managed to miss the "cataclysm" as well, having cashed in a campaign biography he had written for Lincoln for an appointment as vice consul in Venice. While Lincoln directed the Army of the Republic and Whitman visited its wounded soldiers in temporary hospital beds in Washington, Howells pushed papers. Twice he could have met Lincoln—once to interview him for the biography, once to thank him for the appointment—and he avoided both opportunities ("the greatest chance of my life in its kind"). When Howells returned from Venice, Lincoln was dead, and the best Howells could do was to attend one of Whitman's popular lectures on the dead president. Cohen's conclusion is shattering: "Whitman and Lincoln are now twined together, possibly the two greatest missed opportunities of Howells's life, the two hands he could have taken hold of had he wished, as he later did, for a life more connected with the suffering of his own time."

As Cohen's map of interconnectedness enters the twentieth century, another criterion for inclusion in *A Chance Meeting* emerges more clearly. Under Mathew Brady's scrutiny, the eleven-year-old Henry James with his nine buttons had had the feeling that he and his family were "somehow *queer.*" Cohen interprets James's unease to mean that beyond their obvious idiosyncracies (Irish descent, Swedenborgian persuasion, rootless wanderings), the James family "were different because they were American," and that James's uneasiness "presaged his lifelong struggle to define a place for an American artist in a world where history and taste belonged to Europe." Since, as she puts it, Henry James "did in fact grow up to be rather more queer than otherwise," Cohen allows herself a bit of linguistic sleight of hand; like the young Henry James, she associates being queer—though not in the way he meant it—with being American.

One could make a plausible argument that much of mainstream American literature is the legacy of gay and lesbian writers. It is an argument that Cohen makes only by implication. Even leaving aside the giants Cohen does not include (Melville at one end, Frank O'Hara, Merrill, and Ashbery at the other), she is able to marshal a compelling parade beginning with Henry James and Whitman and moving on to Jewett, Stein, Cather, Hughes, Hart Crane, Elizabeth Bishop, John Cage, Merce Cunningham, Jasper Johns, Robert Rauschenberg, James Baldwin. But Cohen is less interested in some alchemical affinity between same-sex inclinations and artistic creativity than she is in the webs of friendship and family spun among her mainly childless writers and artists. Cohen has a nuanced sympathy for these hard-to-name alliances: the "Boston marriage" of Annie Fields and Sarah Orne Jewett; the father-and-son bond between the Harlem Renaissance painter Beauford Delaney and the fatherless James Baldwin; the mother-daughter bond between Marianne Moore and the motherless Elizabeth Bishop; the oddly configured Woojums family, established during Gertrude Stein's triumphant lecture tour of the United States in 1935, in which "Van Vechten was Papa Woojums, Stein was Baby Woojums, and Toklas was Mama Woojums." She is alert to the ways in which such relationships constituted safety nets for vulnerable psyches. Katherine Anne Porter, surely the least "nurturing" of women, provided safe haven for Hart Crane during his crack-up in Mexico, and James Baldwin sheltered Delaney during Delaney's escalating paranoia.

I think that there is a utopian dream behind Cohen's family tree of "intertwined lives." To the idea of literary influence she offers as a countermodel Gertrude Stein's idea that "each American chooses a tradition, collects, in some sense, his or her own sensibility." To the idea—most vigorously advanced by Harold Bloom—that each writer has to wrestle with precursors, forging an identity from this Oedipal struggle, she constructs a more benevolent family romance, in which writers establish temporary refuges in which they can create their work. Temperamentally, Cohen is more Bloomsbury than Bloom, and her Americans have the kind of "only connect" multivalence—both sexual and artistic—that we associate with Carrington and Lytton Strachey and E. M. Forster or, closer to home, with the cluster of artists and writers at Black Mountain College (briefly sketched by Cohen) during and after World War II. For the writers and artists she has "collected," I think her model is largely accurate, and reveals a world of artistic creation based more on cooperation than competition. It means, however, that she instinctively shies away from the patricidal venom directed from Norman Mailer toward Hemingway or James Baldwin toward Richard Wright, and she makes a wide detour around the fiercely competitive and father-killing abstract expressionists.

Cohen has another affinity for Bloomsbury in her gingerly crossing of the line between fact and fiction. For the most part, *A Chance Meeting* sticks to the facts—what Virginia Woolf called the "granite" of biography, as opposed to the "rainbow" of personality—as established in the biographies that serve as her sources. But from time to time, especially at the beginning and end of chapters, she indulges in fanciful invention. She is scrupulous about punctuating these sections with little linguistic flags—"perhaps," "maybe," "might have," "could have been"—and her interesting endnotes add more warnings of such fictional potholes. But the result can be unsettling for two reasons. First, she implies by her warnings that the distinction between biographical fact and fiction is absolute, and that sentences unmarked by maybes and might have beens are trustworthy beyond a reasonable doubt. Every biographer knows that this is not the case, and that biography involves a constant reassessment of the "facts" in light of new evidence or understanding. Second, Cohen sometimes blurs fact and fiction in an uneasy composite. For example, she records a moment when DuBois lifts his hat to Delaney and says, "Evening, Delaney." Her endnote reads in part:

> In 1941, a friend of Delaney's actually witnessed almost precisely this interaction, of Du Bois raising his hat to Delaney in Washington Square park, though Du Bois said, "Good afternoon, Delaney," instead of, "Evening, Delaney." This is reported in David Leeming's biography of Delaney. . . . I took the liberty of moving the scene back a decade.

The conflicted phrasing here, "actually witnessed almost precisely," is symptomatic. The word "liberty," to characterize a scene moved ten years earlier and adjusted from evening to afternoon, is meant to evoke "poetic license," and sound like a modest and pardonable stretch. Such liberties should leave the reader uneasy. As Virginia Woolf remarked of a similar fudging of the facts in Harold Nicholson's *Some People* (1927), "Let it be fact, one feels, or let it be fiction; the imagination will not serve under two masters simultaneously."

In almost every case, Cohen's inventions serve her utopian ends by forging an even tighter web of intimacies than the documentary record alone would support. *A Chance Meeting* makes abundantly clear that Rachel Cohen is herself a "collector"; one might say of her book what Carl Van Vechten said of Gertrude Stein's *Selected Works,* "A Collection is a Collection is a Collection." In *A Chance Meeting,* she has assembled her own ideal family of writers and photographers and artists. Despite her title, she is less of an acolyte of chance than Duchamp or Cage, who collected objects and sounds literally found in the streets. Her wishful manipulations of the factual record are more in the spirit of another artist she admires, Joseph Cornell, who lived on Utopia

Parkway in Queens, and assembled his boxes, little shrines to people he wished he had known, with meticulous care. But then, as Duchamp liked to say, "Your chance is not the same as mine, is it?"

VOLUME REVIEWED

*A Chance Meeting: Intertwined Lives of American Writers and Artists, 1854–1967*
By Rachel Cohen
Random House, 2004

# Acknowledgments

"Emerson at Age 200," *Times Literary Supplement,* July 25, 2003.
"A Face from the Fire: The Enduring Smile of Nathaniel Hawthorne," *Times Literary Supplement,* December 17, 2004.
"Longfellow Lives Again," *Times Literary Supplement,* January 5, 2007.
"The Mystery of Emily Dickinson," *New York Review of Books,* April 8, 1999.
"The Convert" (Emma Lazarus), *New York Review of Books,* February 15, 2007.
"Dark Darker Darkest" (Robert Frost), *New Republic,* January 22, 2007.
"Flawed Perfection" (Edna St. Vincent Millay), *New Republic,* November 5, 2001.
"Deserters" (John Dos Passos), *New Republic,* January 12, 2004.
"Covering Her Century" (Martha Gellhorn), *New Republic,* September 11, 2006.
"The Critter Poet" (Gary Snyder), *New Republic,* March 24, 1997.
"Lowell's Curse," *Agni Online,* September 2006.
"The Ding-Dong of Doom" (William Faulkner), *New Republic,* November 8, 2004.
"The War between the Tates" (Allen Tate), *New Republic,* June 4, 2001.
"The Family Man" (James Agee), *New Republic,* October 31, 2005.
"Love in the Ruins" (Walker Percy), *New Republic,* September 8 and 15, 1997.
"A Sense of Place" (Eudora Welty), *New Republic,* March 3, 1999.
"Poet in the Sun Belt" (Randall Jarrell), *New York Review of Books,* May 1985.
"American Jeremiad" (Denis Donoghue's *The American Classics*), *New York Review of Books,* September 21, 2005.
"Patriotic Gore" (Doctorow's *The March*), *New York Review of Books,* October 20, 2005.
"Friends by Chance" (Rachel Cohen's *A Chance Meeting: Intertwined Lives of American Writers and Artists, 1854–1967*), *New Republic,* March 15, 2004.

Text design by Mary H. Sexton
Typesetting by Delmastype, Ann Arbor, Michigan

Font: Monotype Garamond
Monotype Garamond is based on roman types cut by Jean Jannon in 1615, following the designs of Claude Garamond which had been cut in the previous century. It is a beautiful typeface with an air of informality that works well for setting text.
—courtesy fonts.com